An RL

MW01274219

By Research Teams of

The University of the Witwatersrand
Graduate School of Public
and Development Management
Johannesburg

and

The Human Sciences Research Council
Pretoria

ISBN 0-7969-1919-4

Published by:
HSRC Publishers
134 Pretorius Street
Pretoria 0002
South Africa

Preface

The inauguration of President Thabo Mbeki on 16 June 1999 marks a new era in South Africa's democratic transformation. President Mbeki's government is committed to speeding up the pace of transformation. At his inaugural speech, the new president gave eloquent testimony to this:

> Our nights cannot but be nights of nightmares while millions of our people live in conditions of degrading poverty. Sleep cannot come easily when children get permanently disabled, physically and mentally, because of lack of food. No night can be restful when millions have no jobs, and some are forced to beg, rob and murder to ensure they and their own do not perish from hunger.

The RDP was the ANC and democratic movement's stated means for ensuring peaceful nights and prosperous days.

Clearly much unfinished business lies ahead for the South African government, and as President Mbeki stated in 1998, the RDP remains "the combat orders of our movement as we continue the struggle for the genuine liberation of our people". President Mbeki gave the commitment that government will "further develop and refine the policies and programmes which will ensure that, over time, we achieve the objectives set out in the RDP".

The second democratic government requires an examination of the extent to which the existing approach to development met the commitment of the original RDP Base Document.

To this end the National Executive Committee of the African National Congress commissioned the RDP audit, which was conducted by a team of researchers at the University of the Witwatersrand School of Public and Development Management and the Human Sciences Research Council. A special word of appreciation is due to Minister Jeff Radebe (Head of ANC Policy), Smuts Ngonyama and Cheslyn Mostert for their sterling contribution and advice. I would also like to thank officials from various government departments for their assistance. This book is but one marker of the South African government's continuing commitment to reconstruct and develop a society still torn by conflict and underdevelopment.

Professor Yvonne Muthien
Executive Director: Democracy and Governance
Human Sciences Research Council
June 1999

An RDP Policy Audit

Table of Contents

List of Acronymns

ABET	Adult Basic Education and Training
ANC	African National Congress
CBPWP	Community-Based Public Works Programme
CGE	Commission for Gender Equality
COSATU	Congress of South African Trade Unions
CSIR	Council for Scientific and Industrial Research
CSS	Central Statistical Service
DCD	Department of Constitutional Development
DLA	Department of Land Affairs
DPW	Department of Public Works
DTI	Department of Trade and Industry
DWAF	Department of Water Affairs and Forestry
GDP	Gross Domestic Product
GEAR	Growth, Employment and Redistribution
IBA	Independent Broadcast Authority
IDT	Independent Development Trust
MECs	Members of Executive Council
NEDLAC	National Economic Development and Labour Council
NGOs	Non-Governmental Organizations
NURCHA	National Urban Reconstruction and Housing Agency
OBE	Outcome-Based Education
PHC	Primary Health Care
RDP	Reconstruction and Development Programme
SADC	South African Development Community
SA-EU	South African-European Union
SANCO	South African National Civic Organisation
SACP	South African Communist Party
SDIs	Spatial Development Initiatives
SMMEs	Small, Medium and Micro Enterprises
TPP	Ten Point Plan
VAT	Value Added Tax

Chapter One:
Introduction to the RDP Audit

This booklet assesses the first democratic South African Government's policies, legislation and delivery performance against the directives offered by the 1994 *Reconstruction and Development Programme* (RDP). The booklet focuses on the core directives in the RDP's Chapters Two-Five, which encompass the four areas of key concern: "Meeting Basic Needs", "Developing our Human Resources", "Building the Economy," and "Democratising the State and Society". (The RDP's first chapter is an introduction, while Chapter Six, on "Implementing the RDP", has few concrete policy directives and the final chapter is a brief conclusion.)

Each of the core RDP chapters sets out a broad problem statement associated with the subject at hand, followed by a vision and objectives. To a large extent, these introductory sections of each chapter offer thematic approaches which in this booklet are considered in broad terms. It is in the subsequent sections dealing with 34 different issue areas, that it is possible to establish precise mandates that government had in the wake of the first democratic election in April 1994.

The RDP itself went through six drafts in 1993-94. At the "Conference on Reconstruction and Strategy" in January 1994, the African National Congress, Congress of South African Trade Unions, SA Communist Party, SA National Civic Organisation, National Education Crisis Committee, and many other Mass Democratic Movement and related organisations made final amendments and approved the document as the "policy framework" and programme around which the ANC would contest the elections. The RDP booklet was issued in March 1994, and carried the endorsement by ANC President Nelson Mandela that it

represents a framework that is coherent, viable and has widespread support. The RDP was not drawn up by experts — although many, many experts have participated in that process — but by the very people that will be part of its implementation. It is a product of consultation, debate and reflection on what we need and what is possible.[1]

As expressed by Mandela at the ANC victory celebration on 2 May 1994,

> We have emerged as the majority party on the basis of the programme which is contained in the *Reconstruction and Development* book. That is going to be the cornerstone, the foundation, upon which the Government of National Unity is going to be based. I appeal to all leaders who are going to serve in this government to honour this programme.

Has the programme been honoured? To help the ANC National Executive Committee establish the extent to which the RDP mandate has been implemented through the national government's policies, laws and performance, *an RDP Audit* was conducted by researchers associated with the University of the Witwatersrand Graduate School of Public and Development Management and the Human Sciences Research Council in 1998-99, covering some 36 areas of sectoral policy, legislation and implementation. The Audit raw data took the form of a dense set of four tables (covering one RDP chapter each) with five columns — Issue, RDP Directive, Government Policy, Legislation, and Implementation — and several hundred issues.

This booklet presents a condensed version of the *RDP Audit*, with extensive endnotes that reflect the precise wording associated with the RDP and government policies, laws and delivery announcements. A typical paragraph begins with the issue area in bold type, a statement of the RDP directive (the first endnote reflects the precise wording), and whatever readily available, documented information from departments, ministries or other government sources that has a bearing on the issue in question.

With this information, readers can draw their own conclusions about how in various departments, the 1994-99 government succeeded in turning a broad electoral mandate into concrete policies and laws.

Chapter Two: Meeting Basic Needs

2.1 INTRODUCTION

The RDP's Chapter Two has more concrete policy directives than any other, reflecting the enormous apartheid backlog in meeting South Africa's basic needs. This chapter was also the most diverse in its authorship, drawing in hundreds of suggestions from the dozens of organisations and social movements with interests and expertise in areas of basic need.

2.2 VISION AND OBJECTIVES

The RDP made its highest priority "attacking poverty and deprivation",[2] and each of the eleven issue areas discussed below (2.3-2.13) provides details on how this was to be accomplished. However, several other cross-cutting themes were important components of the Meeting Basic Needs objectives, including affirmative action, gender equity, population and migration, and social/economic rights.

2.2.1 Affirmative action

The RDP called for affirmative action for "black people, women and rural communities" and in particular "vulnerable groups such as farm workers, the elderly and the youth".[3] Many policies were adopted (some specifically noted in later sections) to promote affirmative action, beginning with the *White Paper on Reconstruction and Development*.[4] A *White Paper on Affirmative Action* was completed by the Department of Public Service Administration in 1998, specifying mandatory requirements for the development and implementation of state affirmative action programmes. Regarding society more broadly, government's policy has included "anti-discriminatory measures to protect individuals combined with measures to encourage institutional and cultural change by employing organisations; [and] accelerated training and promotion for individuals from historically disadvantaged groups in this context ... with strong legal protection against discrimination and harassment"[5]. Addressing rural inequality, government established new "structures of local government and local coordination" and promoted "fair and equitable access to social welfare".[6] Disability issues received increasing attention in the Integrated National Disability Strategy.[7] Youth programmes are discussed in Chapter Three, below. To some extent, affirmative action initiatives were codified in law. In the workplace, the 1998 *Employment Equity Act* promoted "equal opportunity and fair treatment through the elimination of unfair discrimination; and ... positive measures to redress the disadvantages in employment experienced by black people, women and people with disabilities, in order to ensure their equitable representation in all occupational categories and levels in the workforce"[8]. As for implementation, there are no universally-accepted statistics available on the extent to which affirmative action has been achieved throughout the South African state and society, but in more precise areas discussed below, more concrete information is presented on the implementation of this broad objective.

2.2.2 Gender equality
The RDP insisted that women's concerns deserve "particular emphasis", beginning with a need to "recognise and address "gender inequities".[9] The extent to which the RDP itself represented an advanced statement of women's equality should itself be questioned and debated, but more importantly, government's concrete policies, laws and implementation in several areas are discussed below. An emphasis on women's concerns is mainly dealt with by government through the Commission on Gender Equality, whose aim, "as set out in section 119 of the *Constitution*, is to promote gender equality and to advise and make recommendations to Parliament or any other legislature with regard to any laws or proposed legislation which affects gender equality and the status of women".[10]

2.2.3 Population and migration
The RDP called for more attention to population and migration issues, including a committee to be established in the RDP Ministry.[11] A *White Paper on Population Policy* was published in 1998, mandating the President to oversee population policy, to liaise with the Cabinet Committee for Social and Administrative Affairs on population issues, to locate the National Population Unit in the Deputy President's Central Planning Unit, to take into consideration regional concerns about migration, and to ensure a high profile for National and Provincial

Population Units (the latter under the wing of provincial welfare MECs).[12]

2.2.4 Poverty statistics

The RDP called for the development of more sophisticated social statistics, in particular with regard to gender, race, income, rural/urban differences and age, and mandated the establishment of demographic maps to illustrate geographical location.[13] This mandate was accepted by several national departments (and appears in several white papers, including the *White Paper on Reconstruction and Development*, *White Paper for Social Welfare*, *White Paper on Population Policy*, and *Towards a National Health System*). From the outset the United Nations Development Programme's Human Development Index was given a high priority by Statistics South Africa (formerly Central Statistical Service). The Departments of Welfare and Health established statistical systems that focus on poverty, while the *White Paper on Population Policy* stipulated a disaggregation of data by gender, geographical area, age and other attributes.[14]

2.2.5 Social and economic rights

The RDP called for South Africa to sign and implement the International Covenant on Economic, Cultural and Social Rights and related conventions.[15] This was accomplished in 1994, and in 1996 South Africa also signed the African Charter on Human and People's Rights, and drafted a protocol for the African Charter on the establishment of an African Court of Human and People's Rights. In addition, South Africa's *Constitution* establishes social and economic rights, as described in Chapter Five.

2.3 JOBS THROUGH PUBLIC WORKS

2.3.1 Jobs for women and youth

To begin, the RDP highlighted the need for women and youth to become central beneficiaries of public works programmes.[16] This was established as policy in the *Public Works Green Paper* (1996) and *White Paper* (1997).[17] By the end of 1997, the Community-Based Public Works Programme (CBPWP) was responsible for 1 112 projects which provided 1,43 million days of work, of which 41% were accounted for by women and women-headed households[18] (although women were paid consistently less than men).[19] Youth payments were not measured.

2.3.2 Good wages and working conditions
The RDP also mandated public works projects to pay adequate wages and ensure good labour standards.[20] Policy papers endorsed this position[21] (with the exception of the 1997 *Rural Development Framework*),[22] and the Department of Public Works codified it in the Nedlac *Agreement on Job Creation in the Construction Industry*,[23] but debates continued about how far this had been (and could be) implemented. Evaluations of public works programmes indicated a large variance in wages paid, but on average the 1997 monthly wage was just over R500.[24] Formal construction industry wage rates were in the order of R50 per work-day (over twice as much as CBPWP workers received).

2.3.3 Community empowerment
In addition, community empowerment was an important RDP objective for public works programmes.[25] This was confirmed in the *Green* and *White Papers*,[26] but due to the difficulty in measuring such empowerment, the only data kept relate to training and skills development. The success of the programmes varied, with the percentage of workers receiving training ranging from 14% to 80%.[27] However, out of the initial R250 million CBPWP budget, a large share (R100 million) went to NGOs (of which a quasi-NGO, the Independent Development Trust, received R70 million).[28]

2.3.4 A national programme
The community programmes were meant, according to the RDP, to fit within a broader national programme.[29] Such a programme — the National Public Works Programme — did indeed encapsulate the CBPWP and other activities (such as transformation of the construction industry). Policy papers for the National Public Works Programme incorporated quite broad objectives (maintenance of public buildings; creating jobs and education/training opportunities; creating community assets; and providing relief during natural disasters).[30] There remained, however, questions about the national programme's implementation (with some evidence of corruption by officials in at least one major province, the Eastern Cape).

2.3.5 Rural bias

The RDP specified that these opportunities should be biased in favour of rural people.[31] This seems to have been accomplished (albeit at low wage levels),[32] with additional funds from the fast track poverty alleviation programme directed to rural areas of KwaZulu-Natal, the Northern Province and the Eastern Cape.[33]

2.3.6 Funding sustainability

It is worth noting that for a period in 1995-97, there was indeed some question as to whether the CBPWP would continue (it was not necessarily anticipated to do so in the 1996 *Green Paper*, because of weak performance and overlap of functions with other departments). But by 1997-98, there was more certainty about the CBPWP's future (even if funding allocations did not meet expectations).[34] For a recent R274 million allocation to the CBPWP (in 1998-99), Minister Radebe estimated that 60 000 temporary jobs would be created within a year along with 6 000 sustainable jobs, and there would be empowerment of 600-700 communities (involving 4 800-5 600 training opportunities for residents) in development management. At less than R5 000 per temporary job, this is considered an extremely good return on investment.[35] However, the RDP's calls for a Community Fund and for interrelationships with other development planning processes[36] appear to have gone largely unheeded.

2.4 LAND REFORM

The RDP put great emphasis on land reform, citing land as "the most basic need for rural dwellers" and aiming "to redistribute 30 per cent of agricultural land" by 1999.[37] Although the actual amount was a tiny fraction of the target, 814 rural land-related projects were implemented in 1997, improving the lives of 20 224 small farmers and their families, with more rapid delivery expected in 1998.[38] Policies adopted to support land reform targeted land redistribution, restitution (for those unjustly removed from their rural or urban land), and tenure reform, along with various other technical support and infrastructural services.[39]

2.4.1 Land redistribution

With respect, firstly, to land redistribution, the RDP envisaged acquisition of "land already on sale and land acquired by corrupt means from the apartheid state or mortgaged to state and parastatal bodies"; the need to "expropriate land and pay compensation as the *Constitution* stipulates"; recovery of "land acquired [by recipients] from the apartheid state through illegal means"; and the use of "land outside of the historically black areas".[40] A *White Paper on South African Land Policy* emerged in 1997 from a 1996 *Green Paper* (which stated that quantifiable targets were not feasible),[41] but existing laws proved inadequate for land redistribution processes.[42] However, the 1997 *White Paper* made provision for virtually all forms of land acquisition for redistribution.[43] In terms of implementation, though, progress was extremely slow; by the end of 1997 only about 25 000 households were beneficiaries of the various methods of land redistribution.[44]

2.4.2 Resources for land redistribution
One issue raised consistently in this regard was whether the Department of Land Affairs had been allocated sufficient budgetary resources to redistribute more than a nominal amount of land (a matter which the RDP also explicitly raised).[45] Not only was a small and (in real terms) declining amount budgeted,[46] the maximum amount of state subsidy was set at R15 000 (often not enough for an individual, even in combination with other settlers through a group grant, to purchase a viable piece of land).[47] Moreover, subsidised interest rates for land development were explicitly rejected by the Department of Land Affairs[48] (as well as by the Strauss Commission on rural credit), although the Land Bank ultimately adopted a different view. While the RDP advocated a land tax to promote land sales and gain further resources for rural infrastructure,[49] it was opposed as national policy by the Katz Tax Commission (which recommended municipalities tax land at a maximum of 2%).[50]

2.4.3 Land restitution
With respect, secondly, to land restitution, the RDP mandated an accessible, efficient Land Claims court to assess and redress forced removals dating to the 1913 *Land Act*.[51] The *White Paper on South African Land Policy* confirmed these intentions.[52] However, partly because of personnel problems in the Land Claims Commission, partly because of budgetary constraints, and partly because of the enormous complexity involved, only a tiny fraction of the 30 000 claims received by late 1998 had been resolved.[53]

2.4.4 Security of tenure

With respect, thirdly, to security of tenure, the RDP stressed its importance given how apartheid had uprooted millions from traditional farming areas.[54] Tenure rights were indeed established as policy [55]and in law (the 1997 *Extension of Security of Tenure Act* as well as the 1996 *Communal Property Associations Act* for the purpose of social ownership).[56] Policy was established for labour tenants, for farmworkers[57] and for land invasions that led to evictions.[58] In particular, the RDP highlighted how difficult it was for women to gain rural land security, due to traditional tenure arrangements and matrimonial laws.[59] Firm resolve to address gender discrimination was cited in the *White Paper*,[60] and implementation was supported by the establishment of a new Gender Sub-Directorate in the Department of Land Affairs.

2.4.5 Rural infrastructure

The RDP also mandated technical and infrastructural services for rural settlers, especially water supply,[61] in the light of the fact that even in late 1998 18 million people were without basic water supply and another 27 million had no basic sanitation. When translated into an investment programme (mainly by the Department of Constitutional Development in its *Municipal Infrastructure Investment Framework*), levels of rural infrastructure provision were far lower than those available in urban areas (due to larger geographic distances and hence higher costs, as well as lower incomes of rural beneficiaries).[62] In addition, the Department of Water Affairs and Forestry promoted rural water projects (see 2.6, below).

2.4.6 Capacity-building

Finally, rural capacity-building was highlighted in the RDP.[63] Translated into policy, there was some ambivalence expressed in the (Ministry of Reconstruction and Development's) *Rural Development Strategy* of 1995.[64] In terms of the implementation of capacity-building, the Department of Water Affairs and Forestry built up a large capacity in the area of institutional and social development for rural water projects.[65]

2.5 HOUSING AND SERVICES

2.5.1 Housing as a human right
One of the central RDP directives was the establishment of housing as a human right,[66] which was codified in the 1994 *White Paper*[67] and the 1996 final *Constitution*.

2.5.2 Delivery and budget targets
An extremely ambitious target was set of one million houses for 1994-99, to be paid for through generous budgetary allocations (5% of the state budget).[68] The ambitious goals were confirmed in a 1994 *White Paper* entitled *A New Housing Policy and Strategy for South Africa*.[69] (By 1995, however, the huge housing backlog, poverty and fiscal constraints were identified in an RDP Ministry *Urban Development Strategy* as prohibitive factors for the goal of universal housing access.)[70] Judging the implementation of the policy is less straightforward, however. On the one hand, it is evident that national budgetary resources allocated to national and provincial housing departments never came close to 5% (and indeed averaged closer to 1,5% over the 1994-99 period). On the other hand, estimating the numbers of houses built is more complicated. For while in July 1998, the Department of Housing stated that 596 059 of the promised one million low-cost houses had been completed, and the numbers of total subsidies approved had risen to 792 552,[71] definitions of what constituted a "house" remained up for debate.

2.5.3 Housing standards
The RDP offered explicit standards for an acceptable quality of housing, subject to community negotiation.[72] By 1998, the Housing Minister herself cited community anger about the quality of housing projects, inadequate construction standards in many of the houses delivered, the need for new minimum guidelines,[73] and reversed the *White Paper*'s antipathy to setting standards.[74]

2.5.4 Nature of housing subsidy
The precise character of the housing subsidies envisaged in the RDP (largely oriented to blending public-private funds and to promoting social, not individual, housing consumption)[75] was not endorsed in policy[76] (nor hence in law or implementation). It was generally acknowledged that the R15 000[77] maximum grant for housing (for households with less than

R1 500 per month income) could not finance sufficient covered space — in addition to an internal wet core and other facilities anticipated in the RDP — and that a "top-up" loan provided by a financial institution would be required.

2.5.5 Housing finance

Notwithstanding a 1994 "Record of Understanding" with the major banks, throughout the late 1990s most financial institutions appeared reluctant to grant housing credit to housing subsidy recipients (those that did often used a recipient's pension as collateral, a practice unprecedented for white borrowers). Housing finance mandates in the RDP (particularly the prohibition of "redlining" or geographical lending discrimination, and the desire for lower interest)[78] were not implemented in policy (and indeed were reversed insofar as state mortgage guarantees were denied to many dozens of townships, and low-value bonds were allowed to carry higher interest rates).[79] (However, on occasion, policy measures were threatened to prevent housing finance discrimination or at least improve disclosure.)[80] In addition, the handling of housing bond defaults in the interests of consumers (in part to promote social ownership and in part to allow defaulters who had lost their jobs to remain in their houses through demand-side mechanisms) was specified in the RDP in part because levels of default on late 1980s township houses had reached 40%.[81] But housing policy took a different route,[82] based on the establishment of several new institutions which aimed to normalise the home mortgage lending environment.[83] Nevertheless, typically only 15% of housing subsidy recipients received bank loans to top up the housing grant each year.

2.5.6 Building materials

In addition to commercial housing finance, the RDP also argued for a major state-led transformation in the construction and building materials industries,[84] but instead, policy favoured industry self-regulation.)[85]

2.5.7 Infrastructure standards

With respect to the quality of household infrastructural services, many of the post-1994 houses did not contain sanitary facilities and a household energy supply, as the RDP had mandated. To some extent this reflected decisions made in local settings to spend the R15 000 on a better dwelling rather than infrastructure; however, policy (established by the Department of Housing, RDP Ministry, and Department of Constitutional Development) also mandated relatively low standards.[86]

2.5.8 Entrepreneurial and community empowerment

There were other RDP housing directives. The RDP stressed empowerment of black entrepreneurs,[87] and although this was not considered a priority in housing policy,[88] in practice the uneven commitment by large established developers ensured some smaller contractors would gain increased business.[89] Likewise, the RDP anticipated that communities would be empowered,[90] which was confirmed by the *White Paper* (though with a qualification).[91] Assessing community empowerment implementation is extremely difficult and subjective, for some very good examples (the National Homeless People's Federation's many projects, for instance) of state support[92] did not outweigh the fact that traditional community organisations (such as civic associations) generally fared poorly in terms of gaining access to state (and donor) resources and capacity-building.

2.5.9 Housing legislation

The RDP also made explicit provisions for legislation in several areas of housing, including construction standards, tenants' and squatters' rights, community reinvestment by banks, evictions, consumer protection, land restoration, community participation in development, and anti-discriminatory protection.[93] These have been reflected unevenly in government policy and law since 1994, particularly in the 1997 *Housing Act*.[94]

2.5.10 Housing design

The RDP called for more sensitive housing design for household members (women, the elderly, disabled people) usually ignored by architects.[95] This proposal was partially codified in policy insofar as discrimination was concerned,[96] and more firmly addressed in law.[97] Disabled people were given special support in the Deputy President's *Integrated National Disability Strategy*, and by 1998 the Minister acknowledged lack of progress to date but committed more subsidy resources in future.[98] (Less progress could be reported on other groups' housing and community design requirements.)

2.5.11 Urban land for housing

As for state access to increased (and better-located) urban land for housing, the RDP made an ambitious call to break up land monopolisation,[99] which was to some extent addressed through the *Development Facilitation Act* of 1995[100] and other institutional mechanisms.[101] But given Constitutional property rights (hence the difficulty of land expropriation), the limited taxation of municipal land, and intense opposition from higher-income prospective neighbours (and their bankers) to Provincial Housing Board applications for well-located low-income settlements), most housing projects were "peri-urban" in character, on the outer edges of existing settlements. The distant geographical location of most post-1994 settlements pushed up the costs of infrastructure, but because land costs were less expensive and acquisition procedures usually easier, far-away locations were favoured by developers.

2.5.12 Housing tenure

Diverse forms of tenure were anticipated in the RDP,[102] which although codified in the 1994 policy[103] and 1997 law[104] (as well as in the 1998 *Housing Rental Act*, which protects tenants),[105] it was only at the Jobs Summit in 1998 that a realistic mass-rental housing programme was established by the state.

2.5.13 Hostel refurbishment

Hostels were also mandated for transformation in the RDP.[106] This was endorsed in policy[107] and some progress was made towards upgrading approximately a third of the country's 180 major hostels.[108]

2.5.14 Rural housing

Finally, rural housing was also emphasised in the RDP.[109] Although policy endorsed rural housing,[110] the policy mechanisms were not amenable,[111] leading to a reliance for implementation (particularly regarding farmworkers) upon a foreign donor[112] and promised changes in future policy.[113]

2.6 WATER AND SANITATION

2.6.1 Right to water
Underlying the RDP commitment to household water access was its depiction as a human right.[114] This right was considered in the 1994 *Water Supply and Sanitation Policy White Paper*,[115] given more power through the 1996 *Constitution*, made law in the 1997 *Water Services Act*[116] and indeed through the 1998 *National Water Act* became a law that operationalised the right in a National Water Reserve, superseding other (e.g. riparian) rights to water.[117]

2.6.2 Water projects
Implementation began and, although serious questions have been raised about rural water project sustainability, an enormous effort has been made by the Department of Water Affairs and Forestry to implement the right to water, with at least three million people having had (new) access to water at some point during the 1994-99 period.[118]

2.6.3 Water access targets
The concrete RDP goal was a short-term supply of 20-30 litres per person each day within 200 metres of the person's residence, and 50-60 litres in the medium-term.[119] However, because emergency short-term measures (e.g. sending government water tanker trucks to rural areas or squatter camps) were not universally implemented, millions of urban and most rural South Africans remained without the promised short-term water supply.[120] Moreover, water policy codified the short-term supply goals as the (only measurable) objective,[121] which led to the construction of many rural water projects (by government, private contractors and NGOs alike) that were too small (in engineering terms) to sustain demand as it rose beyond more than 25 litres per person per day (and as many rural people illegally attached their own yard or household piping into systems designed generally for only communal standpipes).

2.6.4 Definition of lifeline water supply
The key problem in sustaining many of the rural projects appeared to be affordability and the definition of a "lifeline" amount of water to be provided to consumers. Whereas the RDP mandated cross-subsidies — whereby big users would pay more for progressively larger consumption — and a lifeline supply (albeit with confused wording as to urban/rural

payment expectations, in relation to the operating and maintenance costs of water systems),[122] the definition adopted in the *Water Supply and Sanitation Policy White Paper* and the 1996 *National Sanitation Policy White Paper* was that the lifeline charge (for 25 litres) must be high enough to pay for operating and maintenance costs.[123] In contrast, when the national water reserve was defined in the 1997 *White Paper on a National Water Policy for South Africa*, the word "free" was associated with the need for national redistribution in order to support local lifeline services[124] (although the 1997 *Rural Development Framework* still insisted that national water cross-subsidies were impossible).[125]

2.6.5 Budgetary resources, pricing and disconnection

Government's ability to realise its citizens' right to water is, of course, dependent upon budgetary resources, something acknowledged in the 1994 *Water Supply and Sanitation Policy White Paper* (which unsuccessfully argued for a 2,24% allocation of the budget).[126] But in addition, addressing affordability requires institutional alignment within government, given municipal discretion in water pricing (partly guaranteed by the *Constitution*, and partly ensured through the Department of Constitutional Development's own policy guidelines on water and infrastructural services pricing). Broadly speaking however, the 1997 *White Paper on a National Water Policy for South Africa* and the 1997 *Water Services Act* both allowed the national minister to retain a great deal of discretionary power over both national and local water pricing[127] (not subsequently invoked). Notwithstanding the Constitutional provisions and lifeline supply policy, if consumers cannot afford to pay water bills, water disconnection has been deemed permissible under the 1998 *National Water Act*,[128] a matter not yet tested in the courts. Such cutoffs have occurred in many municipalities facing fiscal constraints, reportedly affecting hundreds of thousands of consumers.

2.6.6 Drought preparedness

In addition, the RDP cited the responsibility of the Department of Water Affairs and Forestry to address threats of drought,[129] a matter taken seriously in policy (although the 1995 *White Paper on Agriculture* and 1995 *Rural Development Strategy* were less willing to support drought relief in cases of poor risk management than the 1994 *Water Supply and Sanitation Policy White Paper* (which recognised the location of poor people in drought-prone areas).[130] Surveillance and monitoring of droughts (and in relation to water management more generally) were established in water legislation[131] and implemented through an InterMinisterial Committee.[132] In addition, the RDP stressed rural capacity-building,[133] something confirmed in policy[134] (including systems of private sector participation where rural municipalities are not capable of providing services).[135]

2.7 ENERGY AND ELECTRIFICATION

2.7.1 Alternative energy supplies
The RDP mandated a wide variety of urgent approaches to the expansion of household energy access, including better (more health and ecology-conscious) use of wood and coal resources as well as lower prices for paraffin and gas.[136] These were largely affirmed in policy (especially the 1996 *White Paper on Forestry* and the 1998 *White Paper on Energy Policy*).[137]

2.7.2 Electrification programme
Expansion of the electricity grid, including urgent access for schools and clinics, was a particularly high priority of the RDP.[138] Although the *South African Energy Policy Discussion Document* noted the problems associated with electrifying rural areas and schools,[139] subsequent policy documents endorsed the RDP household electrification targets.[140] By the end of 1997, nearly 60% of the population had access to electricity, in the wake of several years of more than 300 000 connections[141] (largely thanks to Eskom's own programme).[142]

2.7.3 Cross-subsidies and pricing
As ever, the RDP predicted that sustainability would depend on large-scale capital investment, creative financing and a recognition of low-income consumers' affordability constraints[143] (particularly in rural areas).[144] As in the case of water, this led to a debate over whether, as the RDP mandated, affordability problems should be solved through "cross-subsidies from other electricity consumers". Such cross-subsidies were opposed in the 1997 *Discussion Document on a Minerals and Mining Policy for South Africa* and the 1998 *White Paper on the Energy Policy of the Republic of South Africa*[145] (although they were mooted as an option in the 1997 *Rural Development Framework*).[146]

2.7.4 Sustainability of rural electrifictaion

Notwithstanding a real decline in electricity prices,[147] payment constraints soon led to a slowing of the pace of rural electrification. Because of affordability constraints, the *White Paper on Energy Policy* concluded, "Large-scale over-investment in rural electrification occurs while many urban areas remain unelectrified."[148] In fact, compared to the R12 billion in investments envisaged by the RDP from 1994-99, relatively small investments were made by Eskom and by municipal authorities.[149] One way of resolving the issue was to establish lower levels of minimum energy standards for low-income rural areas, which was endorsed in the 1995 *Rural Development Strategy* and codified in the 1997 *Municipal Infrastructure Investment Programme*.[150]

2.8 TELECOMMUNICATIONS

2.8.1 Telephone access

Another important area of infrastructure commitment was telecommunications, where an RDP commitment was made to universal access (a telephone outlet nearby) for all South Africans.[151] This was affirmed (and strengthened to promote affordable universal service — a phone in every dwelling) in the 1996 *Green Paper on Telecommunications Policy*[152] and in Telkom's own policies.[153] Also in 1996, the *Telecommunications Act* codified this in part through the establishment of a Universal Service Agency.[154] Telkom itself expanded its own grid by more than 250 000 units per year.[155] The RDP goal of providing telephones to all schools and clinics by 1996[156] was not met, though the *Green Paper* confirmed the broad objective.[157]

2.9 TRANSPORT

2.9.1 Expansion of public transport

The RDP emphasised the need to expand affordable public transport options, especially rail.[158] The Department of Transport's early policy papers — such as *Working Documents for Land Transport Bills Cross-Boarder Road Transport Bill* — instead reassessed state ownership of transport services and emphasised corporatisation of municipal services,[159] including rail.[160] The *Working Documents* policy targets for transport access were ambitious, and more detailed than those offered in the RDP.[161]

2.9.2 Transport resources

While subsidies to bus and rail remained substantial (R2 billion per year), and while registered use of public rail transport increased by slightly more than the growth in population,[162] the aggregate amounts available declined. Indeed, the transport budget was several billion rands per year short in terms of capital spending (particularly for new roads) due to fiscal constraints.[163]

2.9.3 Regulation of private transport

The RDP aimed to disincentivise individual automobile use by higher taxes and larger public transport subsidies.[164] Taxes and constraints on auto use were endorsed in the 1995 *Urban Development Strategy*, but subsidies were discouraged (a user-pays principle was recommended).[165] Formal transport policy was silent on means of effecting an incentive shift. The RDP also mandated stronger regulation of private transport.[166] However, policy favoured self-regulation,[167] with the exception of taxi transport which attracted an increased state role.[168] *The National Road Traffic Act* tightened other transport laws.[169]

2.9.4 Transport planning

The RDP stressed decentralised control of transport planning[170] yet at the same time more comprehensive, integrated planning.[171] Accountability was affirmed in the 1996 *White Paper on National Transport*,[172] as was integrated transport planning in the 1998 document *Moving South Africa*.[173] But notwithstanding the RDP proposal for a single transport agency to coordinate planning and financing,[174] which was affirmed in policy,[175] provincial capacity constraints proved to be serious barriers.[176] Some implementation was facilitated by the Department of Transport's role in the Spatial Development Initiatives.[177]

2.9.5 Special transport needs

The RDP mandated additional transport support for people with special needs,[178] as well as special attention to rural transport.[179] Although changes in transport policy for disabled people, women, children, scholars and pensioners were not specified, the commitment to rural areas was repeated in policy documents like the 1996 *Green Paper on National*

Transport Policy, *Rural Development Strategy* and *Rural Development Framework* (albeit at a low standard for roads).[180]

2.10 ENVIRONMENT

2.10.1 Environmental rights
The RDP considered a good environment to be a human right, and insisted on participatory policy processes to ensure that environmentalists and government agreed on how this should be realised.[181] Indeed, not only were environmental rights confirmed in the *Constitution*[182] and policy papers such as the *Green Paper on the Environment*; so too were participatory policy processes.[183]

2.10.2 Environmental impact assessments
The RDP also aimed to build environmental impact assessments into development projects,[184] in part through environmental management legislation and regulation.[185] This was confirmed in the *Green Paper*,[186] and in a 1997 amendment to the *Environmental Conservation Act*, environmental impact statements became compulsory for a "wide range of development activities"[187] (notably, for the first time, large dams).[188]

2.10.3 Waste management
With respect to waste management, the RDP promoted prevention and citizen watchdogging.[189] This was confirmed in the *Draft White Paper on Integrated Pollution and Waste Management*, including a commitment to "prevention and minimisation of waste generation and hence pollution at source".[190]

2.10.4 Environmental education
The RDP mandated more environmental education,[191] which was translated into policy[192] and programmes such as the Environmental Education Curriculum Initiative and the Broadening Participation Initiative.[193] Workplace environmental safety and health were also endorsed in the RDP,[194] in the *Constitution* and in environmental policy[195] (as well as Department of Labour policy).[196]

2.10.5 Marine resources management

The RDP environmental mandate included marine resources,[197] and a Marine Fisheries Policy emerged amidst other environmental policies.[198] Hotly debated on the West Coast where access to fishing is vital for livelihoods, the policy assured participation through a panel on access rights.[199]

2.10.6 Environmental disclosure

More generally, the RDP mandated increased transparency and disclosure,[200] which was translated into policy through the *Green Paper*'s call for "open disclosure, accessibility and effective dissemination of environmental data and information".[201]

2.11 NUTRITION

2.11.1 Nutritional rights

The RDP was extremely ambitious about food security, mandating complete coverage of food programmes within three years, as well as programmes to identify malnutrition.[202] The 1996 *Constitution* and the *White Paper for the Transformation of the Health System in South Africa* affirmed nutrition as a basic human right.[203] In addition to RDP "Mandela sandwiches" for schoolchildren, implementation took the forms of the 1997 National Integrated Nutrition Programme, a National Nutritional Surveillance System and 240 community-based nutrition projects.[204]

2.11.2 Food tax and price control

The RDP also mandated an end to Value Added Tax on basic food and price controls on bread,[205] neither of which were endorsed in either policy[206] or the national budget (aside from retaining bread and maize exemptions).

2.11.3 Food and agricultural regulation

RDP mandates to transform marketing boards, food-related monopolies, and tariffs in the interests of consumers[207] were modified by the 1998 *Agricultural White Paper for South Africa*.[208]

2.12 HEALTH CARE

2.12.1 Health system transformation

The RDP called for a complete transformation of the health system.[209] The 1997 *White Paper for the Transformation of the Health System in South Africa* confirmed the RDP framework to this end.[210] A great deal of legislation was passed to transform institutions and practices.[211]

2.12.2 Funding for health transformation

The RDP suggested a major budget shift from curative care to PHC,[212] which was confirmed in Department of Health policy and budgeting.[213] Construction of primary clinics received a major share of new health funding.[214] Rural health services were in particular need of increased resources, according to the RDP.[215] This is recognised in the policy document *Towards a National Health System* as well as in the *Rural Development Framework*.[216]

2.12.3 Implementation of health system changes

Implementation was uneven. For example, the RDP's promotion of community participation in health care and community health workers[217] was partially endorsed in policy (community workers were excluded in the policy document *Restructuring the National Health System for Universal Primary Health Care*),[218] but implementation was often limited to community consultation on programmes rather than actual delivery.[219] District Health Authorities were endorsed by the RDP as key implementing agents,[220] and this was carried through into policy (noting the possible involvement of accredited private providers)[221] and implementation.[222]

2.12.4 Free primary health care

The RDP's conception of a national health care programme was premised on the Primary Health Care (PHC) approach and made provision for free primary care in many instances.[223] Preventive and promotive health programmes for children were encouraged.[224] The Department of Health's subsequent policy was strongly oriented to PHC[225] and did (immediately) make free primary care available to pregnant women and children under six, and in 1996 expanded the coverage to include (for permanent residents) "all personal consultation services, and all non-personal services provided by the publicly funded PHC system".[226] But implementation at provincial level was uneven, with many provinces still limiting their free services to pregnant women and young children in 1999. Preventive and promotive programmes for infants and children were, however, quite strongly supported.[227]

2.12.5 Maternal and child health
In relation to maternal and child health, specific RDP mandates included indirect support (such as transport) and ambitious free coverage targets,[228] which were mainly endorsed in policy[229] and quite effectively implemented.[230] Six months of (paid) maternity leave (and some paternity leave) was endorsed in the RDP,[231] but this was lowered to four months unpaid leave in the document *Employment Standards Statute: Policy Proposals*[232] and then in the *Basic Conditions of Employment Act.*[233]

2.12.6 Reproductive rights
Access to abortion was promised in the RDP,[234] and this was confirmed in policy,[235] in the 1996 *Choice of Termination of Pregnancy Act*[236] (notwithstanding extensive challenge from the Religious Right) and in 1997 implementing regulations.[237]

2.12.7 Health workers
The RDP called for redeployment of health workers,[238] which in policy was translated, in part, into a legal requirement that recent graduates do community service.[239] This was implemented in 1998 to augment the use of Cuban and other foreign doctors in rural settings.[240] More appropriate PHC-oriented training was also mandated in the RDP[241] and confirmed in the *National Human Resource Development Policy.*[242]

2.12.8 Essential drugs
Finally, the RDP emphasised the need for better access to essential drugs.[243] Government established an Essential Drugs List as policy in 1996,[244] legislated the *Medicines and Related Substances Control Amendment Act* in 1997,[245] and proceeded with implementation[246] notwithstanding subsequent constitutional debates surrounding intellectual property rights and the importation of generic drugs.

2.13 SOCIAL SECURITY AND SOCIAL WELFARE

2.13.1 Scope of social security

Given racial and geographic discrimination in welfare and pension allocation, the RDP called for a special focus on the needs of domestic workers, agricultural workers, seasonal workers, workers who are disabled, women, the homeless, and families living in rural and informal settlements.[247] These objectives were recognised in the *Draft White Paper for Social Welfare*[248] and in law (e.g. the *Welfare Laws Amendment Act* and *Not-for-Profit Organisations Act).*[249] However, severe fiscal constraints reduced the per capita amount available for some grants (the Child Support Grant witnessed massive increases in beneficiaries, but the resulting initial cuts in per capita grants were, after public protest, partially reversed).[250]

2.13.2 Empowerment

But rather than simply expanding existing charity programmes, the RDP highlighted the need for empowerment,[251] which was rephrased as "community development" in policy.[252] This entailed welfare projects more directly aimed at fighting poverty, as well as other reforms to grants systems fraught with corruption.[253]

2.13.3 Consultation and intersectoral planning

Coordination of welfare policy and law through consultative processes was recognised as necessary in the RDP[254] and in the *Draft White Paper.*[255] In practice this took the form of the National Interim Consultative Committee on Developmental Social Services.[256]

2.13.4 Pensions

Provision was also made in the RDP for transforming the state pension system.[257] Government policy partially endorsed RDP suggestions, and further advocated that all people in formal employment belong to a compulsory retirement scheme, that social assistance be continued, and that savings systems be promoted to supplement retirement income.[258]

2.13.5 Child/youth welfare

The welfare of children and youth was also given prominence in the RDP, with many suggested policies.[259] Some were endorsed as formal policy in the *Draft White Paper*,[260] and numerous practical programmes and protective laws were established.[261]

2.13.6 Social welfare personnel

Finally, the RDP envisaged a retraining and dramatic increase in social welfare personnel.[262] Training and job equity were recognised as policy priorities in the *Draft White Paper*.[263]

Chapter Three: Developing our Human Resources

3.1 EDUCATION AND TRAINING

3.1.1 Compulsory school education for all

The RDP established ambitious schooling targets, including education for at least ten years, with all classes having 40 or fewer students.[264] Government mandated that from ages seven to fifteen, schooling would be compulsory in the 1995 *White Paper on Education and Training*[265] and the 1996 *South African Schools Act*.[266] But this right was, as ever, subject to available financial resources. Procedures for school governing bodies to augment their resources through setting (and waiving) student fees were established in the document *Norms and Standards for School Funding*.[267] Government legislated in the *South African Schools Act* that education should be free of charge to a student if annual school fees are more than 10% of the parents' income (with partial fees exemption in cases of between 3,3% and 10%).[268] One of the Presidential Lead Projects was the Culture of Teaching and Learning Project, which aimed to improve the quality of school facilities.

3.1.2 Prioritisation of women and youth

The RDP commitment to education highlighted the needs of women and youth, especially in rural areas.[269] Educational biases — particularly against girls in mathematics and science — were identified for removal in the *White Paper*,[270] the 1996 *National Education Policy Act*[271] and rural policy strategy documents.[272] In addition, Youth Colleges are being created by provincial departments to cater for out-of-school youth.

3.1.3 Educational governance

Democratic school governance was advocated in the RDP, with roles for parents, teachers and students.[273] Provisions appeared in the *South*

African Schools Act[274] (including funds for training),[275] and implementation appears to have been nearly universal.[276]

3.1.4 Qualifications framework
The establishment of the South African Qualifications Authority was mandated in the RDP[277] and affirmed in the *White Paper*.[278] Implementing agencies (the National Standards Bodies and Education, Training and Quality Assurance Bodies) were set up and the National Qualifications Framework was established in 1997.[279]

3.1.5 Early childhood development
The RDP emphasised public funding and standards for educare.[280] While the *White Paper* confirmed state responsibility for "curriculum frameworks and related advice on teaching methodology", the policy concluded that "responsibility for provision" would lie "with non-government, community-based and private providers, resource and training agencies."[281] However, there was a degree of public support for pilot Early Childhood Development projects.[282]

3.1.6 Adult basic education
The RDP argued that Adult Basic Education and Training (ABET) should be "centrally included" in development projects, based on partnerships between various roleplayers.[283] Such partnerships were confirmed in the *White Paper*.[284] A separate ABET policy was agreed upon by late 1997, followed by a curriculum process and the development of a recognised qualification.[285]

3.1.7 Special education
The RDP argued that disabled students required special educational support.[286] The *White Paper* established a National Commission on Special Needs in Education,[287] which in 1997 made recommendations for special education policy, programmes and projects.[288]

3.1.8 Curriculum reform
Though not specified in detail, curriculum reform was promoted in the RDP.[289] The *White Paper* advocated a National Institute of Curriculum Development and more attention to science and mathematics.[290] A new national "Curriculum 2005" geared towards outcomes-based education was established in 1997.[291]

3.1.9 Further education

After a period of compulsory education, the RDP mandated access to further (certificated) education that would blend with training opportunities.[292] Subject to available resources, expanded pre-employment training, vocational training, skills development and remedial courses were endorsed in the *White Paper*, the 1997 *National Youth Policy* and the 1998 *Skills Development Act*.[293] A National Committee on Further Education was also established.[294]

3.1.10 Higher education

The RDP insisted on a "representative and expert higher education commission" to resolve various problems in tertiary education.[295] The National Commission on Higher Education was appointed in 1995[296] and led (by order of the 1997 *Higher Education White Paper* and *Higher Education Act*) to the appointment of a Council on Higher Education.[297] The *Act* gave the Council important advisory powers, especially through its Higher Education Quality Committee.[298] In addition, the *National Youth Policy* stressed information technology centres for access to distance education.[299]

3.1.11 Teachers, educators and trainers

The RDP saw a need to overhaul training of educators, a more appropriate industrial relations system, and better salaries and conditions of service.[300] Advice on the teaching of teachers would be provided by the Technical Committee on the Revision of Norms and Standards for Educators[301] (which produced *Norms and Standards for Educators* in 1998) and by the Committee for Teacher Education Policy.[302] As for conditions of service, the 1998 *Employment of Educators Act* established a South African Council of Educators to define educator rights and responsibilities.[303]

3.1.12 Skills training

The RDP insisted that training programmes be restructured and expanded, and incorporate (amongst other components) prior learning and experience.[304] Some of government's policies were based on National Training Board recommendations,[305] some were built into Curriculum 2005,[306] and others followed from new labour skills upgrading policies, considered in Chapter Four.

3.2 ARTS AND CULTURE

3.2.1 Resources for community arts facilities
In order to promote "the production and the appreciation of arts and culture", the RDP advocated subsidisation for community arts centres to be located across South Africa, and consistent support from formal, democratic Arts Councils in each region.[307] This was endorsed in principle (albeit in the context of fiscal restraint) in the *White Paper on Arts, Culture and Heritage*.[308] A first tranche of R50 million was budgeted by the Department of Arts, Culture, Science and Technology for 43 projects in 1997, of which R22 million had been spent on 15 of the projects by October 1998.[309]

3.2.2 Accessible heritage facilities
The RDP called for resources to promote access to the heritage of South Africa's "many different (cultural) strands".[310] This objective was confirmed in the *White Paper* and the 1996 *National Heritage Act*,[311] and the 1998 Legacy Project aims to develop heritage sites.[312]

3.2.3 Education in arts and culture
Amongst RDP mandates for arts/culture education were its promotion within national school curricula (at all levels), teacher training, and better arts facilities.[313] The *White Paper* confirmed this as policy, and expanded it to include community libraries and resource centres.[314] The Department of Arts, Culture, Science and Technology began working with the Department of Education's National Standards Body to implement improved arts education in the schools.[315]

3.2.4 Arts/culture links to development
The RDP advocated concrete linkages — hence more thorough-going support — of arts and culture to health, housing, tourism and other areas of development.[316] This was broadly confirmed in the *White Paper*,[317] and the 1997 Cultural Industries Growth Strategy began to serve as a basis for implementation.[318]

3.2.5 Diversity in languages
The RDP advocated "utilisation of all the languages of South Africa" and promoted the Pan South African Language Board.[319] This mandate was confirmed in the *White Paper* and made law even earlier, in the 1995 *Pan*

South African Language Board Act.[320] A Multilingualism Campaign was launched in 1998 and the *Act* was strengthened.[321]

3.2.6 Existing arts/culture institutions
The RDP insisted that all publicly funded and parastatal culture and arts structures (which were beneficiaries of apartheid cultural support) be democratised within two years.[322] The *White Paper* confirmed the gradual appointment of more representative boards and the opening of their facilities, but also reported on their defunding.[323]

3.2.7 International exchange
The RDP promoted global intercultural exchanges,[324] which was endorsed in the *White Paper* (with special reference to the region).[325] In 1997, 70 arts and culture exchanges were funded by the Department of Arts, Culture, Science and Technology.[326]

3.2.8 Film and audio-visual industry
The RDP mandated a statutory national body to promote the film and audio-visual industry.[327] Following the 1996
Film Development Strategy,[328] the 1997 *National Film and Video Foundation Act* established an arms-length funding agency to this end.[329]

3.2.9 Tax incentives
To promote arts/culture investment, the RDP advocated tax breaks,[330] but this was not deemed possible in the *White Paper.*[331]

3.3 SPORT AND RECREATION

3.3.1 Access to sport and recreation
The RDP mandated accessible, affordable, developmental sports and recreation, particularly in rural areas.[332] This was confirmed in the 1995 *Getting the Nation to Play White Paper,*[333] and the National Department of Sport began erecting facilities in rural areas in 1996.[334]

3.3.2 Special needs of youth
The RDP advocated the prioritisation of facilities in places "where there are large concentrations of unemployed youth", and that special attention be paid to differing levels of abilities.[335] This prioritisation was confirmed in *Getting the Nation to Play* and the *National Youth*

Policy.[336] Progress in implementing the construction of 126 facilities was made, based on a R50 million allocation in 1996.[337]

3.3.3 Coaching and drug control
The RDP advocated the strict control of drugs through an independent national sports agency, and the establishment of a national academy for training coaches and managers.[338] These were confirmed in the *White Paper*.[339] Feasibility studies began on a national sports academy.[340] The *White Paper* recommended a code of ethics for sport and recreation,[341] and the 1997 *South African Institute for Drug-Free Sport Act* established an institute to control drugs and educate sportspeople.[342]

3.4 YOUTH DEVELOPMENT

3.4.1 Employment and reconstruction
The RDP called for a national youth service programme (and legislation and an institution) that would ensure youth had a productive role in South Africa's development (while not undermining permanent workers).[343] The ideas of National Youth Service and Youth Career Guidance Centres were confirmed in various policy documents, including the *White Paper on Reconstruction and Development*, the Department of Public Work's *White Paper*, the *White Paper for Social Welfare* and the *National Youth Policy*.[344] Indeed in addition to the latter policy, the *National Youth Commission Act* was passed in 1996,[345] and was followed by a *National Clearing House for Youth Employment and Entrepreneurship* publication and a *Green Paper on National Youth Service* in 1998.[346]

3.4.2 Children
The RDP mandated the new government to sign the International Convention on the Rights of the Child and promote child welfare in development.[347] Parliament ratified the Convention in 1995, but the Cabinet's Interministerial Steering Committee which favoured a national programme for children recommended against in order to more consistently thread children's interests through the RDP.[348] The Department of Welfare promoted children's interests in the *Not-For-Profit Organisations Act* and the *Welfare Amendment Act* as well as through programmes.[349]

Chapter Four: Building the Economy

4.1 INTRODUCTION

4.1.1 Character of the economy

The RDP's principles for economic policy included "democracy, participation and development". The RDP carefully avoided overt ideological bias when describing "the leading and enabling role of the state, a thriving private sector, and active involvement by all sectors of civil society". With regard to nationalisation or privatisation, according to the RDP, "the balance of evidence" would be the basis for judgement on a case-by-case basis.[350] As President Mandela expressed it in 1998, "We shall privatise where necessary. But we shall also set up new state enterprises where market imperfections and failures play themselves out to undermine social programmes."[351] Since 1994, a few sectors saw increased state ownership or intervention (e.g. in mineral and water rights), but the *White Paper on Reconstruction and Development* set the tone by promoting the sale of state assets for the purpose of building the RDP Fund,[352] and in 1996, the *National Framework Agreement*[353] and *GEAR* described a variety of means of restructuring state assets.[354] The largest single private sector participation was the 30% stake offered in Telkom (for R5,7 billion) in 1997 (other state assets for sale included radio stations, resorts, airlines, forests and diamond mines).[355] In some cases (such as water services), legislation (the *Water Services Act*) and agreements with organised labour suggested that "all known public sector providers" be given an opportunity to bid for a state contract prior to private outsourcing or privatisation.[356]

4.1.2 Objectives

The RDP objective of building "a strong, dynamic and balanced economy" included many components, of which the first listed was to "eliminate the poverty, low wages and extreme inequalities in wages and wealth generated by the apartheid system, meet basic needs, and thus ensure that every South African has a decent living standard and economic security".[357] The 1996 *Growth, Employment and Redistribution* (*GEAR*) macroeconomic framework did not focus on these latter, points but instead prioritised objectives such establishing "a competitive platform for a powerful expansion by the tradable goods sector; a stable environment for confidence and a profitable surge in private investment; a restructured public sector to increase the efficiency of both capital expenditure and service delivery; new sectoral and regional emphases in industrial and infrastructural development; greater labour market flexibility; and enhanced human resource development".[358] One RDP goal was reducing inequality in all government programmes,[359] which was partially endorsed in *GEAR* particularly through the removal of structural and racial workplace barriers.[360]

4.1.3 Targets
Two goals of the RDP were 5% annual GDP growth and the creation of as many as half a million (non-agricultural) jobs per year by 1999.[361] Likewise, *GEAR* anticipated a 6% GDP growth rate and 400 000 jobs per year by 2000.[362] Neither set of targets would be reached: annual real GDP growth peaked at 3,5% in 1995 before falling to around 0,5% in 1998, and approximately 500 000 net (non-agricultural) jobs were lost from 1994-98.

4.1.4 Economic policy negotiations
The RDP advocated a corporatist approach to policy-making, involving "the democratic government, the trade union movement, business associations and the relevant organisations of civil society".[363] This was endorsed in the *White Paper on Reconstruction and Development*, and in *GEAR* in the form of a "national social agreement" (and more restraint in collective bargaining).[364] The National Economic Development and Labour Council (NEDLAC) was established and the *NEDLAC Act* passed in 1994, but although numerous sectoral accords were developed,[365] the a national social agreement binding all parties to macroeconomic policy remains elusive.

4.1.5 Human resources development
The RDP stressed training of workers as a central economic strategy,[366] which was endorsed in *GEAR*,[367] and, through the *Skills Development Act*, mandated a small levy on payrolls.

4.2 INTEGRATING RECONSTRUCTION AND DEVELOPMENT

4.2.1 Location of economic activity

The RDP called for attention to the implications of macro-economic policy on the geographic location of economic activity, and advocated spatial development that was informed by existing problems such as "the excessive growth of the largest urban centres, the skewed distribution of population within rural areas, the role of small and medium-sized towns, and the future of declining towns and regions, and the apartheid dumping grounds[368]. The *Rural Development Framework* attempted to locate rural economic development within a macroeconomic policy context,[369] while the *Urban Development Strategy* discounted large cities as an issue and opposed measures that would "artificially induce or restrain growth in a particular centre, region or tier"[370]. Apartheid policies had attempted such inducement and restraint, and while the RDP attacked apartheid-era decentralisation subsidies, these were considered so vital to many impoverished areas that their redirection within local communities was recommended.[371] Instead, a new Regional Industrial Location Strategy phased out the decentralisation subsidies, and in 1996 replaced them with a tax holiday and other industrial incentives based on regional location, job creation and priority industries.[372] Spatial Development Initiatives soon became the major source of subsidies for (and planner of) new regional location trends.[373]

4.2.2 Local economic development

The RDP called for support (and where necessary, subsidies) to promote community-controlled local economic development.[374] This objective was endorsed in the *Urban* and *Rural Development Strategies*[375] and is being implemented by the Department of Constitutional Development (although financial support is not specified).

4.2.3 Rural development

The RDP's visions of rural economic development were to a large extent grounded in meeting the backlog of basic needs, including land and infrastructural services,[376] and with support (rural financial services, in particular)[377] to small and micro enterprises.[378] An expanded set of objectives were established in the *Rural Development Framework*,[379] including local service centres to assist entrepreneurs.[380] Finance would be provided, according to the *Rural Development Strategy*, but — with the exception of the Land Bank — preferably through (non-subsidised) guarantee schemes rather than direct state lending.[381]

4.2.4 Rural capacity-building and training

The RDP advocated support for local government and civil society capacity-building and organising, including the promotion of locally-based Community Development Officers.[382] Capacity-building support was offered in the *White Paper on Reconstruction and Development*, but aside from noting potential funding from the National Development Agency, the *Rural Development Strategy* and *Rural Development Framework* were ambivalent.[383] The RDP also promoted extensive training and retraining for rural community and agricultural workers.[384] These were endorsed in the *Rural Development Framework*[385] and the *Policy Document on Agriculture*.[386]

4.3 INDUSTRY, TRADE AND COMMERCE

4.3.1 Industrial policy

The RDP's strategy for industrial growth was multifaceted. It promoted greater technological capacity, and aimed to make South Africa "a significant exporter of manufactured goods", while at the same time rooting industrial development in expanded "infrastructure to urban, peri-urban and rural constituencies" so as to "support and strengthen those internationally competitive industries that emerge on the basis of stronger internal linkages, meeting the needs of reconstruction and raising capacity utilisation".[387] *GEAR* focused primarily on promoting an "outward-oriented industrial economy" based on "more labour-intensive components of industry".[388]

4.3.2 Export promotion

In a context of more rapid integration into the world economy, the RDP mandated export promotion yet, at the same time, more equitable sharing of the costs of adjustment to freer trade.[389] Targeting of potential "winner" export industries was advocated in *GEAR*,[390] and implemented not only through SDIs and industrial cluster support (see above) but also through the Industrial Development Corporation.[391]

4.3.3 Competition policy

To promote domestic competitiveness, the RDP advocated "strict anti-trust legislation" (to apply also to parastatal agencies), in part based on a "commission to review the structure of control and competition" in the economy.[392] Before the commission had been established, in 1997 *Proposed Guidelines for Competition Policy* were issued and subjected to debate within NEDLAC, and parastatals were also included.[393] These objectives were codified in the 1998 *Competition Act*.[394]

4.3.4 Regional trade

On trade within Southern Africa, the RDP called for "more balanced and less exploitative trade patterns"[395]. Government policy (especially *GEAR*) was more concerned with simple expansion (not balancing) of regional trade.[396] To this end, the *Protocol on Trade in the Southern African Development Community* promoted liberalisation (with the end goal of a Free Trade Area for the region), partly through cross-border Spatial Development Initiatives.[397] However, complaints mounted from neighbouring countries about South Africa's huge and growing net regional trade surplus.

4.3.5 Trade and tariffs

The RPD acknowledged the need for lower tariffs, but called for "reducing protection in ways that minimise disruption to employment and to sensitive socio-economic areas" (including Southern African regional interests). The bias against smaller exporters should be reversed, according to the RDP, through measures such as "short-term export finance to small business".[398] *GEAR* acknowledged the need for "long-term survival strategies ... for certain sensitive sectors" but mainly promoted the rapid reduction of tariffs and export subsidies.[399] However, the Department of Trade and Industry retained the ability to introduce tariffs as part of its industrial policy toolkit.[400]

4.3.6 Black economic empowerment

The RDP confirmed that a "central objective" was "to deracialise business ownership and control completely", even if that required the supply of capital from state and parastatal institutions and affirmative action in tendering.[401] Some such support was given through the establishment of a National Empowerment Fund, provisions for black empowerment in the

Competition Act, and policy aimed at promoting joint (black empowerment) ventures with overseas firms.[402]

4.3.7 Foreign investment

The RDP called on foreign investors to create jobs, transfer technology and knowledge, and provide opportunities for worker participation.[403] *GEAR* stressed concessions to be made by the South African government (and workers).[404] Such investment promotion attracted R32 billion in foreign direct investment from 1994-98.[405]

4.3.8 Black small business development

The RDP provided an extensive set of suggestions for promotion of emergent small businesses (especially those run by women), including state provision of infrastructure and skills, pressure on financial institutions to expand their lending to black-owned enterprises, a transformation of the various state business-promotion agencies, and generous procurement policies for black businesses (particularly in social and economic infrastructure investment).[406] The Department of Trade and Industry established a variety of new institutions in terms of this mandate,[407] and — through the 1996 *National Small Business Act* — a National Small Business Council.[408] Many of these institutions were open for business by 1997,[409] although they did not gain immediate support from, for example, the banking fraternity.[410] (In its 1998 *Financial Access for SMMEs* policy, the Department of Trade and Industry encouraged guaranteed municipal procurement contracts to serve, in turn, as a collateral base for banks,[411] but this does not appear to have been attractive to lenders.) Moreover, tendering by the state and parastatal agencies was uneven,[412] and notwithstanding good support from the Department of Public Works in its "Ten Point Plan" and the *Green Paper on Public Sector Procurement Reform in South Africa,* there remained many barriers to small black business involvement.[413]

4.3.9 Gender and small business

Gender equality was an RDP priority[414] and was confirmed not only by the Department of Trade and Industry in the 1995 *White Paper on National Strategy for the Development and Promotion of Small Business in South Africa,*[415] but also by several other departments in the *First South African Report* of the *Convention for the Elimination of all Forms of Discrimination against Women.*[416]

4.3.10 Local service centres

The RDP called for the doubling of satellite centres to provide entrepreneurs with assistance.[417] This was endorsed in the *White Paper*[418] and resources were made available by 1997 to dramatically expand the Ntsika service centre support programme.[419]

4.3.11 Technology and SMMEs

The RDP suggested that state technology resources be directed to SMMEs, including "appropriate and sustainable technologies for the rural areas".[420] To this end, the CSIR became more active in these areas,[421] the Department of Trade and Industry Competitiveness Fund to promote SMME technology was established,[422] and a Technopreneur Programme was piloted in several colleges to complement the Technology and Human Resources in Industry Programme.[423]

4.3.12 Technology and gender

The RDP encouraged the promotion of girls' and women's opportunities in technology-related fields.[424] This was confirmed in the *White Paper on Science and Technology*, *the Education White Paper* and the *Green Paper for the Introduction of Technology Education*.[425]

4.3.13 Import of technology

The RDP feared dependence upon foreign technology and made provision for local training and maintenance, as well as limits on royalties and fees.[426] This was endorsed in the *Green Paper on Public Sector Procurement Reform in South Africa*.[427]

4.3.14 Military to civilian technology conversion

The RDP advocated the conversion of military to civilian technological utilisation.[428] This was initially considered "not tenable" by the *White Paper on Science and Technology*,[429] yet with the forthcoming privatisation of Denel and its first financial loss in 1997, a reorientation of its business towards commercial activities was planned.[430] However, the Department of Trade and Industry has also provided resources aimed at making defence-related industries more competitive.[431]

4.3.15 Private sector technology needs

The RDP mandated the establishment of a "strong coordinating agency" for technology support to "key stakeholders".[432] Such cooperation was

endorsed in the *White Paper on Science and Technology*, and *GEAR*
mandated the Department of Trade and Industry's technology transfer
programme to promote "access by firms to needed technologies".[433]

4.3.16 Commerce policy
The RDP's agenda for wholesale and retail trade included more
"geographically balanced and accessible distribution, lowered costs of
distribution, modernised linkages between production and distribution, and
greater participation by black people in the distribution chain".[434] This
has not been translated into policy to date.

4.4 RESOURCE-BASED INDUSTRIES

4.4.1 Minerals ownership
Arguing that "the minerals in the ground belong to all South Africans,
including future generations", the RDP called for "the return of private
mineral rights to the democratic government".[435] Although an early
Discussion Document on a Minerals and Mining Policy for South Africa
as well as the October 1997 *White Paper: Mineral and Mining Policy for
South Africa* vested "the right to prospect and to mine for all minerals" in
the state, the latter also confirmed existing users' rights to "the
continuation of current prospecting and mining operations in accordance
with the 'use-it and keep-it' principle"[436] in part because of "the
constitutional constraints of changing the current mineral rights
system".[437]

4.4.2 Minerals beneficiation
The RDP called for a raised "level of mineral beneficiation through
appropriate incentives and disincentives" in order to create jobs and
produce "more appropriate inputs for manufacturing."[438] Subsequent
policy called on beneficiation for "the maximum benefit of the entire
population" (including downstream linkages) and advocated "lower royalty
rates" and other tax concessions for firms that engaged in
beneficiation.[439] But limited job creation in beneficiation projects
continued to be of concern.

4.4.3 Local buyers of raw materials
While the RDP advocated that government should consider encouraging
companies to "sell to local industries at prices that will enhance their

international competitiveness",[440] subsequent policy discouraged government intervention. In the case of SA firms' sale of minerals, steel and other products overseas at prices below those offered to South African producers (which have attracted international sanctions), the *White Paper* rebutted, "All measures which restrict the sale of South African minerals on foreign markets will be opposed."[441]

4.4.4 Economic democracy in mining
The RDP advocated worker participation and "workplace democracy" through negotiation and meaningful "financial participation by workers in mining companies".[442] The *White Paper* committed government to a "wider spread of ownership" of mines, and stated that government would "encourage real worker participation in the management of all mines".[443] Particularly in relation to problems faced by the gold industry, government helped establish a Gold Crisis Committee with a strong labour input, whose purposes included "reviewing proposed retrenchment notices submitted by the industry to the committee, and recommending other alternatives".[444]

4.4.5 Alleviating structural decline
In cases of mining exhaustion or declines in mineral prices that would lead to mine closure, the RDP recommended a careful phasing out and "reskilling and training of workers for other forms of employment".[445] The *White Paper* confirmed that "Government will endeavour to ameliorate the social consequences of sizeable downscaling and mine closure".[446] As an example, the Gold Crisis Committee "saved up to 42% of the jobs that were threatened".[447]

4.4.6 Mineworker rights
The RDP aimed to substantially upgrade the rights of mineworkers.[448] The *Discussion Document* endorsed improved working conditions and better enforcement, improved access to mineworker education and training, and improved housing and living conditions.[449] The June 1996 *Mine Health And Safety Act* confirmed these rights in law, provided for worker representatives, and established a Mine Health and Safety Council.[450] In 1997, the law took effect, the Council was established, amendments were agreed between labour and mining firms, and a 10% reduction in fatalities was recorded that year.[451]

4.4.7 Mining and the environment

The RDP called for tougher legislation and comprehensive environmental impact studies prior to new mining activity.[452] The *Discussion Document* instead stipulated the "maintenance of balanced and responsible standards with regard to the interface between mining and the environment that are based on local needs and requirements".[453] However, environmental legislation[454] and other financial provisions regulate this interface.[455]

4.4.8 Regional cooperation in mining

The RDP called for a regional investment facility to help develop Southern African mineral resources.[456] Although endorsed in the *Discussion Document*, this evolved into *White Paper* advocacy of the "comprehensive dismantling of foreign exchange controls", removal of "barriers to the movement of labour, capital, goods and services ... cross-border mineral processing" and "regional cooperation in technology development".[457]

4.4.9 Small-scale mining

Although the RDP called for more support to small-scale mining — financial/technical aid and access to mineral rights — it insisted on good "environment, health and safety and other working conditions".[458] Most of these provisions were endorsed in the *White Paper*.[459]

4.4.10 Agricultural objectives

The RDP argued for state services "including marketing, finance and access to cooperatives" (for "small and resource-poor farmers, especially women") but at the same time the removal of "unnecessary controls and levies as well as unsustainable subsidies" so that agriculture could provide "affordable food to meet the basic needs of the population" as well as "household food security".[460] The *Agriculture White Paper* agreed on the need to "improve national as well as household food security" and at the same time, a variety of subsidised support and marketing systems oriented to white farmers were dismantled, and others set up for small black farmers.[461]

4.4.11 Farm labour

The RDP called for labour law to be applied to commercial farming ("with specific provisions").[462] The *White Paper* included other goals, such as "organisation, good labour relations, the appropriate training of farm workers and finding a balance between labour and mechanisation".[463] The 1995 *Labour Relations Act* applies to farm labour,[464] security of tenure has been improved for labour tenants thanks to the 1997 *Security of Tenure Act*,[465] and a variety of other initiatives have been taken to improve farmworker living conditions.[466]

4.4.12 Agricultural efficiency
The RDP endorsed "efficient, labour-intensive and sustainable methods of farming", including drought risk management.[467] These were endorsed in the *White Paper*.[468]

4.4.13 Agricultural beneficiation
The RDP recommended "additional processing and value-adding activities derived from agriculture" (including goods for the tourist industry),[469] which were endorsed in the *White Paper* and *Policy Document on Agriculture*[470] and began to be implemented.[471]

4.4.14 Institutional arrangements for fisheries
The RDP made various recommendations for restructuring departments associated with fisheries and forestries (as well as a Coastguard),[472] but these were not adopted in the 1997 *Marine Fisheries Policy for South Africa*.[473]

4.4.15 Forestries regulation
With respect to forestries, the RDP recommended stricter land use regulation in sensitive areas.[474] This was endorsed in the 1996 *Green Paper for Environmental Policy for South Africa*[475] and soon led to a National Forestry Action Programme,[476] which in turn has led to some forests (particularly in fragile ex-homeland areas) being targeted for decommissioning.

4.4.16 Mass tourism
The RDP emphasised the need to develop a local mass tourism market, particularly by supporting black entrepreneurship.[477] The *White Paper on Development and Promotion of Tourism in South Africa* endorsed mass market tourism by the previously neglected.[478] The *White Paper* also endorsed training programmes to promote black entrepreneurship in tourism.[479]

4.4.17 Eco- and cultural tourism

In addition to South Africa's extensive natural resources, the RDP advocated that "cultural and political heritage" also be marketed to tourists.[480] This was reflected in the *White Paper*'s commitment to "responsible tourism"[481] and in various heritage projects.[482]

4.4.18 Community role in tourism

The RDP recommended different kinds of state support for community-based tourism, including "finance, management skills, upgrading of tourist service skills, language proficiency and connections with marketing infrastructure".[483] The broad concept (as well as training programme adaptation to communities) was endorsed in the *White Paper* as part of its conceptualisation of responsible tourism.[484]

4.4.19 Regional approach to tourism

The RDP proposed more active regional relationships in the tourism sector,[485] which the *White Paper* endorsed.[486]

4.4.20 Tourism and the environment

The RDP mandated environmental impact analysis for tourism projects.[487] The *White Paper* endorsed ongoing social and environmental audits,[488] and the *Environmental Conservation Act* makes such assessments compulsory.[489]

4.5 UPGRADING INFRASTRUCTURE

4.5.1 Electrification and SMMEs

In addition to meeting basic household consumption needs, the RDP advocated making the same "cheap electricity" enjoyed by large corporations available to small businesses.[490] The *South African Energy Policy Discussion Document* recognised the importance of electricity,[491] but pricing for small users remained much higher per kilowatt — hour than for large users.

4.5.2 Goals of telecommunications

In addition to universal telecommunications access (see Chapter Two), the RDP mandated that the "basic infrastructural network must remain within the public sector" and that a regulatory authority be established.[492] In 1996, the *Telecommunications Act* gave Telkom ongoing public responsibility and rights, and a South African Telecommunications Regulatory Authority was established.[493]

4.5.3 Transport regulatory review

The RDP called for a review of all transport systems and their mode of regulation.[494] This was begun in 1995.[495] The 1996 *White Paper* broadened the review beyond the National Transport Commission, Road Transportation Boards and other existing regulators, and advocated the setting up of a Maritime Safety Agency, Aviation Safety Agency, and Road Agency for primary roads.[496]

4.6 REFORM OF THE FINANCIAL SECTOR

4.6.1 Goals of financial regulation

High amongst the RDP's many goals in the financial sector were accountability, transparency and extending financial services to those who presently do not have access to these services.[497] These objectives were partially addressed in the 1998 Department of Trade and Industry policy document, *Financial Access for SMMEs*.[498]

4.6.2 Prohibition of financial discrimination

The RDP suggested a variety of anti-discriminatory measures for the financial sector, covering race, gender, location and other non-economic factors.[499] Some of these were confirmed as possibilities in the 1994 *Housing White Paper*[500] as well as in *Financial Access for SMMEs*.[501] However, the RDP mandate to consider removing the Usury Act exemption was contradicted in *Financial Access for SMMEs*.[502]

4.6.3 Housing bank, guarantee and low bond rates

The RDP envisaged a "Housing Bank to ensure access to wholesale finance" (backed by a Guarantee Fund), which would be subsidised to lower the interest rate for home loans.[503] The *Housing White Paper* placed emphasis on commercial banks and deemed a Housing Bank "necessary" but set up a fund (the National Housing Finance Corporation) to on-lend wholesale funds (at market rates).[504]

4.6.4 Community banking

The RDP suggested that the state "encourage community banking", by changing regulations (while protecting consumers) and placing accounts in community banks.[505] The document *Financial Access for SMMEs* confirmed the need to review the *Mutual Banks Act* and consider deposit insurance.[506]

4.6.5 Pension and mutual funds
The RDP called for pension/mutual funds to be more accountable to members, and for Mutual Funds boards to be transformed.[507] The 1996 *Pension Funds Amendment Act* protected pension members.[508]

4.6.6 Reserve Bank
The RDP recognised the Reserve Bank's insulation from "partisan interference" but argued that in order to carry out its developmental duties a new board of directors was necessary (to include trade unions and civil society).[509] The final (1996) *Constitution* maintained the need for the Reserve Bank to operate "independently and without fear, favour or prejudice",[510] and the 1996 *South African Reserve Bank Amendment Act* legislated only that board members would be elected half by government and half by shareholders (mainly commercial banks).[511] In terms of accountability, an existing law mandates the Reserve Bank governor to report regularly to parliament.[512]

4.6.7 Capital flight
The RDP called on government and the Reserve Bank to intervene more actively against "illegal capital flight"[513] than they had earlier, under existing exchange controls.[514]

4.7 LABOUR AND WORKER RIGHTS

4.7.1 Workers' constitutional rights
The RDP mandated that the *Constitution* contain worker rights to organise, strike and gain access to relevant employer information (and it also opposed any right of employers to lock out workers).[515] Aside from information access (provided for in the 1995 *Labour Relations Act*), such rights were included in the *Constitution* (the lock-out clause was excluded)[516] and in the 1997 *Basic Conditions of Employment Act*.[517]

4.7.2 Living wage
The RDP had ambitious objectives for workers, including a living wage, a healthy and safe working environment, collective bargaining, minimum

wage regulation, affirmative action, education, training, technological development, and provision of services and social security.[518] Various initiatives were taken to these ends. For example, following the Labour Market Commission, the *Growth, Employment and Redistribution* policy recommended a minimum wage on a sector-by-sector basis (with subminimum wages for trainees),[519] but within the context of what the 1996 *Green Paper* on *Policy Proposals for a New Employment Standards Statute* first termed "regulated flexibility".[520] Other initiatives were also contained in the *Basic Conditions of Employment Act.*[521]

4.7.3 Collective bargaining

In its endorsement of collective bargaining, the RDP mandated that industrial bargaining agreements "should be extended through legislation to all workplaces in that industry".[522] Such agreements were given more weight in the *Labour Relations Act* — especially for conclusion of collective agreements, enforcement of agreements and prevention of labour disputes — but *GEAR* noted that the Minister of Labour's "discretion to extend or not to extend agreements should be broadened to permit the Minister to bring labour market considerations into play".[523]

4.7.4 Workplace empowerment

The RDP advocated various rights to promote worker participation and empowerment,[524] many of which were included in *Labour Relations Act* provisions for the workplace forum.[525]

4.7.5 Access to information

The RDP called for amendments to company and tax law so as to provide workers more information about their employers.[526] The *Labour Relations Act* limited this to "all relevant information" for the workplace forum to engage in joint decision-making.[527]

4.7.6 Use of incentives

The RDP envisaged the use of state incentives, tenders, subsidies and similar mechanisms to advance "worker rights, human resource development and job creation".[528] These were endorsed through mechanisms such as tax benefits for labour-intensive regional investments, the *National Youth Policy* and the procurement policy.[529]

4.7.7 Affirmative action
Affirmative action was endorsed by the RDP, in part to "address the disparity of power between workers and management".[530] Workplace measures in policy and law included the *Policy Proposals on Employment and Occupational Equity,*[531] the *White Paper on Affirmative Action in the Public Sector*[532] and the *Employment Equity Act.*[533]

4.7.8 Prohibition of sexual harassment
The RDP called for legislation and education to end sexual harassment.[534] The *Green Paper on Policy Proposals for a New Employment and Occupational Equity Statute* and the *Labour Relations Act* prohibited sexual harassment or related forms of discrimination.[535]

4.7.9 International conventions
The RDP mandated the government to ratify International Labour Organisation convention related to freedom of association, collective bargaining and workplace representation.[536] These were recognised in Department of Labour policy[537] and ultimately ratified.[538]

4.8 SOUTHERN AFRICAN REGIONAL POLICY

4.8.1 Regional relations
The RDP endorsed "African integration as laid out in the Lagos Plan of Action and the Abuja Declaration" and advocated joining not only the Southern Africa Development Community, but other regional fora.[539] Indeed South Africa led SADC in 1998,[540] and in a variety of regional fora promoted regional cooperation.[541]

4.8.2 Regional trade and industrialisation
The RDP called for "more balanced trade" and "industrial development throughout the region".[542] Although South Africa's regional trade surpluses grew,[543] there were prospects for a regional free trade agreement[544] and for recognising Southern Africa's development needs within the framework of the SA-EU trade agreement.

4.8.3 Regional worker relations
The rights of workers across the region to organise were defended in the RDP.[545] This was ultimately, however, a matter for individual countries to decide upon.

4.8.4 Regional cooperation

The RDP envisaged regional technical and scientific cooperation in areas including agricultural, environment and health.[546] This cooperation expanded into areas such as tourism development.[547]

Chapter Five: Democratising the State and Society

5.1 INTRODUCTION

The RDP was about "democratising power".[548] The *White Paper on Reconstruction and Development* declared democracy as "an active process enabling everyone to contribute to reconstruction and development".[549] The 1996 *Constitution* declared as a fundamental goal the creation of "a united and democratic South Africa".[550]

5.2 THE *CONSTITUTION*

5.2.1 Socio-economic rights
The RDP mandated the authors of the final *Constitution* to ensure that "social, economic, environmental and peace rights are more fully embodied in the Bill of Rights".[551]
Provisions enshrined in the *Constitution* included rights to a healthy environment, adequate housing, health care (including reproductive care), food, water, social security and access to a basic (and further) education.[552]

5.2.2 Gender equality
The RDP argued that the *Constitution's* "fundamental equality of men and women ... must override customary law".[553] That equality was confirmed in the *Constitution*.[554] In 1995, South Africa signed the International Convention for the Elimination of Discrimination Against Women.[555] The *Commission on Gender Equality Act* was passed in 1996, giving power to investigate and evaluate all sectors of society.[556]

5.2.3 Property rights
The RDP did not endorse property rights fully, and instead argued for "the regulation of the use of property when this is in the public interest"

and also mandated "a right to restitution for victims of forced removals".[557] According to the *Constitution*, "Property may be expropriated only in terms of law of general application for a public purpose or in the public interest and subject to compensation", and a "community dispossessed of property after 19 June 1913 as a result of past racially discriminatory laws or practices is entitled ... either to restitution of that property or to equitable redress".[558]

5.2.4 Central state power
The RDP called for "sufficient central government powers so as to coordinate and implement the RDP effectively".[559] (The RDP function was initially located in the office of the President.) Among the President's responsibilities, according to the *Constitution*, are "developing and implementing national policy [and] coordinating the functions of state departments and administrations".[560]

5.3 NATIONAL AND PROVINCIAL ASSEMBLIES

5.3.1 Legislative procedures
The RDP mandated extensive changes in the national and provincial assemblies, including legislative procedures, the operating procedures of standing committees, inputs from interested parties, and a members' Code of Conduct.[561] These were confirmed in the *Constitution*, and in laws such as the *Public Protector Act 23 of 1994*, the *Executive Members' Ethics Act 62 of 1998* and the *Remuneration of Public Office Bearers Act 20 of 1998*.[562]

5.4 NATIONAL AND PROVINCIAL GOVERNMENT

5.4.1 Redistribution to provinces
The RDP mandated the Financial and Fiscal Commission to develop formulae so that "all provinces receive an equitable share of revenue collected nationally."[563] This was confirmed in the *Constitution*, with the proviso that the equitable share be used to "provide basic services and perform the functions allocated ..."[564] Legislation included the 1996 *Borrowing Powers of Provincial Governments Act*, the 1997 *Intergovernmental Fiscal Relations Act*, and the 1997 *Financial and Fiscal Commission Act*.[565]

5.4.2 Institutional change
The RDP called for "RDP structures" at all levels of government and "restructuring of present planning processes" and rationalisation of delivery systems.[566] This mandate was repeated in the 1994 *RDP White Paper*, although many RDP structures were dissolved following the 1996 closure of the national Ministry in the President's Office.[567]

5.5 SECURITY FORCES

5.5.1 Security force control
The RDP called for non-partisan security forces under civilian control and answerable to parliament.[568] This was confirmed in the *White Paper on National Defence for the Republic of South Africa*.[569] By 1997, the Department of Defence had transferred the Head of Department role and Accounting Officer function from the control of the Chief of the National Defence Force, to the Secretary for Defence, who is accountable to parliament.[570]

5.5.2 South Africa's defence
The RDP called for the defence force's "size, character and doctrines" to be "appropriate", given reconstruction and development priorities.[571] The *White Paper on National Defence* confirmed that (instead of the military), "The RDP is the principal long-term means of promoting the security of the citizens and thereby, the stability of the country."[572] The Defence Review confirmed the "primarily defensive nature" of the Department of Defence.[573]

5.5.3 Police reform
The RDP mandated the police to gain "representivity and gender and human rights sensitivity", and to be more accountable to communities.[574] The Independent Complaints Directorate was one means by which the *National Crime Prevention Strategy* envisaged the police service's transformation.[575]

5.6 THE ADMINISTRATION OF JUSTICE

5.6.1 Judicial system reform
The RDP called for a more accessible, affordable, credible, legitimate judicial system with a professionalised Attorney-General's office, simplified language and procedures, more appropriate public defenders, rights of appearance in court for paralegals, and a fund for women's legal aid.[576] The National Directorate of Public Prosecutions was established to professionalise prosecutions, although language and procedures have not changed and paralegals do not have status. The Legal Aid Board is being overhauled and the legal aid system is transforming from a judicare system to one with a greater emphasis on public defenders. In terms of the Industrial and Labour courts, the RDP anticipated that NEDLAC would have a role in appointments.[577] The *Constitution* gives the courts a strong foundation with respect to promoting their "independence, impartiality, dignity, accessibility and effectiveness".[578]

5.7 PRISONS

5.7.1 Prison administration and prisoner rights
The RDP, concerned about the "present military command structure" of prisons, mandated a transformation in staffing.[579] The Department of Correctional Services demilitarised and changed the character of prison management hierarchies and reported success with affirmative action.[580] The RDP also highlighted prisoners' human rights, their "full constitutional protection" and the need to rehabilitate prisoners.[581] These were codified and amplified in the *White Paper on the Policy of the Department of Correctional Services in the New South Africa,*[582] the 1998 *Correctional Services Act*[583] and the 1997 *Abolition of Corporal Punishment Act.*[584] By way of implementation, a new disciplinary code was introduced, and copies of the *Constitution* and human rights training were made available to prison managers. Meeting prisoners' basic needs — "right to life, food, clothing, medical care, hygienic facilities and contact with family" — as well as access to education (especially literacy) and training programmes, are now considered mandatory.[585] The RDP also attacked existing disciplinary codes in prisons, including solitary confinement and dietary punishment.[586] However, the *Correctional*

Services Act made provision for solidarity confinement, if ordered by an Inspecting Judge.[587]

5.7.2 Imprisoned children

The RDP demanded reform of practices that lead to the mistreatment of children in prison.[588] A ban on imprisoning unconvicted children was confirmed in the *White Paper*,[589] although the norms for brief detention of children (and exceptions for imprisonment) were set out in the 1996 *Correctional Services Amendment Act*.[590] Special needs of children in detention were legislated in the *Correctional Services Act*.[591] By way of implementation, the Department of Correctional Services is promoting correctional institutions and programmes for child and youth offenders.[592]

5.7.3 Pregnant women and infants

The RDP also mandated better treatment of pregnant prisoners and mothers in prison with children.[593] The Department of Correctional Services' *White Paper* committed the department to providing a mother and child unit where children (below the age of five) receive "food, clothing, health care and facilities for the sound development of the child".[594] The department began implementation and also drafted a prison care policy based on the international Convention on the Rights of the Child.[595]

5.7.4 Public and state monitoring of prison conditions

The RDP insisted on public oversight and an independent watchdog to be informed about and take action on unacceptable prison conditions.[596] The *White Paper* welcomed the role of the Public Protector to this end, and the *Correctional Services Act* created the Judicial Inspectorate of Prisons to monitor conditions and receive complaints.[597]

5.8 RESTRUCTURING THE PUBLIC SECTOR

5.8.1 Public sector restructuring and affirmative action

The RDP called for an "extensive programme of affirmative action" in the civil service, including a "defined quota of all new employees" from previously disadvantaged racial and gender groups, to achieve representivity within two years.[598] The *Constitution* mandated that "public administration must be broadly representative of the South African people, with employment and personnel management practices based on ability, objectivity, fairness and the need to redress the imbalances of the past to achieve broad representation".[599] A *White Paper on Affirmative Action* was completed by the Department of Public Service Administration in 1998, specifying mandatory requirements for the development and implementation of state affirmative action programmes. And the 1998 *Public Service White Paper* set the management quota level — for the year 2000 — at 50% black and 30% (of new recruits) women (as well as 2% of all employees being disabled workers).[600] The Department of Public Service and Administration's *Public Service Staff Code* requires monitoring of and reporting on progress made.[601] The RDP also mandated the Public Service Commission to oversee affirmative action, as well as a Code of Conduct.[602] The *Public Service Commission Act* confirmed these responsibilities,[603] and the 1997 Presidential Review Commission and the *Batho Pele White Paper on Public Service Delivery* set about implementing the programme.[604]

5.8.2 Public service training
The RDP envisaged transformation of the Civil Service Training Institute as well as opening such training to NGO development workers.[605] This mandate was confirmed in the 1994 *White Paper on Reconstruction and Development*,[606] and partially in the 1997 *Green Paper* and 1997 *White Paper on Public Service Training and Education*, which established a Public Service Education and Training Authority to oversee training programmes.[607]

5.8.3 Worker participation
The RDP mandated a new public sector labour relations policy aimed not only at ending "corruption, mismanagement and victimisation in public institutions" but also promoting "participation of public sector workers and their organisations in decision-making".[608] Employer accountability to workers was endorsed in the *Green Paper on Policy Proposals for a New Employment and Occupational Equity Statute* and given institutional support through the Public Service Co-ordinating Bargaining Council.[609]

5.8.4 Parastatal reform
The RDP called for parastatals, public corporations and advisory boards to be restructured, with formal civil society representation (mandated by "appropriate organisations").[610] The RDP also demanded tighter

accountability.[611] Some restructuring of parastatals was mandated through the 1996 *National Framework Agreement*,[612] which included regulatory reform.[613]

5.8.5 Development funding
The RDP advocated that development funds "should vest in a competent and legitimate government agency".[614] *GEAR* noted progress in reforming public development finance institutions[615] and a National Development Agency was established (following the Transitional National Development Trust) to channel funds to civil society development organisations.

5.9 LOCAL GOVERNMENT

5.9.1 Local government
The RDP called for local government to be democratic, non-racial and non-sexist, and for councillors to adopt a developmental attitude.[616] The *Constitution* confirmed the importance of the municipal sphere of governance.[617] In addition to the 1993 *Local Government Transition Act*, a variety of Department of Constitutional Development policy documents on local government included the 1995 *Towards a White Paper on Local Government in South Africa: A Discussion Document*, the 1997 *Green Paper on Local Government*, the 1998 *White Paper on Local Government*, and the 1998 *Support Framework for Implementing the Local Government White Paper*, which together provided a vision of democratic local government.

5.9.2 Final local government arrangements
The RDP insisted that due to their unrepresentative character, "councils of local unity" should be removed from the final *Constitution*.[618] The *Constitution* defined the sphere of local government without the *Local Government Transition Act* compromises.[619] Although the 1996 *Local Government Transition Amendment Act* confirmed the unrepresentative ward system,[620] the 1998 *Municipal Structure Act* made no provision for its retention after 1999.[621]

5.9.3 Amalgamation and boundary demarcation
The RDP called for a rationalisation of local governments from more than 800 to around 300, with demarcation of boundaries that link wealthier to

poorer municipal areas.[622] The *White Paper on Local Government* confirmed the amalgamation process,[623] and detailed instructions were provided to the Municipal Demarcation Board in the *Local Government: Municipal Demarcation Act*.[624]

5.9.4 Rural local government

The RDP envisaged rural areas ("including traditional authority areas") having democratic local government, with a strong role for Rural District Councils.[625] As the *Rural Development Strategy* put it, "Local authority structures will form the crucial first link with communities."[626] Specific rural local government functions were described in the *Rural Development Framework*.[627] The role of traditional leaders was delimited in the *Council of Traditional Leaders Act*[628] and the *Municipal Structures Act*,[629] but promoted through the National Council of Traditional Leaders (founded in 1997).[630]

5.9.5 Metro government

The RDP called for "strong metropolitan government" in major urban centres to better coordinate local economic activity.[631] The *Municipal Structure Act* set out the metropolitan government ("megacity") option,[632] and the *White Paper on Local Government* specified Greater Johannesburg, Greater Pretoria, Cape Town, Durban, Lekoa-Vaal and Kayalami as metropolitan governments.[633]

5.9.6 Local government financial legacy

The RDP recognised that the enormous (R1,8 billion) Black Local Authority debt would have to be written off, and that municipal financing would immediately change from the apartheid segregation model to "one city, one tax base",[634] These objectives were provided for in the 1994 *Agreement on Local Government Finances and Services*[635] and the *White Paper on Reconstruction and Development*, as well as a variety of specific Department of Constitutional Development policies (listed above).[636]

5.9.7 Local services

Notwithstanding other provisions for national-level redistribution through cross-subsidisation (of water and electricity, described in Chapter Two), the RDP also argued that locally, "the total body of consumers should be responsible for the cost of the service, including capital improvements" but this was meant to "allow for cross-subsidisation of new consumers" through "progressive" tariffs "to address problems of affordability". In addition, municipalities were to receive "inter-governmental transfers from central and provincial government".[637] A constitutional provision enforced the municipal responsibility for meeting constituents' basic services needs.[638] If not through national cross-subsidisation, to some extent the necessary funds were provided on the basis of the 1998 Department of Finance policy, *The Introduction of an Equitable Share of National Raised Revenue for Local Government*.[639]

5.9.8 Municipal workers

The RDP called for rationalisation of municipalities to occur after consultation with municipal trade unions, and indeed that such unions should enjoy centralised bargaining.[640] Centralised bargaining became general policy for labour-management relations,[641] with the *Local Government White Paper* specifying the role of the South African Local Government Bargaining Council.[642]

5.9.9 Local government training

The RDP called for transformation of bodies such as the Training Board for Local Government Bodies, the Institute of Town Clerks and the Institute of Municipal Treasurers and Accountants.[643] Such transformation was not specified in local government policy or law.

5.9.10 Women in local government

The RDP called for municipalities to speed up gender equity by establishing a women's portfolio and by using contracting capacity to promote women's interests.[644] These did not become formal policy.

5.9.11 Participation of civil society

The RDP called for transparency and public participation,[645] which the *Constitution* confirmed.[646]

5.10 CIVIL SOCIETY

5.10.1 Resources for and organisation of civil society

The RDP was ambitious in envisaging the expansion of civil society organisations (and their own need to increase their accountability to constituents), calling on the state to provide "capacity-building assistance ... funded through a variety of sources ... Every effort must be made to extend organisation into marginalised communities and sectors like, for instance, rural black women".[647] These provisions were confirmed by the *White Paper on Reconstruction and Development*,[648] but although a Transitional National Development Trust and National Development Agency were founded, a great many civil society organisations suffered large funding cuts (and organisational demobilisation) after 1994.

5.10.2 Role in policy-making
The RDP argued that "mass organisations must be actively involved in democratic public policy-making", including "international trade and loan agreements".[649] The *White Paper on Reconstruction and Development* agreed to a civil society role "in planning and policy-making through a variety of advisory boards, commissions, forums and other venues".[650]

5.10.3 Social and economic rights
To promote social and economic constitutional rights, the RDP advocated that the Human Rights Commission have "wider popular involvement" and an extended brief so as "to ensure that social and economic rights are being met".[651] This was endorsed by the *Constitution*.[652]

5.10.4 Forums
The RDP considered multipartite socio-economic forums "an important mechanism for broad consultation on policy matters", although inherited forums were to be restructured at national, provincial and local levels.[653] This respect for forums was confirmed in the *White Paper on Reconstruction and Development*[654] and in legislation such as the *NEDLAC Act*.

5.11 A DEMOCRATIC INFORMATION PROGRAMME

5.11.1 Information policy
The RDP envisaged "open debate and transparency in government" — including "exchange of information within and among communities and between the democratic government and society as a two-way process" — as well as more developmental media, yet without a heavy-handed state imposing "unwarranted intervention".[655] Both the *White Paper on Reconstruction and Development*[656] and the final *Constitution*[657]

affirmed this right, and the *Open Democracy Bill* was drafted in 1998.[658] In 1994 the RDP Ministry established a National Information Management System. The South African government hosted an Information Society and Development Conference in 1996 and launched a National Information Technology Forum for stakeholders. In addition, the *Science and Technology White Paper* created instruments to enable the Democratic Information Programme, including an IT Foresight Exercise, an Innovation Fund, and the *Legal Deposits Act*. Finally, the Department of Trade and Industry continued to develop its IT Industry Strategy project.

5.11.2 Media diversity

The RDP sought to correct numerous biases in the existing public media, calling for "new voices at national, regional and local levels, and genuine competition rather than a monopoly of ideas". Among the concrete suggestions to improve media diversity were granting "resources needed to set up broadcasting and printing enterprises at a range of levels; training and upgrading, and civic education to ensure that communities and individuals recognise and exercise their media rights", as well as anti-monopolisation measures against media groups.[659] Such diversity and affirmative action were endorsed, in principle, in telecommunications policy[660] and the *Competition Act* was passed in 1998 which applies to the media. The Department of Communications endorsed education and training in a policy, *The Information Society and the Developing World: A South African Approach.*[661] In addition, the Independent Broadcasting Authority granted licences in part based on improving the diversity of media holdings, and Government Communications promoted community-based media through the expansion of tele-centres and by launching a Media Development Agency which will address issues of media diversity and community media development.[662]

5.11.3 SA Communications Service

The SA Communications Service was mandated by the RDP to provide "objective information about the activities of the state" as well as facilitate freedom of information.[663] The Government Communication and Information System was inaugurated in 1998 to this end.[664]

5.11.4 Regulatory institutions

The RDP mandated several new regulators, including an Information Development Trust, Independent Broadcasting Authority, Public

Broadcaster Board, and voluntary regulatory mechanisms for private media.[665] Broadcasting regulation was affirmed in the *Constitution*.[666] The 1996 *Telecommunications Act* established the SA Telecommunications Regulatory Authority (whose responsibilities have included the development of a new Frequency Spectrum system, Internet policy, the Joint Economic Development Programme of MTN and Vodacom, the 30% privatisation of Telkom, and licences for a third cellular phone network). Notwithstanding fraud at the Independent Broadcasting Authority (IBA) uncovered in 1997, the IBA had in 1995 conducted the "Triple Enquiry Study" to develop regulations on cross ownership and control of media, local content issues, and the Public Broadcasting Service Mandate. The IBA also licensed South Africa's first private commercial television, granted licences to 160 Community Radio stations, drafted a new Public Service Broadcasting charter, established a policy for an advertising Code of Conduct, and drafted a satellite broadcasting policy paper. The 1999 *Broadcasting Act* establishes new rules for broadcasting. Also in 1999, the State IT Agency was launched as the central mechanism for procuring, purchasing and developing standards, and harmonising all government and public sector IT needs.

Chapter Six: Conclusion

The RDP as a tool of government policy was formally downgraded in March 1996 (the RDP Ministry was closed and the RDP Fund returned to the Ministry of Finance for disbursal). Yet over two years later (in a speech given to the SA Communist Party Congress), ANC President Thabo Mbeki made clear the durability of the original programme as ANC policy:

> The tasks thrown up by the society we inherited are clear enough. Working together we identified them in the *Reconstruction and Development Programme.* They remain, still, as we elaborated them in that *Programme* and therefore constitute the combat orders of our movement as we continue the struggle for the genuine liberation of our people. They also continue to require that we further develop and refine the policies and programmes which will ensure that, over time, we achieve the objectives set out in the RDP.[667]

There are many ways of determining whether RDP "orders" were followed. For example, as the preceding pages often demonstrated, fiscal constraints posed a recurrent barrier to the RDP's implementation. Although the government controlled nearly R1 trillion (R1 000 billion) in expenditures over the five fiscal years from 1994-99, a great deal of spending was non-discretionary. The initial strategy of establishing an RDP Fund — which from 1994-96 amounted to nearly R15,5 billion[668] — was in part meant to ensure that state resources could be redeployed.

But following funding flows is often a sterile exercise, compared to a comparison of the mandates given in the RDP and the policies, laws and delivery record of the first democratic government. The previous pages (and the following notes) have attempted to make such a comparison, but without undertaking the impossible task of providing any kind of "score" or mark, subjective or otherwise.

Still, it must be stated that there are areas not only of convergence between RDP directives and government policy/laws/delivery, but also of divergence. In public administration and political science, there are usually four capacity-related reasons for divergence between promises and reality: lack of "political will," lack of financial/fiscal resources, lack of administrative capacity, and logistical difficulties. In addition, it may also have been the case in some or many areas of the RDP that political leaders and officials "learned by doing", realising upon taking office that some of the RDP policy directives were simply not the optimal approach to solving South Africa's problems.

Whatever the reason, some directives did, and some did not, become policy; some policies did, and some did not, have the necessary legislative codification; and some policies and laws were implemented well, and others were not. Because of the subjectivities involved, however, no final judgment can be made by the researchers involved — as to the overall success of South Africa's first democratic government in adopting, legislating and implementing RDP policy directives, that judgement belonged to the voters on June 2, 1999, and will be made by the new ministers and officials who can now better assess their inheritance.

Notes

1. African National Congress (1994), "Preface," *Reconstruction and Development Programme*, Johannesburg, Umanyano Publications.

2. **2.2.2** Attacking poverty and deprivation is the first priority of the democratic government, and the RDP sets out a facilitating and enabling framework to this end.

3. **2.2.6** A programme of affirmative action must address the deliberate marginalisation from economic, political and social power of black people, women and rural communities. Within this programme, particularly vulnerable groups such as farm workers, the elderly and the youth require targeted intervention.

4. Priorities will include such things as Affirmative Action programmes in the civil service at all levels and priority demands... Affirmative Action policies will be used to end discrimination on the grounds of race and gender and to address the disparity of power between workers and employers, as well as between urban and rural areas... Parties to collective bargaining will be encouraged to negotiate Affirmative Action policies to address discrimination and the disparities of power between workers and employers... The Government of National Unity aims not only to stamp out racism wherever it persists, but to establish a proactive, sensible Affirmative Action programme. All levels of Government will be expected to implement a policy of Affirmative Action to ensure that the public service is representative of all the people of South Africa, in racial, gender and geographical terms. Such a policy will be negotiated with trade union representatives of public sector employees. Fair employment conditions, codes of conduct and prohibition on racism and sexism in the workplace are also envisaged. An all-embracing, integrated framework for Affirmative Action is also being established so as to assist both public and private sector organisations. This approach will extend beyond employment opportunities, into many other aspects of socio-economic life, including gender and geographical inequalities. (*White Paper on Reconstruction and Development*, 2.4.9,3.11.3,3.11.4,5.4.1)

5. *Employment and Occupational Equity: Policy Proposals*, p.30

6. *Rural Development Strategy*, p.14

7. Policy objectives: The unemployment gap between non-disabled and disabled job seekers must be narrowed. 2. Conditions must be created to broaden the range of employment options for disabled people so as to provide them with real possibilities of occupation choice. 3. The vocational integration of people with disabilities must be facilitated, whatever the origin, nature or degree of the disability(ies). The following strategies must be adopted in order to meet policy objectives:- People with disabilities should be provided with a range of employment opportunities aimed at meeting different needs and offering real possibilities for occupational choice... inter-sectoral collaboration... personnel training...

The creation of work opportunities for people with disabilities through the development and maintenance of small, medium and micro-enterprises should form a key component in a comprehensive employment strategy for people with disabilities. (*Integrated National Disability Strategy*, 1)

8. *Employment Equity Act*, Chapter 1

9. **2.2.7** The role of women within the RDP requires particular emphasis. Women are the majority of the poor in South Africa. Mechanisms to address the disempowerment of women and boost their role within the development process and economy must be implemented. The RDP must recognise and address existing gender inequalities as they affect access to jobs, land, housing, etc.

10. *Web Page of the Commission on Gender Equality*, http://cge.org.za

11. **2.2.8** In particular, the impact of any programme on the population growth rate must be considered. A population committee should be located within the national RDP implementing structure. Policies on international migration must be reassessed bearing in mind the long-term interests of all of the people of the sub-continent.

12. The objectives of this policy are to enhance the quality of life of the people through: the systematic integration of population factors into all policies, plans, programmes and strategies at all levels and within all sectors and institutions of government; implementing an interdisciplinary and integrated approach in designing and executing programmes; reviewing the nature and impact of all forms of international migration on sustainable development in order to formulate and implement an appropriate policy... Since the problem of international migration literally cuts across borders, solutions have to be sought in the context of the Southern African region, and even beyond. The Department of Home Affairs, has initiated a comprehensive policy formulation process which focuses on various contentious issues pertaining to international migration. [I]t requires a multi-sectoral policy approach [involving] all relevant stakeholders in both the public and private sectors... The President as Head of State will oversee the implementation of the population policy and will report on progress with its implementation as part of an annual national development report. The Cabinet Committee for Social and Administrative Affairs will ensure coordination and political commitment at the highest political level to integrating population and development concerns as part of the national development strategy... In the meantime it has been decided that the National and Provincial Population Units will remain attached to the departments responsible for the welfare function. Since their functions are different from those of welfare, and involve servicing many sectoral departments, they will therefore operate as separate entities with a unique mandate and functions. Their budgets and priorities will be approved and monitored separately from those of the welfare components. The National Population Unit will collaborate closely with the Central Planning Unit in the Office of the Deputy President in order to facilitate the incorporation of the population policy as part of the national development strategy. Similarly, Provincial Population Units will collaborate closely with the units responsible for provincial development planning. The Cabinet Committee on Social and

Administrative Affairs will make it clear to all relevant departments that the population units offer a service to all of them. (*White Paper on Population Development*, 2.3.5,3.4,3.5.1,4.2,4.4)

13. **2.2.9** The lack of accurate statistics to quantify and locate the problem of poverty underlines the need for a national unit to monitor poverty and deprivation in an ongoing manner, and guide further interventions. The unit must develop and evaluate key indicators for measuring the success of the RDP. It must pay special attention to women's legal, educational and employment status and the rates of infant and maternal mortality and teenage pregnancy. Indeed, monitoring and gathering of all statistical data must, where relevant, incorporate the status of women and their economic position with specific reference to race, income distribution, rural and urban specifics, provincial dimensions, and age particularities (for example, women pensioners and young women). It is also necessary to develop a more acute demographic map of our people, both as to where they are presently located and, more importantly, where they could move so as to facilitate supply of infrastructure and services.

14. Statistical indicators–including appropriate modifications of the United Nations Development Programme's Human Development Index (HDI)–will be measured and reported regularly... The CSS, acting together with the Human Sciences Research Council (HSRC), will be directed to develop an HDI for South Africa. Whereas many indicators are still to be developed, a higher profile will accompany concrete goals and upgrading of existing measures for factors such as child mortality, reduction in epidemics, rates of adult literacy, provision of low-income housing, employment equity in both public and private sectors, incidents of family violence, provision of child care services and the provision of infrastructure, among other things. (*White Paper on Reconstruction and Development*, p.37) The national Department of Welfare in collaboration with all stakeholders will develop a National Information System for Social Welfare in order to inform policy formulation, planning and monitoring... Indicators of poverty and vulnerability will be based on data which provides a breakdown along racial, gender, sectoral and spatial lines. This sort of disaggregation of information is necessary in order to effectively address the inequities of the past. (*Draft White Paper for Social Welfare*, p.26)
Major strategies of the [population] policy: Ensuring that all data collected, the analyses of such data and the findings of pertinent research studies are, to the extent possible: a. disaggregated by sex to permit the application of gender-sensitive planning techniques and the construction of gender indicators; b. disaggregated by geographical area, age and other attributes, in order to inform policy making and planning at local levels; and c. made available in formats that comply with the needs of users... It will remain essential to maintain data sets disaggregated by race for the foreseeable future in order to monitor the success of corrective action in the quest for social justice. (*White Paper on Population Policy*, 2.1,3.5.24)
A comprehensive NHISSA (National Health Information System) will be developed... to support the health care delivery system. (*Towards a National Health System*, p.80)

15. **2.2.10** The first democratic South African government should sign and implement the International Covenant on Economic, Cultural and Social Rights (and related conventions) and establish a domestic equivalent of a high-profile Covenant review committee and reporting procedure.

16. **2.3.1** All job creation programmes should cater particularly for women and youth. Implementing agencies should include representatives from women's and youth organisations.

17. Affirmative action in public works projects will entail providing increased access to child care facilities and more actively preventing discrimination and sexual harassment, with the aim of increasing the involvement of women workers... [T]he target groups for the CBPWP are the rural poor, women, youth and disabled people. (*Public Works White Paper*, 2.2.4, 2.3.4.1)

18. *Annual Report*, National Department of Public Works, 1997, p.10

19. The proportion of women (18%) paid less than the monthly equivalent of R250 was nearly double that of men (10%). At the upper end of the wage spectrum, the proportion of men (19%) paid more than the equivalent of R751 per month was more than six times greater than that of women (3%). The explanation is largely cultural. The work done by women was reportedly "less demanding" (physically) than work done by men. Fetching and carrying and "helping men" were among the most commonly reported types of work done by women. (*Responding to the Poor: Evaluation of the CBPWP*, p.10)

20. **2.3.4** All short-term job creation programmes must ensure adequate incomes and labour standards... **2.3.9** Such programmes must not abuse labour standards nor create unfair competition within sectors of the economy.

21. The DPW is committed to taking necessary steps to halt and reverse the casualisation of labour in the construction industry. Regarding wage rates, the DPW endorses a minimum floor and a common wage order, covering all those engaged in construction activities, and taking account of regional and project-specific variations. Payment linked to productivity as opposed to time spent on the job is proposed for categories of work for which labour may be substituted for machines in order to create jobs. (*Public Works White Paper*, 3.3.3.3.5)

22. There is ample evidence in South Africa and internationally that public works programmes offering survival wages generally provide relief effectively to those most in need; only people genuinely in need offer themselves for work. (*Rural Development Framework*, p.38)

23. The DPW is party to Nedlac's *Agreement on Job Creation in the Construction Industry*, which proposes a sectoral accord between the major social partners, regarding wages, benefits and minimum standards for workers on public works programmes to curtail the use of labour brokers and casual labour in the industry. The DPW will implement the

regulatory framework, including a Wage Board establishing a wages framework, collective bargaining forums, wages linked to the local economy, a monitoring inspectorate to ensure maintenance of standards, and appropriate training, capacity building and information sharing. (*Public Works White Paper*, 3.3.3.3.3)

24. The 1996 evaluation reported an average equivalent monthly wage of R325, with a working week of five days. The 1997 evaluation reported in more detail on the range of equivalent monthly wages paid--from a low of about R176 to more than R750. Within this range, 45% of both men and women were paid the monthly equivalent of between R450 and R750. Using aggregate data on total employment, total expenditure and the share of expenditure on labour (with associated caveats), the equivalent monthly wage derived in 1997 was R520. (*Responding to the Poor: Evaluation of the CBPWP*, p.10)

25. **2.3.4** All short-term job creation programmes must... link into local, regional or national development programmes, and promote education, training and community capacity and empowerment... **2.3.6** A further component of the public works programme must be provision of education and training and the involvement of communities in the process so that they are empowered to contribute to their own governance. Assets created by a public works project must be technically sound.

26. The DPW is committed to redress uneven geographical development by increasing both the provision of public services as well as asset creation through new public facilities in underdeveloped areas. This will entail extensive interaction with other government departments and local community organisations of various sorts, and capacity-building support so that communication and consultation is a two-way process... The DPW will also ensure that all its capital projects are structured to provide technical and entrepreneurial training, and targeted to promote local resources and utilisation of construction-related small enterprises. (*Public Works White Paper*, 2.5, 2.3.2.3)

27. As of December 1996... a total of 148 523 temporary jobs have been created and 21 050 people trained in technical and life skills. (*Annual Report*, Department of Public Works, 1996, p.10)
The 1997 survey revealed that 80% of workers reported they acquired life long skills. 5% said there were some many job opportunities in their communities for them. (*Responding to the Poor: Evaluation of the CBPWP*, p.8)

28. *Responding to the Poor: Evaluation of CBPWP*, p.9.

29. **2.3.5** There must be a coordinated national public works programme to provide much-needed infrastructure, to repair environmental damage, and to link back into, expand and contribute to the restructuring of the industrial and agricultural base.

30. The DPW will continue to adopt forward planning of public sector construction projects in the context of the state's multi-year budgeting so as to counteract the cyclical nature of construction demand. Although the PWD has been given the responsibility for

implementing the NPWP, it is a programme of the entire government. (*Public Works Green Paper*, p.3)

The DPW is committed to the implementation of public works programmes to achieve the following specific objectives: reduce unemployment; provide education and training; empower communities through providing job opportunities, transferring skills and creating community assets in a manner which builds communities' capacity to manage their own affairs; provide relief and temporary livelihood support to threatened communities during times of disaster, through maintaining the local economy by bringing funds into the area, preventing involuntary sale of household and productive assets, and rebuilding infrastructure and building work that reduce vulnerability to disaster. (*Public Works White Paper*, 3.1.4)

31. **2.3.7** The public works programme must maximise the involvement of women and youth in the poorest rural households and most deprived regions to create assets such as water supply, sanitation and clinics. This must have significant socio-economic benefits, particularly with respect to production which meets women's basic needs (such as child care facilities).

32. Deliberate government action to give rise to real wage increases in rural areas... would be achieved by a labour-intensive investment programme, for which obvious targets would be those that reduce drudgery and increase health and productivity... It is essential that rural women are targeted for employment, to have the greatest impact on poverty. These should initially be concentrated in those rural areas with the greatest production and export potential. Programmes must offer a fairly low wage that ensures that only the poorest benefit. (*Rural Development Strategy*, p.10)

33. *Annual Report,* Department of Public Works, 1997, p.10.

34. The DPW is committed to the continuation of the CBPWP for at least the next 15 years. For 1997/98, R300 million has been requested, and for 1998/99, R1 billion. The DPW is determined to enhance the CBPWP by introducing world-class targeting, monitoring, and institutional arrangements to ensure that the programme benefits the poorest of the poor, women, the aged, youth, children, rural dwellers and the disabled. As such it will not be treated as a short-term programme but as one of the business lines of the department. (*Public Works Toward the 21st Century White Paper*, 3.3.4.3, 3.3.4.4)

The package of Special Employment Programmes will be dramatically expanded over the next few years [to include] Clean Cities Campaign, Working for Water, Land Care Campaign, Municipal Infrastructure Programme, Welfare Programmes, and the Community-Based Public Works Programme. (*Creating Jobs, Fighting Poverty, An Employment Strategy Framework*, 3.3)

35. Shortcomings and problems with the initial programme were identified around monitoring and evaluation, the possibility of improved targeting procedures, and the need to realign the programme around the concept of clustering. Corrective measures have been implemented through the pilot projects under last year's R85m Rural Anti-Poverty Programme. The success of these pilots has led me to instruct my department to continue

the programme for the allocation granted by government in terms of the R274m given my department. (Jeff Radebe, Minister of Public Works, *Contribution to the Jobs Summit*, 30 October 1998)

36. **2.3.8** The public works programme must coordinate with and link to other job creation and labour-intensive construction initiatives. A community development fund could be set up within the context of a national public works programme to make resources available to communities. Care must be taken to ensure that disbursements from such a fund are carefully controlled and relate to local and regional development plans.

37. **2.4.2** A national land reform programme is the central and driving force of a programme of rural development... **2.4.3** The RDP must implement a fundamental land reform programme. This programme must be demand-driven and must aim to supply residential and productive land to the poorest section of the rural population and aspirant farmers. As part of a comprehensive rural development programme, it must raise incomes and productivity, and must encourage the use of land for agricultural, other productive, or residential purposes... **2.4.14** The land reform programme, including costing, implementing mechanisms, and a training programme, must be in place within one year after the elections. The programme must aim to redistribute 30 per cent of agricultural land within the first five years of the programme.

38. *Annual Report*, Department of Agriculture, 1997, p.3.

39. At present, the central thrust of land policy is the land reform programme. This has three aspects: land restitution, land redistribution and tenure reform... The provision of support services, infrastructural and other development programmes, is essential to improve the quality of life and the employment opportunities resulting from land reform. [The objective is] land reform which results in a rural landscape consisting of small, medium and large farms; one which promotes both equity and efficiency through a combined agrarian and industrial strategy. (*White Paper on South African Land Policy*, 2.1)

40. **2.4.6** The land redistribution programme will realise its objectives in various ways, including strengthening property rights of communities already occupying land, combining market and non-market mechanisms to provide land, and using vacant government land... **2.4.7** The redistribution programme should use land already on sale and land acquired by corrupt means from the apartheid state or mortgaged to state and parastatal bodies. Where applicable, it will expropriate land and pay compensation as the *Constitution* stipulates. Land acquired from the apartheid state through illegal means must be recovered after due process of investigation. The land reform programme must include land outside of the historically black areas. All legal provisions which may impede the planning and affordability of a land reform programme must be reviewed and if necessary revised.

41. Over the next ten years, rights in land will be secured for a significant proportion of eligible citizens... the scale of the proposed distribution is not yet quantifiable. (*Green Paper on South African Land Policy*, pp.1,26)

42. *The Provision of Certain Land Settlement Act*, 126 of 1993, provides the legal mechanism through which land redistribution takes place. Several shortcomings of the *Act* have been noted and a process has been initiated to have the *Act* amended. (*Annual Report*, Department of Land Affairs, 1997, p.149)

43. The government is committed to a land reform programme that will take place on a willing-buyer willing-seller basis where possible. However, where this is not possible, the state must be able to expropriate land required in the public interest; public interest includes "the nation's commitment to land reform." Where land is acquired for land reform through purchase or expropriation, the state is obliged to pay "just and equitable" compensation [the definition of which] makes it clear that it will not permit profiteering or undue capital gains at the expense of the public... [The government's approach] depends largely upon voluntary transactions between willing-buyers and willing-sellers, which should result in dispersed land acquisition and settlement, as against block settlement in designated areas. Expropriation will be used as an instrument of last resort where urgent land needs cannot be met, for various reasons, through voluntary market transactions... The concept of willing-buyer willing-seller is only effective if potential buyers are able to walk away and buy elsewhere... The role of government in the land valuation process is that of facilitator, provider of information and a guardian of the principles set out above. The DLA is therefore required to appraise all land transactions concluded under the Land Reform Programme... The DLA believes that land reform beneficiaries should be exempted from transfer duty. A ruling has been obtained that VAT should be zero-rated on service procured with government grants where the seller is a VAT vendor... Different groups of beneficiaries have to pay different amounts, depending on the status of the seller... Land reform beneficiaries acquiring land on a group basis do not qualify for limited exemptions from transfer duties which apply only to individual purchases. (*White Paper on South African Land Reform*, 3.5, 4.4, 4.6.1, 3.3)

44. Projects submitted for purposes of redistribution can be categorised into: group settlement with some production[;] group production; individual production; commonage schemes; on-farm settlement; share equity schemes; rapid land release in an urban context; others that hinge upon policy innovation... In 1997, the redistribution programme reached take-off. Both the number and scope of projects designed by the Minister increased, some 150 projects in total had been designated in 1997. This year's total included 12 126 households and some 95 260 hectares of land. The progress made in 1997 matched the progress made in the previous three years taken together. (*Annual Report*, Department of Land Affairs, 1997, pp.149,151)

45. **2.4.8** The democratic government must provide substantial funding for land redistribution. In addition, beneficiaries must pay in accordance with their means.

46. During the 1997/98 financial year, the Department of Land Affairs (DLA) spend R391 million on restitution, redistribution, tenure reform, auxiliary and associated services, appropriation, and registration of deeds trading account. (*Annual Report*, Department of Land Affairs, 1997, p.331)

47. [I]f there are to be grants for land acquisition, then they should be modest so that as many eligible people benefit as possible... [T]he allocation per qualifying beneficiary has been set at R15 000. The level of the subsidy will be kept under review. This subsidy level means that [the Grant] alone will not provide the resources necessary for a person to enter the commercial farming sector... The R15 000 Settlement/Land Acquisition Grant is essentially a capital grant. It is intended for land purchase, investment in infrastructure, home improvements, livestock, machinery and fencing... The allocation of the grant will be registered on the same national data base as the National Housing Subsidy. A household may apply for both, and in any order, but cannot qualify for more than R15 000. For groups, average household income must be less than R1 500 per month. Although a means test for groups will not be applied as a matter of routine, in certain cases an investigation may be conducted... Grants awarded to applicants who have applied as a group must be disposed of according to collective decision-making... (*White Paper on South African Land Policy*, 3.2, 3.11)

48. [S]ubsidised interest rates for land purchase increase the demand for land and hence increase the market price for land, without increasing its productive worth. Hence a subsidy on interest rates results in higher land prices and rate of indebtedness and this outcome is not desirable. The Strauss Commission clearly proposed that interest rate subsidies for land acquisition should not be considered. (*White Paper on Land Reform*, 4.23.3)

49. **2.4.8** A land tax on rural land must be based on clear criteria, must help to free up underutilised land, must raise revenues for rural infrastructure, and must promote the productive use of land.

50. The Sub-Committee [of the Commission of Enquiry into Certain Aspects of the Tax Structure of South Africa (Katz Commission)] stated that such a tax should be levied at a local government level. It did not recommend the implementation of a national land tax on agricultural land. The sub-committee proposes that all land (ie, privately owned land, state-owned land and tribal land and land used for any purpose) within the jurisdiction of local councils be included in the tax base and levied on the improved market value of the land, to a maximum of 2% per annum for all land in all jurisdictions. (*White Paper on South African Land Policy*, 3.4)

51. **2.4.13** To redress the suffering caused by the policy of forced removals, the democratic government must, through the mechanism of a land claims court, restore land to South Africans dispossessed by discriminatory legislation since 1913. This court must be accessible to the poor and illiterate. It must establish processes that enable it to take speedy decisions. In order for this court to function effectively, constitutional rights to restitution must be guaranteed... **2.4.14** The land restitution programme must aim to complete its task of adjudication in five years.

52. The government has set itself the following targets: a three-year period for the lodgement of claims, a five year period for the Commission and the Court to finalise all claims, a ten year period for the implementation of all Court orders... Restitution can take

the following forms: restoration of the land from which claimants were dispossessed; provision of alternative land; payment of compensation; alternative relief including a package containing a combination of the above, sharing of the land or special budgetary assistance; priority access to state resources in the allocation and the development of housing and land in the appropriate development programme. (*White Paper on South African Land Policy*, 4.13, 4.14.4)

53. Eighteen [restitution] cases were resolved by the end of 1997, allowing some 27 000 people to recover approximately 150 000 hectares of land. (*Annual Report*, Department of Land Affairs, 1997, p.121.)

54. **2.4.4** The land policy must ensure security of tenure for all South Africans, regardless of their system of land-holding... **2.4.10** A democratic government must ensure secure tenure rights for all South Africans by adopting a tenure policy that recognises the diverse forms of tenure existing in South Africa. It must support the development of new and innovative forms of tenure such as Community Land Trusts and other forms of group land-holding.

55. Tenure reform must move toward rights and away from permits. Tenure reform must build a unitary non-racial system of land rights for all South Africans. Tenure reform must allow people to choose the tenure system which is appropriate to their circumstances. [I]t is accepted that both group based and individually based ownership systems play valuable roles under different circumstances. All tenure systems must be consistent with the *Constitution*'s commitment to basic human rights and equality... In order to deliver security of tenure a rights-based approach has been adopted. A procedure is being developed which involves all stakeholders in situations of overlapping rights in the process of putting forward concrete proposed solutions. Apart from registering individual ownership, the *Communal Property Act* provides one vehicle for group ownership. (*White Paper on South African Land Policy*, 4.16, 4.18)

56. *The Extension of Tenure Security Act*, 62 of 1997 was passed into law on 28 November 1997. The *Act* provides for tenure security in two ways:
it gives occupiers who lived on someone else's land on or after 4 February 1997 with permission of the owner, a secure right to live on and use that land; and it provides for ways in which occupiers can strengthen these rights with financial help from the state, in some cases becoming owners. (*Annual Report*, Department of Land Affairs, p.140)
[B]alanced with the rights of the owner or person in charge, an occupier shall have the right— (a) to security of tenure... (*Extension of Security of Tenure Act*, p.6)
[The purpose of the *Communal Property Associations Act* is] to enable communities to form juristic persons, to be known as communal property associations in order to acquire, hold and manage property on a basis agreed to by members of a community in terms of a written constitution; and to provide for matters connected therewith. (*Communal Property Associations Act* No. 28 of 1996, Introduction)

57. [For farmworkers, off-farm settlement options] entail the purchase of land and establishment of housing and service infrastructure close to existing farm employment. [On-farm] settlement options range from schemes in which agreements between parties cover investment in farm worker housing and amenities only, to schemes in which investment includes equity shares in the farming enterprise as a whole. Options include... a contractual agreement between the state, farmworker and the farm owner in which the farmworker and his/her family use the grant to enhance the housing stock and/or non-bulk service provision on the farmer's land... an equity share-holding agreement. (*White Paper on South African Land Policy*, 4.9.1., 4.9.2)

58. Evictions as a solution to land invasion are a measure of last resort and should only be considered after all other alternative solutions have been explored, including commitments to organised groups of landless people for the delivery of land within specific time frames (*White Paper on South African Land Policy*, 4.8.1).

59. **2.4.4** The land policy... must remove all forms of discrimination in women's access to land... **2.4.11** Women face specific disabilities in obtaining land. The land redistribution programme must therefore target women. Institutions, practices and laws that discriminate against women's access to land must be reviewed and brought in line with national policy. In particular, tenure and matrimonial laws must be revised appropriately.

60. It is essential that gender equity be ensured in the land redistribution and land reform programme so that women achieve a fair and equitable benefit. This requires the following: The removal of all legal restrictions on participation by women in land reform, (including) reform of marriage, inheritance and customary law which favor men and contain obstacles to women receiving rights to land; Clear mechanisms on both project planning, beneficiary selection and project appraisal to ensure equitable benefit from the programme for women and men; Specific provision for women to enable them to access financial and support services; Specific mechanisms to provide security of tenure for women, including the possibility of registering assets gained through land reform in the name of women as direct beneficiaries; Training in gender awareness and participatory gender planning for all officials and organisations involved in implementing the land reform programme; Develop a partnership with NGOs/CBOs who are often a key source of support to women. (*White Paper on South African Land Policy*, 4.11)

61. **2.4.9** Rural infrastructure, support services and training at all levels must be provided to ensure that land can be utilised effectively. Within this, water provision must take priority, followed by provision of basic health care... **2.6.7** Water supply to nearly 100 per cent of households should be achieved in the medium term, and adequate sanitation facilities should be provided to at least 75 per cent of rural households.

62. A preliminary financing scenario [concerning rural infrastructure, not land reform] can be put forward, based on the... assumption [that] local infrastructure [is] to be financed from a "basic services" subsidy, set at say R4 000 per household, and forming a first tranche of other possible subsidies such as the Settlement Grant... Rural households would

still have the right to the full subsidy they qualify for over time... (*Rural Development Strategy*, p.35).

The principle promoted in the MIIF is that all South Africans living in municipal areas should have access to at least a basic minimum level of service. While the same principle applies, different standards are called for in rural areas due to the dispersed character of human settlement. However, in areas where the settlement has no economic rationale, does not form part of the urban fabric, and appears dependent on transport and other subsidies for survival, then government should commit itself only to a basic minimum level. (*Municipal Infrastructure Investment Framework*, p.12)

63. **2.4.12** The programme must include the provision of services to beneficiaries of land reform so that they can use their land as productively as possible. Assistance must include support for local institution building, so that communities can devise equitable and effective ways to allocate and administer land.

64. Dealing with communities: There is great need for caution in assuming that local structures are representative or competent. Yet without true representation, projects break down, and issues of maintenance, user charges and levies do not get resolved. Furthermore, departments have found that NGOs sometimes bring with them their "history" as a local level, which often creates adverse reactions. Some departments have also found communities demanding payment for attendance at meetings, even though the end result is supposed to be a community-owned asset such as a water system. Thus many government departments are having to learn caution and patience. They have also found that they often need to maintain a close watch on local level management, and to assist communities with prioritisation, mediation and facilitation. Formal structures by which the state can keep assisting with these processes are an absolute necessity. (*Rural Development Strategy*, p.18)

65. *Annual Report*, Department of Water Affairs and Forestry, 1997, p.27.

66. **2.5.4** The RDP endorses the principle that all South Africans have a right to a secure place in which to live in peace and dignity. Housing is a human right.

67. The challenge facing South Africa in housing, is to develop a strategy in the short term to direct scarce and insufficient State housing and other resources together with private, non-State resources, to ensure that all those in need... are able to progress towards the realisation of an effective right in housing. (*White Paper: A New Housing Policy and Strategy for South Africa*, p.22)

68. **2.5.2** At minimum, one million low-cost houses should be constructed over five years. These units should specifically be intended for low-income households and should include the rural areas... **2.5.5** The democratic government is ultimately responsible for ensuring that housing is provided to all. It must create a policy framework and legislative support so that this is possible, and it must allocate subsidy funds from the budget--to reach a goal of not less than five per cent of the budget by the end of the five-year RDP.

69. Government's goal is to increase housing's share in the total State budget to five percent and to increase housing delivery on a sustainable basis to a peak level of 350 000 units per annum, within a five year period, to reach the target of the Government of National Unity of 1 000 000 houses in five years. (*White Paper: A New Housing Policy and Strategy for South Africa*, p.21)

70. The required annual delivery rate, relatively high proportion of poor households and budgetary constraints do not allow sufficient subsidy money per household to enable the construction, at State expense, of a minimum standard complete house for each household not able to afford such a house. (*Urban Development Strategy*, p.20)

71. *Nomvula* Housing Database, Department of Housing, August 1998.

72. **2.5.7** As a minimum, all housing must provide protection from weather, a durable structure, and reasonable living space and privacy. A house must include sanitary facilities, storm-water drainage, a household energy supply (whether linked to grid electricity supply or derived from other sources, such as solar energy), and convenient access to clean water. Moreover, it must provide for secure tenure in a variety of forms. Upgrading of existing housing must be accomplished with these minimum standards in mind... **2.5.8** Community organisations and other stakeholders must establish minimum basic standards for housing types, construction, planing and development, for both units and communities.

73. Feedback from some communities has confirmed that some of the units produced do not provide adequate shelter and living space for families. There are a number of reasons for this:
* lack of sufficient information for beneficiaries on housing related issues like size, costing of material and ability to read plans which are vital in making informed decisions about their options regarding sizes of units...
* some contractors and developers have taken advantage of the unrestrictive and loose definition of norms and standards, coupled with the fact that these were left to the discretion of the operatives on the ground.
The rationale behind this was mainly to produce a groundswell of innovation and creativity in encouraging people to produce units of good value. This has led to unscrupulous developers skimming off and producing units that are substandard in terms of providing adequate living spaces for families... We did not have strict specifications that clearly defined the basic parameters within which housing development would take place. A document stipulating these specifications has been drafted and is under discussion... The minimum size of a house to be built with a government subsidy is currently under discussion and this will take into abnormal geo-technical or topographical conditions of the area. The maximum amount of 15% of the subsidy will be allocated to cater for this. The provincial housing boards may with approval of the MEC for housing in the province, deviate from these standards only if there are reasonable circumstance which justify this. (*Speech by Minister Sankie Mthembi-Mahanyele*, Parliamentary Media Briefing Week, 6 August 1998)

74. There are always cost implications for the setting of standards. As a general rule it should be stated that the higher or more restrictive the standard, the higher the cost to the community as a whole. (_White Paper: A New Housing Policy and Strategy for South Africa_, p.58)

75. **2.5.14** Government funds and private sector funding must be blended in order to make housing finance affordable. A national bank and a national home loan guarantee fund must be initiated to coordinate subsidies and financing most efficiently... Mechanisms (such as time limits on resale, or compulsory repayment of subsidies upon transfer of property) must be introduced to prevent speculation and downward raiding. Subsidies... must be paid directly to individuals, groups or community-controlled institutions.

76. A capital subsidy approach, based on the current subsidy scheme will be maintained... Following extensive investigations... it was concluded that an institution tasked with unlocking housing finance at the wholesale level at scale and on a sustainable basis, has become necessary... Government therefore is currently finalising the detailed design of a National Housing Finance Corporation... The State has insufficient resources to meet the needs of the homeless on its own and recognises that sustained, substantial investment in housing from sources outside the national fiscus will be required. Housing policy will therefore need to recognise the fundamental pre-condition for attracting such investment, which is that housing must be provided within a normalised market and thus attract maximum private investment. The challenge is achieving a balance between State intervention and the effective functioning of the housing market with vigorous and open competition between suppliers of goods and services to end users. (_White Paper: A New Housing Policy and Strategy for South Africa_, pp.24,30,49)

77. In 1998, the grant was increased to R16 000, still far below the inflation-adjusted 1994 grant.

78. **2.5.15** End-user finance and credit must be made available for diverse tenure forms, community designs and housing construction methods. Commercial banks must be encouraged, through legislation and incentives, to make credit and other services available in low-income areas; 'redlining' and other forms of discrimination by banks must be prohibited... Interest rates must be kept as low as possible.

79. It is recognised that the reinstatement of a habitable public environment has to be a precursor to a resumption of private investment... Government will therefore recognise... those areas where conditions are progressively becoming conducive to viable development and will at an identified stage signal to the private sector that investment and the provision of credit is viable and required, through making housing subsidies and mortgage indemnity cover available in such areas... The Association of Mortgage Lenders have indicated that the banking industry intends to introduce fixed instalment mortgage loans by the end of 1994. This initiative is encouraged by Government as it is believed that the introduction of such instruments will contribute significantly to meeting the requirements of the market. The principle of pricing for risk and cost is likely to result in a higher interest rate

on such bonds than the prevailing bond rate. (*White Paper: A new Housing Policy and Strategy for South Africa*, pp.33,48)
Mortgage Indemnity Scheme: Government is to indemnify financial institutions for losses within certain limits. This will apply where normal contractual rights to access and attached securities provided for mortgage loans cannot be exercised due to a breakdown in the due process of law. (*Urban Development Strategy*, p.29)

80. An agreed code of conduct for mortgage lending will require banks to apply credit criteria on a non-discriminatory basis. (*Urban Development Strategy*, p.29)

81. 2.5.15 Locally controlled Housing Associations or cooperatives must be supported, in part to take over properties in possession of banks due to foreclosure. Unemployment bond insurance packages and guarantee schemes with a demand-side orientation must be devised.

82. Existing Properties in Possession: Where no payments are being made by occupants, and financiers are unable to obtain relief in accordance with court orders and contractual rights, actions taken will have to be consistent with those of the Mortgage Indemnity Scheme... Rightsizing: A service organisation, SERVCON, has been established which will help borrowers to downsize/rightsize their accommodation to suit their affordability level. (*Urban Development Strategy*, p.29)

83. The Mortgage Indemnity Fund (MIF) was formed in June 1995... to encourage mortgage lenders to resume lending at scale in the affordable housing market in a sustainable manner in neglected areas in the country... [G]overnment has facilitated granting 133 158 loans with a value of R9.2 billion between June 1995 and December 1997... The mission of [The National Housing Finance Corporation] is to ensure the development and appropriate funding of institutions providing affordable housing finance at the retail level... The NHFC group has granted 25 facilities totalling R327 million by 31 December 1997 (up from R25 million in December 1996) and has disbursed R225 million (up from R1.5 million) to intermediaries. It is estimated that these facilities will deliver 250 000 loans to households through the intermediaries... There are two points of focus for [the National Urban Reconstruction and Housing Agency's] loan guarantee: guarantees for Bridging finance... Guarantees for End user finance... 55 projects for bridging finance guarantees (with a total value of R20.7 million) by the end November 1997. These projects will produce 14 275 houses at a cost of R229 million. By the end of December 1997, 4700 houses in the projects had been built... Servcon [Housing Solutions] has been offering a payment normalisation programmed... By December 1997, Servcon was administering a portfolio of approximately 22 500 properties comprising Properties in Possession (PIP's) and Non Performing Loans (NPL's) on behalf of the banks. (*Annual Report*, Department of Housing, 1997, pp.51-58)

84. 2.5.19 The costs of housing construction must be kept as low as possible while meeting the proposed standards... The building materials industries must be examined, both to improve productive output and to reduce costs. Cartels, price agreements and market share agreements must end, and consideration must be given to public, worker and community-

based ownership. Community-controlled building materials suppliers must be encouraged, possibly with government subsidies to enhance competitiveness. An enforceable Code of Conduct must be established to guide developers.

85. It is of critical importance that the material and services supply sector to the housing industry impose effective measures of self-regulation and control in order to contain inflationary pressures on the prices of goods and services... As with the suppliers of material and services to the housing sector, self-regulation within the construction sector of construction prices will be a critical element to the success of a large scale national housing delivery programme. (*White Paper: A New Housing Policy and Strategy for South Africa*, p.39)

86. An average national distribution of 55:25:20 between full, intermediate and basic levels of services in municipal areas is considered a realistic target for the infrastructure investment strategy over the next ten years. To comprehend the choices which face decision-makers in this regard, a definition of the types of services under each category and an indication of the target groups of each is necessary: "Basic services" means communal standpipes (water), on site sanitation, graded roads with gravel and open stormwater drains and streetlights (electricity). These services will be targeted at households with an income of less than R800 per month and charged for at between R35 and R50 per month. "Intermediate services" entail water provision through yard taps on site, simple water-borne sanitation, narrow paved roads with no curbs and open drains and 30 amps electricity with prepaid meters for households. These should be affordable to households which earn between R800 and R1700 per month and will cost them between R100 and R130 per month. "Full services" mean house connected water supplies, full water-borne sanitation, paved roads with curbs and piped drains and 60 amps electricity provision. It is anticipated that households in the R1700-R3500 monthly income class could afford "low consumption" costing them between R180 and R220 per month. Households with monthly incomes of above R3500 will be assumed able to pay for "full services at high consumption" at charges between R270 and R350 per month. (*White Paper: A New Housing Policy and Strategy for South Africa*, pp.24-25)

87. **2.5.3** The development of small, medium-sized and micro enterprises owned and run by black people must be incorporated into the housing delivery programme.

88. The growth and support of the emerging (black) construction sector is not seen as a primary housing responsibility and therefore does not justify the allocation of housing funds. (*White Paper: A New Housing Policy and Strategy for South Africa*, p.39)

89. Government policy and the resistance to outside contractors in communities has resulted in the rapid growth of small business contractors. These contractors are sub-contracted by the approved developers, which in the case of small towns, is usually the local authority. Nurcha is actively supporting these contractors... By year-end 1997, Nurcha had approved guarantees for 37 loans to emerging contractors, delivering 2300 homes. Among emerging entrepreneurs assisted by Nurcha were four women contractors. These businesses are notable for energy of their principals and their dedication to the cause

of community upliftment. (*Annual Report*, National Urban Reconstruction and Housing Agency, 1998, pp.12,16)

90. **2.5.6** The approach to housing, infrastructure and services must involve and empower communities... **2.5.18** Role players include civic associations and other community groups... **2.5.21** Beneficiary communities should be involved at all levels of decision-making and in the implementation of their projects. Communities should benefit directly from programmes in matters such as employment, training and award of contracts. Key to such participation is capacity building, and funds for community-based organisations must be made available.

91. Government is committed to a development process driven from within communities... Government will be required to actively provide support for this process... In addition, communities as well as government must be constantly alert to people and organisations who abuse this developmental approach for their own ends, and turn development into a contest for influence. (*White Paper: A New Housing Policy and Strategy for South Africa*, p.23)

92. The National Housing Policy: Supporting the People's Housing Process intends to assist these people to have access to: housing subsidies, and – technical financial, logistical and administrative support regarding the building of their homes on a basis which is sustainable and affordable... Under the interim policy, housing support has successfully been implemented in the following areas: Galeshewe, Kleinskiil, Uitenhage, Queenstown, Ocean View, Victoria Mxenge, Villiersdorp, Integrated Serviced Land Project, Piesang River, and Soshanguve... (*Annual Report*, Department of Housing, 1997, pp.18,20)

93. **2.5.8** Legislation must... be introduced to establish appropriate housing construction standards... **2.5.9** Legislation must be rapidly developed to address issues such as tenants' rights, squatters' rights, the rights of people living in informal settlements, community reinvestment by banks, evictions, consumer protection, land restoration, community participation in development, and anti-discriminatory protection.

94. The Minister must publish a code called the National Housing Code... [Government] must give priority to the needs of the poor in respect of housing development, consult meaningfully with individuals and communities affected by housing development, ensure that housing development provides a wide choice of housing and tenure options, and is economically, fiscally, socially and financially affordable and sustainable, encourage and support individuals and communities, including, but not limited to, co-operatives, associations and other bodies which are community-based, by assisting them in accessing land, service and technical assistance in a way that leads to the transfer of skills and empowerment of community, promote the process of racial, social, economic and physical integration in urban and rural areas, level the playing field [and] prohibit unfair discrimination. (*Housing Act* 1997, p.4)

95. **2.5.9** The democratic government must promote and facilitate women's access to housing and to appropriate community design. The provision of appropriate housing for the elderly and the disabled is also an important priority.

96. It is essential that new policies, strategies and legislative actions by the State should be particularly sensitive to the removal of entrenched discriminatory mechanisms and conventions in respect of gender, race, religion and creed. (*White Paper: A new Housing Policy and Strategy for South Africa*, p.23)

97. National, provincial and local government must promote... measures to prohibit unfair discrimination on the ground of gender and other forms of unfair discrimination, by all actors in the housing development process; the meeting of special housing needs, including but not limited to, the needs of the disabled; the housing needs of marginalised women and other groups disadvantaged by unfair discrimination; the expression of cultural identity and diversity in housing development. (*Housing Act*, December 1997, pp.4,5)

98. The disabled people form one of the most neglected sector of our society in terms of access to goods and services. Up to now, few buildings have been constructed taking their needs into account. Their living spaces are nothing but ideal... It gives me great pleasure to announce that subsidy levels for the disabled will be increased by between 8 percent and 36 percent depending on the severity of the person's disability. The aim is not only to make sure that disabled people are part of the housing consumer loop, but this is a means of enabling them to get appropriate shelter for their needs. Each provincial office will determine its implementation date. (Minister Mthembi-Mahanyele, Parliamentary Media Briefing, 6 August 1998)

99. **2.5.11** Land speculation must be prevented and land monopolies broken up.

100. The (Development Facilitation) Act seeks to promote efficient and integrated land development through a set of general principles as the basis for future land developments. (*Urban Development Strategy*, p.17)

101. The National Development and Planning Commission was launched in September 1997, and Development Tribunals began. (*Annual Report*, Department of Land Affairs, 1997, p.20)

102. **2.5.12** The democratic government must ensure a wide range of tenure options including individual and collective home ownership as well as rental, and facilitate a wide range of housing types. Sufficient affordable rental housing stock should be provided to low-income earners who choose this option... **2.5.13** The democratic government must support the transfer of houses to those who have been denied the opportunity to own houses in the past... **2.5.20** Provincial and local governments should be... particularly active in the delivery of rental housing stock.

103. Subsidy policy will... be designed to provide for the fullest range of tenure options... In addition to the project based subsidy programme already in place, Government will introduce a range of specifically designed lump sum subsidy instruments to support a broad range of innovative housing delivery processes... (including) subsidies for individual ownership purposes... (and) subsidies for collective social and rental housing, directed at institutions supplying such housing. (*White Paper: A New Housing Policy and Strategy for South Africa*, p.42-43)

104. National, provincial and local spheres of government must... provide as wide a choice of housing and tenure options as is reasonably possible. (*Housing Act*, 1997, p. 4)

105. The Minister may introduce a rental subsidy programme, as a national housing programme, instituted in terms of section 3(4)(g) of the *Housing Act*, 1997, to stimulate the supply of housing rental property for low income wage earners in a manner that promotes urban integration and renewal. (2) Parliament may appropriate annually to the South African Housing Fund an amount to finance such a programme... The MEC may... declare by notice in the *Gazette* the regulated area [with the effect that] a. the rent of a dwelling in the regulated area may not be increased... b. a tenant of a dwelling situated in a regulated area may not be given notice to vacate or in any manner whatsoever be induced to vacate the dwelling... c. the MEC must appoint a Housing Rental Tribunal... In advertising housing for rent, or in negotiating a lease of housing with a prospective tenant, or during the term of a housing lease, a landlord may not unfairly discriminate against such prospective tenant or tenant, or the members of such tenant's household or the bona fide visitors of such tenant, on one or more grounds, including race, gender, sex, pregnancy, marital status, ethnic or social origin, colour, sexual orientation, age, disability, religions, conscience, belief, culture, language and birth. (*Housing Rental Act*, 1998, 4-6, Chapter V)

106. **2.5.16** Hostels must be transformed, upgraded and integrated within a policy framework that recognises the numerous interest groups in and around hostels and provides a range of housing options, including both family units and single people... The democratic government must upgrade hostels where residents cannot pay costs.

107. It must be honestly acknowledged that the stated desire to end the marginalisation of hostels and their residents has not yet been given effect. Government undertakes to constantly review its approach to hostels, both public and private, and to do so with the assistance of the residents and workers living in conditions that are often inhumane. (*White Paper: A New Housing Policy and Strategy for South Africa*, p.25)

108. To date [December 1997], 32 of the 182 hostels have been upgraded. There are 25 projects currently under construction. (*Annual Report*, Department of Housing, 1997, p.17)

109. **2.5.17** Rural people have specific concerns around housing, such as tenure forms on trust land; the relationship with the commercial agricultural sector; inadequate or non-existent bulk infrastructure; farm workers housed on the farms; the legacy of apartheid removals and resettlements; access to land, and land claims procedures and processes. In rural areas, problems of ensuring full property and home-ownership rights for women are

likely to be greater. A rural housing action plan must be developed to address this. While recognising that rural incomes are far lower, the democratic government must consider rural housing needs in calculating backlogs, and make provision for gradually improving housing in rural areas. In particular, labour tenants require security of tenure, and legal defence and advice offices must be established to assist farm workers in cases of eviction.

110. State housing policy and strategy should achieve balance in emphasis between urban and rural and take cognisance of the particular characteristics and requirements of rural communities. (*White Paper: A New Housing Policy and Strategy for South Africa*, p.25)

111. Present subsidy policy deals with urban circumstances with freehold or leasehold tenure arrangements as well as with housing provision in formal towns where such tenure can be achieved. Areas where traditional tenure regimes apply are still effectively excluded... Farmworkers are effectively excluded. (*White Paper: A New Housing Policy and Strategy for South Africa*, p.44)
Government intends to extend the Housing Subsidy to rural settlements, but this has yet to happen... Applicants to the Department of Land Affairs often prefer to spend their grant on acquiring productive land ;and to forgo their right to the basic services needed to sustain their health. This could result in requests for a housing subsidy at a later date. While the present system of dual funding is acceptable because it speeds up disbursement of the subsidy, duplicate funding will not be permitted... Government support to housing development tends to be neglected in rural areas. Where rudimentary shelter is in place, housing is often perceived by the authorities not to be a problem. The fact that other basic facilities (potable water, sanitation, etc) are totally lacking tends to be overlooked. Rural households often fail to obtain their place in the queue for the subsidies offered by government. Housing subsidies are usually granted in response to submissions canvassed by developers or better organised urban communities. For these and other reasons, provincial housing allocations tend to be spent in urban and peri-urban areas. Government's intention is to have, as far as possible, a unitary subsidy policy which operates for both rural and urban areas and different types of tenure countrywide. In practice, this has been difficult to implement, due to the differences between rural and urban areas. Although the tenure issue is in the process of being resolved, other differences in needs and capacities between rural and urban areas have been more difficult to overcome. (*Rural Development Framework*, pp.44,47)

112. The Rural Housing Loan Fund (RHLF), set up as a section 21 company with a revolving fund sourced from a DM50 million German government grant... Loans totalling R36 million had been made by the RHLF by the end of October 1997. The average loan to the end-user by non-traditional lenders accessing finance from the RHLF is around R3 000 and assists people in developing a recognised credit history. (*Annual Report*, Department of Housing, 1997, pp.25,26)

113. To give rural households access to housing subsidies and to address their housing needs on the basis of secure tenure, policy guidelines for housing subsidies in rural areas based on the *Interim Protection of Land Rights Act, 1996* were developed... It is envisaged that it will be implemented in 1998. (*Annual Report*, Department of Housing, 1997, p.17.)

114. **2.6.3** The fundamental principle of our water resources policy is the right to access clean water–"water security for all"... **2.6.12** The RDP must undertake a process to involve all relevant parties in updating the *Water Act* to ensure the right of all South Africans to water security.

115. There is a need... to review South Africa's water law entirely. A White Paper to this effect will be presented to parliament... The principle that "water security for all" should supersede all other rights to water will be considered... There is also the need to regulate the exploitation of ground water. (*Water Supply and Sanitation Policy White Paper*, p.35)

116. 2. The main objects of this *Act* are to provide for—(a) the right of access to basic water supply and the right to basic sanitation necessary to secure sufficient water and an environment not harmful to human health or well-being... 3. (1) Everyone has a right of access to basic water supply and basic sanitation. (2) Every water services institution must take reasonable measures to realise these rights. (3) Every water services authority must, in its water services development plan, provide for measures to realise these rights. (4) The rights mentioned in this section are subject to the limitations of this Act. (*Water Services Act*, 1997, pp.6,7)

117. The basic human needs reserve provides for the essential needs of individuals served by the water resource in question and includes water for drinking, for food preparation and for personal hygiene... The Reserve refers to both the quantity and quality of the water in the resource...[and] the Minister is required to determine to Reserve for all or part of any significant water resource... Any entitlement granted a person by or under this *Act* replaces any right to use water which that person may have been otherwise able to enjoy or enforce under any other law [including] to take or use water, to obstruct or divert the flow of water. (*National Water Act*, 1998, pp.15,10)

118. Since its inception in 1994 the Community Water Supply and Sanitation branch of the Department of Water Affairs and Forestry has put money behind 693 projects (12 in RDP Programme 1 314 in RDP Programme 2 and 361 in RDP Programme 3)... Expenditure on construction schemes totalled R406 million of which R218,5 million was off budget. Expenditure took place on nine major projects with R186,6 million being spent on direct labour and R219,4 million on contract work, R30,6 million was spent on equipment rebuilds and new purchases and R2,0 million on contract drilling. (*Annual Report*, Department of Water Affairs and Forestry, 1997, pp.25,52)

119. **2.6.6** The RDP's short term aim is to... provide all households with a clean, safe water supply of 20-30 litres per capita per day (lcd) within 200 metres, an adequate/safe sanitation facility per site, and a refuse removal system to all urban households. **2.6.7** In the medium term, the RDP aims to provide an on-site supply of 50-60 lcd of clean water, improved on-site sanitation, and an appropriate household refuse collection system. Water supply to nearly 100 per cent of rural households should be achieved over the medium term, and adequate sanitation facilities should be provided to at least 75 per cent of rural households. **2.6.8** The long term goal is to provide every South African with accessible water and sanitation.

120. The CWSS Strategic Study (Planning) National Assessment (November 1996)... indicates that 12 million people do not have access to adequate water supply and a further 18 million people have inadequate or no access to sanitation. (*Annual Report*, Department of Water Affairs and Forestry, 1997, p.25)

121. Basic water supply is defined as: Quantity: 25 litres per person per day... Cartage: The maximum distance which a person should have to cart water to their dwelling is 200m. (*Water Supply and Sanitation Policy White Paper*, p.15)

122. **2.6.10** To ensure that every person has an adequate water supply, the national tariff structure must include the following: a lifeline tariff to ensure that all South Africans are able to afford water services sufficient for health and hygiene requirements; in urban areas, a progressive block tariff to ensure that the long-term costs of supplying large-volume users are met and that there is a cross-subsidy to promote affordability for the poor; and in rural areas, a tariff that covers operating and maintenance costs of services, and recovery of capital costs from users on the basis of a cross-subsidy from urban areas in cases of limited rural affordability.

123. The policy of sliding tariff scales is endorsed by the Department of Water Affairs and Forestry... A life-line or social tariff... is to cover basic human needs. The quantity shall not exceed 25 litres per capita per day. The tariff shall be set so as to cover only the operation and maintenance costs... It is... not equitable for any community to expect not to have to pay for the recurring costs of their services. (*Water Supply and Sanitation Policy White Paper*, pp.24,23)
The basic policy of government is that services should be self-financing at a local and regional level. The only exception to this is that, where poor communities are not able to afford basic services, Government may subsidise the cost of construction of basic minimum services but not the operating, maintenance or replacement costs... Grants for capital costs will be available where local authorities are unable to meet the national basic level of service for sanitation. Where households and/or communities wish to have access to services which are more expensive than the basic level, the extra capital and running costs must be met within that local authority area. (*National Sanitation Policy White Paper*, pp.19,15)

124. This [reserve] will be provided free of charge in support of the current policy of Government which is to encourage the adoption of lifeline tariffs for water services to ensure that all South Africans can achieve access to basic services. *White Paper on a National Water Policy for South Africa*, p.4.

125. Only in the electricity sector is there scope for redistribution on a national basis, other than through the national fiscus. (*Rural Development Framework*, p.43)

126. In order to achieve the goal of ensuring that the majority of citizens do have at least basic services within seven years, the annual budget of the new amalgamated Department will need to increase from an estimated R1,6 billion per annum (1,28% of the total budget)

to approximately R2,8 billion (2,24%). (*Water Supply and Sanitation Policy White Paper*, p.20)

127. To promote the efficient use of water, the policy will be to charge users for the full financial costs of providing access to water, including infrastructure development and catchment management activities. To promote equitable access to water for basic needs, provision will also be made for some or all of these charges to be waived. (*White Paper on a National Water Policy for South Africa*, p.4).
The Minister may, with the concurrence of the Minister of Finance, from time to time prescribe norms and standards in respect of tariffs for water services. (2) These norms and standards may—(a) differentiate on an equitable basis between—(i) different users of water services; (ii) different types of water services; and (iii) different geographic areas, taking into account, among other factors, the socio-economic and physical attributes of each area; (b) place limitations on surplus or profit; (c) place limitations on the use of income generated by the recovery of charges; and (d) provide for tariffs to be used to promote or achieve water conservation. (3) In prescribing such norms and standards, the Minister must consider, among other factors... (b) social equity; (c) the financial sustainability of the water services in the geographic area in question; (d) the recovery of costs reasonably associated with providing the water services... (f) the need for a return on capital invested for the provision of water services... (*Water Services Act*, 1997, p.10)

128. Non-payment of water use charges will attract penalties, including the possible restriction or suspension of water supply. (*National Water Act*, 34D, 1998, p.36)

129. **2.6.4** A national drought management system and water reserves are a priority... **2.11.6** South Africa currently lacks an early warning system which can alert central authorities to threats to food and water security. The RDP should establish institutions to collect and monitor nutritional and other key socio-economic and agricultural data.

130. It is when farmers and householders intensify their use of dry areas that they become vulnerable to drought. Government programmes for drought should aim to reduce this vulnerability. They should, however, never compensate rural people for the failed production created by ill-considered intensification of land use in drought prone areas. (*Rural Development Strategy*, p.32)
It is the poor who suffer most because a small change in their circumstances can have a far greater effect on their ability to survive than a similar change in the lives of more affluent citizens. The poor are often forced by their circumstances to occupy land which is prone to disaster... The Department of Water Affairs and Forestry supports the proposal to create an inter-departmental structure to take responsibility for long term national disaster management and mitigation strategies. (*Water Supply and Sanitation Policy White Paper*, p.33)
Drought will be recognised as a normal phenomenon in the agricultural sector and it will be accommodated as such in farming and agricultural financing systems. The Government should not support measures that soften the negative impact on farm incomes caused by poor risk management. (*White Paper on Agriculture*, p.7)

131. The Minister must establish national monitoring systems on water resources as soon as reasonably practicable... [and must] establish national information systems regarding water resources... The objectives of national information systems are... to provide information to water management institutions, water users and the public... (ii) for planning and environment impact assessments; (iii) for public safety and disaster management... A water management institution must, at its own expense, make information at its disposal available to the public in an appropriate manner, in respect of—(a) a flood which has occurred or is likely to occur; (b) a drought which has occurred or is likely to occur... The Minister may establish early warning systems to anticipate such events. (*National Water Act*, Chapter 14, Part 3, p.62)

132. In 1997 the Cabinet established the Inter Ministerial Committee (IMC) for disaster management chaired by the Minister Provincial and Constitutional Affairs...To deal with immediate disaster issues, such as El Nino Phenomenon, an interim Disaster Management Centre for established. (*Annual Report*, Department of Welfare, 1997, p.39)
The Government has also altered its policies on drought relief. In the past, policies tended to weaken farmers' inclination to adopt risk-coping strategies, with a consequent reliance on high-value, high-risk monocultures. The culmination of this tendency was the 1992/93 drought-relief programme which provided R3,8 billion to consolidate and write off debts of commercial farmers. In future, drought will be recognised as a normal phenomenon and farmers will be encouraged to adopt low-risk technologies, rather than plant drought-susceptible crops and maintain inappropriately high numbers of livestock in areas prone to drought. (*Web Page of the National Department of Agriculture*, http://www.nda.agric.za/)

133. **2.6.5** Community organisations must... receive training in water management and must ensure such management is integrated into overall planning... **2.6.9** Particularly in rural areas, the RDP must develop appropriate institutions, including water village committees. Consultation with communities is essential in the provision of water.

134. Training and capacity building for communities... is an important part of the government's strategy. (*Water Supply and Sanitation Policy White Paper*, p.38)... Community involvement is essential for long term success. Urban local governments need to develop the capacity to involve people in local decision-making. In rural areas existing bodies such as Local Development Committees or Water and Sanitation Committees, assisted by local government or water boards where possible, will be involved in promoting sanitation programmes. (*National Sanitation Policy White Paper*, p.10)

135. Community Water Supply and Sanitation (CWSS) works with local government... The Build Operate Train and Transfer (BoTT) approach will soon be used to implement RDP projects in four provinces. (*Annual Report*, Department of Water Affairs and Forestry, 1997, p.26)

136. **2.7.4** Immediate policies to meet energy needs must include a low-smoke coal programme, improved management of natural woodlands, social forestry programmes, commercial woodlots, and support for the transport of wood from areas of surplus to areas

of need. Gas and paraffin prices must be reduced through better regulation and by bringing bulk supplies closer to households.

137. The Department of Water Affairs and Forestry has already redirected its programmes toward RDP goals. This includes the new Community Forestry programme, for example. (*White Paper on Forestry*, 1.2)
Government will promote access to affordable energy services for disadvantaged households, small businesses, small farms and community services... Government will determine a minimum standard for basic household energy services and monitor progress over time. People must have access to fuels that do not endanger their health... Government will promote research into low-smoke fuels as a transitional product that may be utilized as an energy source for remotely located and rural households. Investigations will be made into simple strategies that may be used in order to reduce the production costs... Government will continue to encourage household electrification, whether grid or off-grid, and will introduce safety and performance standards for paraffin retail and paraffin stoves. ...Government expects energy suppliers and the private sector to carry out appropriate research. (*White Paper on the Energy Policy of the Republic of South Africa*, Parts 1,3 and 4)
A *low smoke fuels* programme has been initiated by the DMEA... A *fuelwood security* programme is... needed to ensure the sustainable use of wood resources to provide a cheap and renewable source of energy. The DMEA has launched the Biomass Initiative... Although IP (illuminating paraffin) is widely available throughout the country, there is significant scope for reduction in prices paid by small consumers. Tighter enforcement of regulated prices can reduce excessive mark-ups... Another reason for relatively high domestic LPG (liquid petroleum gas) prices is the high mark-up at the wholesale and retail end of the distribution chain... There is room for oil companies to improve distribution and lower prices. (*South African Energy Policy Discussion Document*, pp.66,72,74)

138. **2.7.7** An accelerated and sustainable electrification programme must provide access to electricity for an additional 2,5 million households by the year 2000, thereby increasing the level of access to about 72% of households (double the present number)... All schools and clinics must be electrified as soon as possible.

139. Option: Provision of electricity to clinics and schools. Time Frame: Focussed effort over 5 years... It is not clear whether having electricity in all schools is a first priority... There is a danger that in the absence of established institutions to undertake large scale solar electrification, ambitious, early targets could lead to poor design, implementation and insufficient maintenance... Fuelwood is likely to remain the primary source of energy in the rural areas. (*South African Energy Policy Discussion Document*, pp.96,66)

140. Option: Large-scale electrification by Eskom and local governments aimed at making 2,5 million connections by the year 2000. Time Frame: Sustained electrification at this level during the next 5 years. (*South African Energy Policy Discussion Document*, p.95)
In line with the target proposed in the RDP, it has been government's intention to ensure the electrification of 2,5 million households by the end of the decade... Grid and off-grid connections will continue to be made at more modest levels after 1999, until all South

Africans have access to electricity... The Minister of Minerals and Energy, together with the Minister of Finance, will establish rolling, five-year national electrification targets on an annual basis (*White Paper on the Energy Policy of the Republic of South Africa*, Part 3)

141. With more than 400 000 electricity connections in 1997 alone, today South Africa has reached a 58% electrification level so millions can have light. (*President Nelson Mandela, Opening of Parliament*, 6 February 1998)

142. In 1994 Eskom undertook to electrify 1 750 000 homes by the year 2000 in terms of its RDP commitment. By December 1997 Eskom had electrified 1 148 000 homes and again was on track to meet its obligations. Eskom has made available 50 million rand per annum until 1999 to be spent on the electrification of schools and other community development activities. (*Ministry of Public Enterprise Budget Vote*, 25 May 1998)

143. **2.7.8** The electrification programme will cost around R12 billion with annual investments peaking at R2 billion. This must be financed from within the industry as far as possible via cross-subsidies from other electricity consumers. Where necessary the democratic government will provide concessionary finance for the electrification of poor households in remote rural areas. A national Electrification Fund, underwritten by a government guarantee, must be created to raise bulk finance from lenders and investors for electrification. Such a fund could potentially be linked to a Reconstruction Fund to be utilised for other infrastructural financing needs. A national domestic tariff structure with low connection fees must be established to promote affordability.

144. **2.7.8** Where necessary the democratic government will provide concessionary finance for the electrification of poor households in remote rural areas.

145. One question is whether the necessary cross-subsidies should be provided only by the high usage domestic customers or whether non-domestic customers should also contribute... Cross-subsidies should have minimal impact on the price of electricity to consumers in the productive sectors of the economy... A suite of capacity-differentiated tariffs with a range of connection fees and tariff structures will therefore be offered to domestic consumers... The average level of domestic tariffs should, be set to recover operating losses incurred in supplying poorer domestic consumers from within the domestic sector. (*White Paper on the Energy Policy of the Republic of South Africa*, Part 3) The national electrification programme is a significant part of the RDP. However, there is opposition to cross-subsidisation in electricity tariffs between different classes of consumers as a means of financing this programme. The view has been expressed that where financial support is required, it should be confined to capital expenditure. It should also be explicit and costs should be borne by the fiscus. (*Discussion Document on a Minerals and Mining Policy for South Africa*, p.22)
The entire industry (generation, transmission, and distribution) must move to cost-reflective tariffs with separate, transparent funding for electrification and other municipal services. (Part3, Industry Finance, *Draft White Paper on the Energy Policy of the Republic of South Africa,* June 1998).

The price of energy services to poor households will, necessarily, have to be subsidised at times since the fulfillment of basic needs remains a higher priority for government than the achievement of cost-reflective prices for this market segment (Energy Sector Policy Objectives, Objective 3, *Draft White Paper on the Energy Policy of the Republic of South Africa,* June 1998). Cross-subsidies should have minimal impact on the price of electricity to consumers in the productive sectors of the economy...A suite of capacity-differentiated tariffs with a range of connection fees and tariff structures will therefore be offered to domestic consumers....the average level of domestic tariffs should, be set to recover operating losses incurred in supplying poorer domestic consumers from within the domestic sector (Part 3, "Electricity pricing" and "Domestic Tariffs and Connection Fees," *Draft White Paper on the Energy Policy of the Republic of South Africa,* June 1998).

The national electrification programme is a significant part of the RDP. However, there is opposition to cross-subsidisation in electricity tariffs between different classes of consumers as a means of financing this programme. The view has been expressed that where financial support is required, it should be confined to capital expenditure. It should also be explicit and costs should be borne by the fiscus (*Discussion Document on a Minerals and Mining Policy for South Africa,* p.22).

New household electrification connections made under the national electrification programme will receive a standard subsidy and there will be no discrimination in subsidy level on the basis of geographic region, supply technology or any other factor (Part 3, *Draft White Paper on the Energy Policy of the Republic of South Africa,* June 1998).

146. Only within the electricity sector is there scope for redistribution on a national basis, other than through the national fiscus. Because of the national electricity grid, and the fact that generation is undertaken almost entirely by Eskom, it is possible to set generation and transmission prices high enough to generate a profit for redistributive purposes to poor households, particularly rural ones. (*Rural Development Framework,* p.43)

147. Eskom made a commitment in terms of the RDP to reduce the real price of electricity by 15% by the end of the year 2000. Eskom is on track to meet this commitment. Honourable Members will be interested to learn that the cumulative real price reduction since 1995 amounted to 11,7% by the end of 1997. (*Minister for Public Enterprise Budget Vote,* 22 May 1998)

148. *White Paper on the Energy Policy of the Republic of South Africa,* Part 3

149. An amount of R300 million is available in 1997 to local authority distributors for electrification of permanently occupied residential dwellings that are situated in legally authorised areas set out by Local Governments for permanent settlement in designated township development areas. This amount has become available and has been approved by the NER Board as a reduction of revenue to Eskom that will contribute towards leveling the playing field between Eskom distributors and local authority distributors. (*Web Page of the National Electricity Regulator,* http://www.ner.org.za/)

150. The partial coverage programme assumes lower coverage levels for... electricity (50% grid, 10% RAPS) than the full coverage programme. Half of the local electricity cost is financed through sector (or utility) borrowing... Based on these assumptions, it can be shown that while the partial coverage programme can be financed through this approach, the full coverage programme cannot. (*Rural Development Strategy*, pp.33,35)

In rural areas, where the lowest capacity grid system cannot be supplied within the capital expenditure limit, this system will provide a natural opportunity for Remote Access Power Supply (RAPS) systems to be supplied. (*White Paper on the Energy Policy of the Republic of South Africa*, Part 3)

151. **2.8.4** The RDP aims to provide universal affordable access for all as rapidly as possible within a sustainable and viable telecommunications system; to develop a modern and integrated telecommunications and information technology system that is capable of enhancing, cheapening and facilitating education, health care, business information, public administration and rural development.

152. The provision of universal access means placing a telephone within people's reach but not in every household, for example, by installing public or community telephones within walking distance of people's houses. The RDP plans to provide universal affordable access as soon as possible... The long term goal of universal service is a telecommunications line in every household at affordable prices. Telecommunications can play an important role in furthering social and economic development in a participatory and democratic fashion... The telecommunications sector must work towards meeting four interrelated objectives: the achievement of universal service, the economic empowerment of historically disadvantaged South Africans, the provision of a wide range of telecommunications services to stimulate and support economic growth in various sectors, and the effective use of telecommunications for social and infrastructural development. The provision of universal services means putting a telecommunications line in every household wanting the service, at affordable prices... The RDP plans to provide universal affordable access as soon as possible. (*Green Paper on Telecommunications Policy*, 1)

153. The telecommunications sector is key to the success of the RDP. Access to communications facilities is not only necessary for the delivery of services in critical sectors such as education and health; it also serves to stimulate the creation of small business and offers a channel of communication to reinforce participation in democratic processes at community, provincial and national levels. It is the essential backbone for development and offers the only opportunity for leapfrogging its relatively slow sequential phases. (*Telkom Web Page*, http://www.sn.apc.org/sangonet/technology/telecoms/white/chap01.htm)

154. There is hereby established a juristic person known as the Universal Service Agency... The Agency shall—(a) strive to promote the goal of universal service; (b) encourage, facilitate and offer guidance in respect of any scheme to provide—(i) universal access or universal service; or (ii) telecommunication services as part of reconstruction and development programmes...; (c) foster the adoption and use of new methods of attaining universal access and universal service... The Agency—(c) shall continually survey and evaluate the extent to which universal service has been achieved... There shall be a

Universal Service Fund, of which the Agency shall keep account... (1) The money in the Universal Service Fund shall be utilised exclusively for the payment of subsidies—(a) for the assistance of needy persons toward the cost of the provision to or the use by them of telecommunication services. (*Telecommunications Act*, 58,59,65,66)

155. Telkom produced 250 000 telephone connections in 1996 and 421 000 during 1997/8. (*The Building has Begun. The State of the Nation: Government's Report to the Nation*, p.26) During the year, we installed a total of 386 426 net new working lines, 275 218 of which were added in underserviced areas. These figures include public payphone growth of 32 335, which was substantially higher than the 18 027 required in terms of the license. The net growth in total and underserviced lines, excluding public phone lines, also exceeded the license target by 15,5% and 4% respectively. First-time service was provided to 461 villages, slightly above the license target. A total of 3 181 new lines were provided to priority customers, namely hospitals, schools, local authorities and libraries, of whom 1 231 were first-time customers. (*Telkom Annual Report*, 1997/8)

156. **2.8.4** Telecommunications services must be provided to all schools and clinics within two years.

157. The RDP has already identified connectivity for schools and health facilities as a priority... The rapid increase of penetration rates, particularly in black urban and rural areas, should be a prime objective of any telecommunications policy. (*Telecommunications Green Paper*)

158. **2.9.3** An effective publicly-owned passenger transport system must be developed, integrating road, rail and air transportation... A future transport policy must: promote coordinated, safe, affordable, public transport as a public service... **2.9.4** the future emphasis must be on the provision of safe, convenient, affordable public transport... **2.9.5** As a first priority, rail transport must be extended.

159. The strategic value of state ownership of infrastructure should be reassessed... The public passenger transport system in South Africa will be based on regulated competition... where public transport services require government funding support, for example for welfare, or traffic management, or strategic reasons, competition will take the form of tendered contacts (competition on routes or networks will then be precluded); where public transport can be rendered as profitable commercial services, on-the-road competition will be encouraged, with competition being regulated through the issuing of permissions... Contracts will only be awarded to privately-owned or corporatised municipal and parastatal bus companies and registered minibus operators to ensure that there is fair competition between competing tenderers. (*Working Documents for Land Transport Bills and Cross-Boarder Road Transport Bill*, pp.16,26,27)

160. Rail operations should be based on operating and maintenance concessions, awarded by transport authorities, based on a transport plan with ownership of infrastructure and rolling stock being retained by transport authorities. The working documents provide for permissions to be issued to public service transport operators for passenger services based

on commercial service contracts, subsidised service contracts, scheduled and unscheduled services, metered taxi services and long distance services. To qualify, operators will have to be registered, be separate legal entities and be liable for taxation. In addition, municipal and State owned undertakings will have to operate on business principles, have no unfair access to financial resources and ultimately be corporatised. (*Working Documents for Land Transport Bills and Cross-Boarder Road Transport Bill*, p.27)

161. Proposals should identify appropriate levels of service for defined customer groups and minimise the costs associated with meeting these requirements... The strategic objectives for land passenger transport (include): To ensure that passenger transport services address user needs, including those of commuters, pensioners, the aged, scholars, tourists and the disabled; To improve accessibility and mobility, limiting walking distances to less than about 2km in urban areas; To ensure that public transport is affordable, with commuters spending less than about 10 percent of disposable income on transport... Transport authorities, in consultation with communities, must define passenger transport needs at affordable fare levels in order to identify and target recipients of mobility support. (*Working Documents for Land Transport Bills and Cross-Boarder Road Transport Bill*, pp.7,22,28-29)

162. A total amount of R967 255 896... was used to subsidise approximately 20 million passenger trips... Services were provided by 35 bus operators with approximately 8 000 buses... An amount of R1 381 703 000 was spent on subsidising approximately 458 million [rail] passenger journeys during the year [96/97] in the six major metropolitan areas. An increase of approximately 3,5% in passenger journeys was registered during the year. (*Annual Report*, Department of Transport, 1996-1997, p.41.)

163. *Moving South Africa* has already detailed... The R3.3 billion annual road underfunding... capital reinvestment below required levels for almost all modes. (*Moving South Africa*, 7.4.2)

164. **2.9.5** Commuters should be encouraged to use public transport, and should be actively discouraged from using cars (via parking, access and fuel levies). The funds so raised must be used to directly benefit the provision of public transport... **2.9.11** Funding for public transport would come both from central government and from local rates and taxes. The (Metropolitan Transport Authorities) must be empowered to impose such levies and taxes as may be appropriate and the funds thus raised must be used primarily to promote public transport.

165. Transportation subsidies alone cost the fiscus in excess of R2 billion a year, and are particularly excessive in providing for the inhabitants of far-flung 'commuter townships'... As far as possible, infrastructure should be funded through user charges and/or investments by the private sector... Unrestrained car usage and subsidised car parking should be contained through the application of policy instruments including strict parking policies, access restrictions for private cars, higher license fees, road pricing and area licensing... The application of funds to transport improvements should be self-sustaining and replicable. To

encourage this, the users of urban transport facilities should pay for all or most of the costs incurred within the limits of affordability. (*Urban Development Strategy*, pp.15,,18-19,24,28)

166. **2.9.3** All privately-controlled passenger transport must be effectively regulated and controlled.

167. The roles and responsibilities of the key stakeholders and service providers will be clearly agreed. This will enable government regulation to be kept to a minimum, while the private sector will be able to build and operate within a competitive environment, be socially and environmentally responsible and self-regulating. (*Working Documents for Land Transport Bills and Cross-Boarder Road Transport Bill*, p.6)

168. Provincial taxi registrars will be appointed to register taxi associations and their members. (*Working Documents for Land Transport Bills and Cross-Boarder Road Transport Bill*, p.6)
The process initiated by the National Taxi Task Team (NTTT) focused on three key target areas: regulation and control; formalisation and training; and the provision of economic assistance to the industry. (*Annual Report*, Department of Transport, 1996-1997, p.38)

169. 3. (1) (a) In each province there shall be—(i) one or more registering authorities; and (ii) persons registered as inspectors of licenses, examiners of vehicles, examiners for driving licenses and traffic officers in accordance with the laws of that province... 32 (1) No person shall drive a motor vehicle in respect of which an operator is registered on a public road except in accordance with the conditions of a permit (to be known as a professional driving permit) issued to him or her in accordance with this Chapter and unless he or she keeps such permit with him or her in the vehicle... 52. (1) The Director General may—(a) prepare a comprehensive research programme to effect road safety in the Republic, carry it out systematically and assign research projects to persons who, in his or her opinion are best equipped to carry them out. (*National Road Traffic Act*, no. 93, 1996)

170. **2.9.3** A future transport policy must: ensure accountability so that the people have control over what is provided.

171. **2.9.3** A future transport policy must: ensure comprehensive land-use/transport planning.

172. Clear guidelines on acceptable, equitable and efficient public involvement processes should be established and followed by planners as well as public interest groups. (*Working Documents for Land Transport Bills and Cross-Boarder Road Transport Bill*, p.18)
Responsive to inputs from customers, key customer groups will be identified, and assessments made of their individual needs and how these can best be met. These will include the users of passenger transport Services, for commuting, educational, business, tourism, and private Purposes, in the urban, rural, regional, and international environment, by All modes. Special customer groups will include the poor, and the disabled. The key customer groups will also include persons sending goods, which Could be high bulk goods like coal and minerals, manufactured products, perishables, or those goods which have

specialised requirements like hazardous materials, in all environments, by any mode. (*White Paper on National Transport*)

173. Transport planning has in the past been highly accommodative or "reactive", leading to the reinforcement of dispersed settlement and land use patterns... A more sustainable approach to the provision of transport infrastructure is required, shifting from accommodative, supply-focused transport approaches to a more balanced approach including pro-active land use and transport demand management as part of the policy package. The Department of Transport must play a more prominent role in relevant decision-making processes and forums on urban and rural development and land use... Policy actions necessary to provide for urban restructuring (densification) and efficient land use/transport interaction include: establishment of structures (all tiers of government) which facilitate integrated planning of infrastructure, operations and land use in a co-ordinated manner; regulation of land use development at a local level so that development approval is subject to conformity with integrated land use/transport plans. (*Working Documents for Land Transport Bills and Cross-Boarder Road Transport Bill*, pp.14,23)
Transport planning for metropolitan transport areas must be integrated with the land development process in the context of integrated development planning in terms of the *Local Government Transition Act*. (*National Land Transport Interim Arrangements Act*, p.4)
2.9.9 The integrated vision for the strategy entails five principal components across all customer groups, based on the underlying assumption that transport is an enabling industry (and the NDOT therefore a provider department), assisting other segments of society in meeting objectives for basic mobility, competitive production, and social integration as effectively as possible. The core of the integrated vision therefore centres on the need to: Provide low systems cost transport; Improve the level of access to the system to ensure basic mobility; Increase service levels and reliability, and reduce transit times; Allow the system to provide customer choice and tailored services and systems to differentiated customers; Create a self-sustaining industry that can upgrade and meet future capacity requirements for all customer groups. (*Moving South Africa*, 6)

174. **2.9.9** For all public transport services to be fully integrated their functioning must be coordinated and financed by one organisation. The organisation should be accountable to the public and responsible for the provision, coordination and funding of all public transport and the infrastructure necessary for public transport (in cooperation with the national public works programme). The organisation should specifically address current problems such as uncoordinated tariff structures, duplication of services, and conflict as a result of different forms of ownership. Minimum norms and standards, policy frameworks and the format of transport plans for national, provincial, urban and rural areas should form an integral part of the responsibilities of this organisation.

175. It is proposed that: The national Department of Transport (DoT) assume the role of coordinator of transport infrastructure for all modes of transport... The DoT should address intermodal integration issues. In this regard, a clear coordinating, information-sharing and integrated planning function should be added to the department. (*Working Documents for Land Transport Bills and Cross-Boarder Road Transport Bill*, pp.12-13)

176. Planning and Infrastructure:... Capacity at [provincial and local government] levels was not in place and, as a result, little progress was made by the provinces towards assuming their assigned functions. (*Annual Report*, Department of Transport, 1996-1997, p.39)

177. The Spatial Development Initiatives (SDI) programme...includes a growing spread of both regional and urban initiatives in a number of our provinces. The seed capital for the projects comes from a R304 million allocation from RDP funds... Department of Transportation participation in Regional SDIs [included] Maputo Development Corridor; Maputo Development Sub-corridor; Lubombo SDI; Rustenberg N4 West; and Wild Coast SDI. (*Annual Report*, Department of Transport, 1996-97, p.62-66)

178. **2.9.3** A future transport policy must take into account the transport needs of disabled people... **2.9.13** The needs of women and children for affordable and safe transport are important. Adequate public transport at off-peak hours, and security measures on late-night and isolated routes, must be provided. Additional subsidies for scholars, pensioners and others with limited incomes will be considered.

179. **2.9.2** Rural areas require more frequent public transport and improved facilities, at an affordable cost. There is inadequate access for emergency services in rural areas, inadequate public transport frequencies and route coverage, poor coordination, and other inefficiencies. Indeed, in many rural areas there is no public transport at all.

180. The partial coverage programme assumes lower coverage levels for... roads (43%)... than the full coverage programme. (*Rural Development Strategy*, p.33)
The strategic objectives for land passenger transport (include): To provide an appropriate and affordable standard of accessibility to work, commercial and social services in rural areas... The need to give attention to rural passenger transport is recognised. Accordingly, a national investigation should be undertaken to develop a guideline and framework of principles for rural passenger transport policy. (*Green Paper on National Transport Policy*, pp.22,30)
There will be a strict upper limit on central government funding; subsidies on water connectors and local connector roads must not exceed R3 000 per household. (*Rural Development Framework*, p.45)

181. **2.10.2** The democratic government must ensure that all South African citizens, present and future, have the right to a decent quality of life through sustainable use of resources... The government must work towards: equitable access to natural resources... a participatory decision-making process around environmental issues, empowering communities to manage their natural environment.

182. **24.** Everyone has the right (a) to an environment that is not harmful to their health or well-being; and
(b) to have the environment protected, for the benefit of present and future generations, through reasonable legislative and other measures... (*The Constitution of South Africa*, p. 11)

183. Policy must promote equitable access to resources and services and build institutional and community capacity for participation in securing more effective environmental management and sustainable use of resources. (*Green Paper on the Environment*, p.36)

184. **2.10.3** Environmental considerations must be built into every decision. To accomplish this, procedures must be set in place which oblige decision-makers to demonstrate what environmental considerations they take into account when considering projects... **2.10.4** Developmental strategies must incorporate environmental consequences in the course of planning.

185. **2.10.4** The democratic government must revise current environmental legislation and administration with a view to establishing an effective system of environmental management. It must make use of environmental auditing, with provision for public disclosure. It must monitor those activities of industry which impact on the environment... **2.10.9** Fines for environmental offenses are inadequate and inconsistent. The South African legal system makes it difficult to obtain *locus standi* in the courts on environmental issues... **2.10.10** The democratic government must rationalise environmental legislation into a cohesive and workable form. It must legislate the right of access to information on environmentally harmful practices. It must also require compulsory environmental impact assessments for all large-scale projects. It must establish an environmental ombuds and criminalise environmental offenses. It must review and conform with international conventions and agreements on environmental issues.

186. The debate around regulatory approaches has become polarised and labels such as "strict liability" and "self-regulation" are used to characterise viewpoints of different sectors. In drafting the *Green Paper* it became evident that, in order to avoid the dangers of extreme positions, it was best not to use these labels. Instead we have attempted to devise a balanced and holistic package of mechanisms to ensure that regulation takes place in a consistent and effective manner... Objective 4: Participation, policy legislation and standards: To carry out a legislative audit and develop relevant and effective policy, legislation and standards through a participative process... Objective 5: Integration of environmental considerations: To review current sectoral policies and governmental responsibilities and decision making functions with a view to coordinating all functions relating to permitting procedures, impact assessment and legislation through agreements between relevant departments at appropriate levels... Private sector environmental audits and audits of projects undertaken by government and parastatals will become mandatory as capacity and resources become available... Government will cooperate with the Department of Justice to establish a method of determining fines linked to cost of living standards and the cost of the offence to the environment... Certain offenses will carry mandatory prison sentences... Objective 24: Information access: To ensure access to information from commerce and industry... Integrated environmental management and planning will be prerequisites for government approval of all activities likely to have an adverse effect on the environment... Objective 38: Implementation of international agreements: To ensure that international conventions and agreements are implemented. (*Green Paper on the Environment*, pp.37,42,44,71,72)

187. A major step forward in the achievement of sound environmental management in South Africa was taken under the *Environmental Conservation Act* (Act 73 of 1989) in September 1997 to make environmental impact assessment compulsory for a wide range of developmental activities. (*Annual Report*, Department of Environmental Affairs and Tourism, 1998, p.46)

188. Impact assessments have been completed for the Letaba, Levuvhu and Mogalakwena river studies... The Environmental Impact Assessment (EIA) for the Lesotho Highlands Water Project Phase 1B has been prepared. An interim *Environmental Action Plan* (EAP) was produced. Following a broad consultation process which will include inputs from the affected communities, the World Bank, Lesotho National Environmental Secretariat and UNESCO, a final EAP will be tabled. (*Annual Report*, Department of Water Affairs and Forestry, 1996-97, p.47,57-58)

189. **2.10.6** Strategies should include: a system of waste management with emphasis on preventing pollution and reducing waste through direct controls, and on increasing the capacity of citizens and government to monitor and prevent the dumping of toxic wastes.

190. The government aims to promote the prevention and minimisation of waste generation and hence pollution at source;... the management and minimisation of the impact of unavoidable waste from its generation to its final disposal;... ensure environmental justice by integrating environmental considerations with the social, political and development needs of all sectors, communities and individuals... The *Draft White Paper* aims to: prevent, reduce and manage pollution of any part of the environment due to all forms of human activity, and in particular from radioactive, toxic and other hazardous substances... To regulate and monitor waste production, enforce waste control measures, and coordinate administration if integrated pollution and waste management through a single government department; To set up information systems on chemical hazards and toxic releases... Public participation is considered a cornerstone for the development of this policy... [The National Waste Management Strategy aims to] develop mechanisms to involve all affected parties, environmental groups, labour, community based organisations, non-governmental organisations, business and industry, monitoring committees, and particularly local, regional, and provincial authorities as appropriate in the enforcement of environmental standards... [and to] promote the education and empowerment of South Africa's people to increase their awareness of, and concern for, pollution and water issues, and assist in developing the knowledge, skills, values and commitment necessary to achieve integrated pollution and waste management. (*Draft White Paper on Integrated Pollution and Waste Management for South Africa*, 1.4,2.2.2,4,5.2)

191. **2.10.6** Strategies should include: environmental education programmes to rekindle our people's love for the land, to increase environmental consciousness amongst our youth, to coordinate environmental education with education policy at all levels, and to empower communities to act on environmental issues and to promote an environmental ethic.

192. Environmental awareness and education projects must be initiated to meet the needs of primary, secondary and tertiary education as well as those of the general public and of workers and management in the public and private sectors. (*Green Paper on the Environment*, p.35)

193. The Department... serves as the coordinator of the Environmental Education Curriculum Initiative (EECI). The aim of the initiative is to facilitate the implementation of [Environmental Education] EE into Outcomes Based Education (OBE)... The Broadening Participation Initiative, operating within Wildlife Society (WLS) structures, led to the development of the publication *Turning Words into Action*–a workbook for communities that aims to foster environmental literacy, knowledge, skills and commitment to acting for a healthier environment, with the main focus on how to start and administer environmental projects. (*Annual Report*, Department of Environmental Affairs and Tourism, 1997-98, p.61)

194. **2.10.6** Strategies should include: the establishment of procedures, rights and duties to allow workers to monitor the effects of pollution, noise levels and dangerous practices both within the workplace and in its impact on surrounding communities and environment.

195. The lead agent [the Department of Environmental Affairs and Tourism] will ensure that the rights of workers to divulge information to the public and to refuse to perform operations that could result in pollution, are protected...[and] will also provide guidelines... for the participation in integrated pollution and waste management issues with industry and business and other stakeholders... especially where it affects employment. (*Draft White Paper on Integrated Pollution and Waste Management for South Africa*, 6.5.2)

196. We said we would change our approach to health and safety. We now have an advisory council for OHS, which includes union representatives. We have tried to increase proactive inspections and general awareness of the importance of occupational health and safety. But we have been hampered by a shortage of staff, especially of skilled staff. Poor working conditions leads to accidents and illness. The human suffering which follows is incalculable. The cost of our economy runs into hundred of million of rands. Latest figures show that in financial year 1996/7 the Compensation Fund paid over R780 million in compensation and medical expenses to accident victims. (*Statement by the Minister of Labour on the Occasion of the Budget Vote: Labour*, National Assembly, Cape Town, 23 April 1998)

197. **2.10.7** Marine resources must be managed and controlled for the benefit of all South Africans, especially those communities whose livelihood depends on resources from the sea.

198. Objective 50: Coastal zone management: To integrate the management and sustainable development and utilization of the coastal marine zone. (*Green Paper on the Environment*, p.47)

199. An extensive consultative process led to the formulation of a draft Marine Fisheries Policy which was presented to Minister Jordan in June 1998. Following that process, an access rights panel was established to amplify the most controversial aspects of the policy– means of future access to marine resources. (*Annual Report*, Department of Environmental Affairs and Tourism, 1998, p.46)

200. **2.10.13** A Commission on the Environment must be established as an independent body to ensure transparency and accountability on the part of agencies dealing with the environment. Such a body must facilitate the gathering, collation and publication of data on the environment. It must also provide an interface between civil society and public agencies responsible for the environment and natural resources.

201. Information management: To strengthen and optimise the capacity of government and civil society to collect, analyse and use multi-sectoral environmental data, information, knowledge and perceptions in decision making and public participation processes; To ensure open disclosure, accessibility and effective dissemination of environmental data and information. (*Green Paper on the Environment*, p.41)

202. **2.11.2** The RDP must ensure that as soon as possible, and certainly within three years, every person in South Africa can get their basic nutritional requirement each day and that they no longer live in fear of going hungry... **2.11.4** Short-term interventions should support nutrition education and the stable, low cost supply of staple foods combined with carefully targeted income transfers and food subsidies... **2.11.6** The democratic government should institute a National Nutrition Surveillance System, which should aim to weigh a statistically significant proportion of children under the age of five years each month to establish their levels of growth and wellbeing.

203. Nutrition for all South Africans should be promoted as a basic human right and an integral component and outcome measure of the country's social and economic development... Nutrition programmes should be integrated, sustainable, environmentally sound, people and community-driven, and should target the most vulnerable groups, especially children and women...A health facility based nutrition programme should be established as an integral part of the PHC package... The community-based nutrition programme should combine the relevant projects of the Primary School Nutrition Programme and the National Nutrition and Social Development Programme. (*White Paper for the Transformation of the Health System in South Africa*, 7.2)

204. The Integrated Nutrition Programme (INP) focuses on addressing the problems of malnutrition as the outcome of interrelated complex, underlying and immediate causes and nutrition programming as an intersectoral, ongoing process of assessment, analysis and action. The National Nutritional Surveillance System (NNSS) will be implemented in 1998 as part of the National Health Information System of South Africa to monitor the nutritional status of pregnant and lactating women, pre-school children and levels of micronutrient deficiency. Sixteen [community-based nutrition] pilot projects were established in four provinces. (*Annual Report*, Department of Health, 1997, pp.22,25)

The Primary School Nutrition Programme will increasingly be integrated with community development and 240 community-based nutrition programmes will be established by March 1999. (*The Building has Begun!*, p.18)

205. **2.11.5** The democratic government must ensure that VAT is not applied to basic foodstuffs, improve social security payments and reintroduce price controls on standard bread.

206. Input and output are now, and will continue to be, determined by market forces, and the government will not intervene directly to influence them... The [*Marketing of Agricultural Products Act, 1996, Act No. 47 of 1996*], is based on the view that state intervention in agricultural markets should be the exception rather than a rule. (*Agricultural White Paper for South Africa*, p.16)

207. **2.11.5** (The democratic government) must enhance the efficiency of marketing so that farmers receive good prices while consumers pay as little as possible. To that end, the government should curb the powers of marketing boards and monopolies, and review the effect of tariffs.

208. Large-scale enterprises will continue to play an invaluable role in the national economy and on the commercial market where economies of scale, bulk sales and branded products are prerequisites for success... Agriculture will still have access to statutory marketing instruments where necessary, but the mandating procedures that provide for inclusiveness, transparency, and accountability will ensure that such measures can only be instituted and maintained if they are in the public interest... Government intervention in agricultural marketing should allow for export marketing arrangements which enhance the welfare of the nation as a whole... Single-desk export marketing arrangements may often be appropriate. (*Agricultural White Paper for South Africa*pp.9,10,12)

209. **2.12.5.2** Reconstruction of the health sector will involve the complete transformation of the entire delivery system. All relevant legislation, organisations and institutions must be reviewed.

210. Restructuring the health sector has the following aims: (a) unify the fragmented health services at all levels into a comprehensive and integrated NHS; (b) reduce disparities and inequities in health service delivery and increase access to improved and integrated services, based on primary health care principles; (c) give priority to maternal, child and women's health; and (d) mobilise all partners, including the private sector, NGOs and communities in support of an integrated NHS (*White Paper for the Transformation of the Health System in South Africa*, 1.1.1)

211. Acts passed in 1997: *Medicines and Related Substances Control Amendment Act, 1997; Medical, Dental and Supplementary Health Service Professions Amendment Act, 1997; Pharmacy Amendment Act, 1997; Nursing Amendment Act, 1997; Dental Technicians Amendment Act, 1997...* Regulations passed in 1997 [relating to]: *Choice of Termination of Pregnancy Act, 1996; Foodstuff, Cosmetics and Disinfectants Act, 1972; Medical Schemes Act,*

1967; Nursing Act, 1978; Health Act, 1977; Human Tissue Act, 1983 (Annual Report,
Department of Health, 1997, pp.84-87)

212. **2.12.11.1** The RDP must significantly shift the budget allocation from curative
hospital services towards Primary Health Care to address the needs of the majority of the
people.

213. Current spending on PHC is projected to increase from R4,768 billion in 1995/6 to
R7,050 billion in 2000/01, representing an average real growth of 8,3% per year... It is
proposed that capital spending for PHC expansion be financed from international
assistance. (*Towards a National Health System*, p.41)

214. During 1997, 204 new clinics were built, 364 new and existing clinics had residential
units added to them, 38 existing clinics were upgraded and 53 mobile clinics were
purchased. The total monetary value of the programme from September 1995 through to
January 1999 is R743 195 146. This is made up of R258 816 491 from the RDP fund and
R495 501 936 from provincial capital funds... On average, four new clinics were completed
each week. Expenditure on this programme in 1997 amounted to R313 586 172. (*Annual
Report*, Department of Health, 1997, p.8)

215. **2.12.1** Health services are fragmented, inefficient and ineffective, and resources are
grossly mismanaged and poorly distributed. The situation in rural areas is particularly
bad... **2.12.8** AIDS education for rural communities, and especially for women, is a
priority... **2.12.9.2** Access to services must be improved by the development of emergency
response centres and appropriate transport and ambulance services, especially in rural areas.

216. Goals and Objectives:... To promote equity, accessibility and utilisation of health
services: increasing access to integrated health care services for all South Africans, focusing
on the rural, peri-urban and urban poor and the aged, with emphasis on vulnerable groups.
(*Towards a National Health System*, p.5)
The target throughout the country is to have one clinic for every 5 000 people, offering
free primary health hcare and ensuring that essential drugs are available at each facility.
These clinics will be supplemented by mobile units serving sparsely populated rural areas.
The Department of Health is committed to the redeployment of trained staff to rural areas
and to improving their working conditions, in order to encourage greater commitment to
the rural areas. (*Rural Development Framework*, pp.60-61)

217. **2.12.5.3** Communities must be encouraged to participate actively in the planning,
managing, delivery, monitoring and evaluation of the health services in their areas...
2.12.5.9 All providers of health services must be accountable to the local communities they
serve through a system of community committees and through the (District Health
Authorities) which must be part of democratically elected local government... **2.12.10.1**
Core teams must be provided for every Community Health Centre and clinic. This will
require incentives to attract staff to underserviced areas and increased training of
Community Health Workers and Environmental Health Officers.

218. Clinic, health centre and hospital committees should be established to permit service users to participate in the management and policy decisions of health facilities... The essential PHC package should be negotiated between the providers and the communities, to ensure that the priorities perceived by the communities are addressed and the communities, have a clear understanding of their entitlements... Representatives of the communities should play a pivotal role in identifying underserved groups, and establish strategies to reach them in partnership with the primary health team. Women should be enabled and supported in playing a major role in local health committees. (*Towards a National Health System*, pp.28-29)

The Department has noted the view that Community Health Workers (CHWs) or their equivalents should be formally incorporated into the basic PHC team, and that existing CHWs should be absorbed into the formal staff structures of the government health services... However, incorporation of this new category of health worker into the government health services would be both complex and costly... It is therefore the Department's view that this category should not be incorporated into the formal health services. (*Restructuring the National Health System for Universal Primary Health Care*, p.18)

219. Through a process of consultation, provincial workshops, and a discussion within the National Consultative Health Forum, the PHC package has been refined. (*Annual Report*, Department of Health, 1997, p.8)

220. **2.12.5.6** The main bodies responsible for ensuring access to and the delivery of health services must be the (District Health Authorities)... In the first phase of the RDP the government must develop at least one model or pilot in each province.

221. The health district will be the building block of the National Health System, and a unified, integrated health management structure at local level, to be known as the District Health Authority (DHA) will play the key administrative role within the publicly funded PHC system... There will be a carefully controlled and gradual shift in the role of the DHA, from that of an integrated funder and provider of care towards a "public purchaser" model in which the DHA will act as a purchaser of care from varying combinations of public and private providers. (*Restructuring the National Health System for Universal Primary Health Care*, p.14)

It is essential that... a District Health System (DHS), in which responsibility for service delivery is entrusted to the district level, be established as soon as possible... Each province will be subdivided into a number of functional health districts. The district will serve both as a provider and purchaser of health services, and select the appropriate strategy on the basis of equity, efficiency and assessment of local conditions... There will thus be an opportunity for the ultimate emergence of some form of provider competition... public health facilities will remain the dominant PHC providers funded by the government for the next few years... accredited private providers will be introduced gradually. (*White Paper for the Transformation of the Health System in South Africa*, 2.0, 2.3.2, 2.6.4)

222. The Department has adopted the District Health System (DHS) as the vehicle for the delivery of primary health care services in the country... The Department has made significant strides in this respect with the demarcation of districts completed in all

provinces (180 districts already demarcated)... All regional managers and 63 (35%) district managers have been appointed, and more than 130 members of regional and district management teams have received management training. (*Annual Report*, Department of Health, 1997, pp.6-7)

223. **2.12.5.8** The whole NHS must be driven by the Primary Health Care (PHC) approach. This emphasises community participation and empowerment, inter-sectoral collaboration and cost-effective care, as well as integration of preventive, promotive curative and rehabilitation services... **2.12.6.1** Health care for all children under six years of age, and for homeless children, must immediately be provided free at government clinics and health centres... **2.12.11.2** Within a period of five years a whole range of services must be available free to the aged, the disabled, the unemployed and to students who cannot afford health care.

224. **2.12.6.3** Preventive and promotive health programmes for children must be improved. Breast-feeding must be encouraged and promoted, and the code of ethics on breast-milk substitutes enforced. A more effective, expanded programme of immunisation must achieve a coverage of 90 per cent within three years. Polio and tetanus can be eradicated within two years.

225. The publicly funded PHC system will, over time, provide a comprehensive package of PHC services to the entire population of the country. This package will include district hospital services, environmental health service and other preventive, promotive and monitoring services, and comprehensive ambulatory services, including access to essential medicines for PHC... In practice, the actual scope of the PHC package will be determined by resource constraints, and may vary between different regions in the country at different points in time. (*Towards a National Health System*, p.9)

226. The goal: basic health care for all South Africans within 10 years... Access to all personal consultation services, and all non-personal services provided by the publicly funded PHC system will be free of charge to all permanent residents at point of service. In addition, where patients bypass PHC facilities and present at public hospitals for outpatient services, payment of an additional charge will be required, except in cases of emergencies, or where public PHC facilities are closed or not available. Finally, as part of a more general policy on user charges in public hospitals, charges will be placed on inpatient hospital care at district level. The main proposed new financial sources are social health insurance and retention in the health services fees collected by public hospitals. (*Towards a National Health System*, p.11)
To improve accessibility to health services, free health care for children and pregnant mothers was introduced in June 1994. This was extended to free PHC services for all South African citizens in 1996. (*Annual Report*, Department of Health, 1997, p.6)

227. Priority areas of programme communication will (include): Breast-feeding: its successful initiation, management and protection, as well as the development of a Code for the Marketing of Breast Milk Substitutes... Legislation relevant to nutrition will be

reviewed, strengthened, implemented and enforced–to protect breast-feeding and for the marketing of infant foods. (*Towards a National Health System*, p.92,94)

228. **2.12.6.2** There must be a programme to improve maternal and child health through access to quality antenatal, delivery and postnatal services for all women. This must include better transport facilities and in-service training programmes for midwives and for traditional birth attendants. Targets must include 90 per cent of pregnant women receiving antenatal care and 75 per cent of deliveries being supervised and carried out under hygienic conditions within two years. By 1999, 90 per cent of deliveries should be supervised. These services must be free at government facilities by the third year of the RDP.

229. The following (maternal, child and women's health) services will be provided free of charge at all public health facilities: Immunisation, family planning, ante-natal care, delivery and post-natal care, treatment of all children under six years of age... Health workers will be trained to improve their skills in the provision of quality, integrated MCWH services. (*Towards a National Health System*, pp.104-105,111).
All health facilities, as far as possible, will render MCWH services on a one-stop, "supermarket" basis. Existing health facilities should review the allocation of available space and, where possible, relocate MCWH services closer to one another... Health workers will be trained to improve their skills in the provision of quality, integrated MCWH services. Health managers will be trained in micro-planning, focusing on improving the coverage and effectiveness of MCWH services. (*White Paper for the Transformation of the Health System in South Africa*, 8.2.1,8.5.1)

230. Independent evaluation of the implementation of the policy of free health care suggested that it has achieved its aims as most clinics report increased attendance; improved attendance at ante-natal and family planning clinics; and nearly three quarters of the health workers surveyed... said that the policy was successful in preventing serious illness or death among pregnant women and children (Evaluation and Free Health Care done jointly by Health Systems Trust and Department of Health). (*Annual Report*, Department of Health, 1997, p.6)

231. **2.12.6.2** There should be established the right to six months paid maternity leave and 10 days paternity leave.

232. An employee is entitled to four months' maternity leave during which her security of employment is protected... Every employee with more than one year's service is entitled to three days paid paternity or child-care leave during the year of the birth of the child. (*Employment Standards Statute: Policy Proposals*, pp.61,62)

233. An employee is entitled to at least four consecutive months maternity leave... No employee may work for six weeks after the birth of her child unless a medical practitioner or midwife certifies that she is fit to do so... An employee who has a miscarriage during the third trimester of pregnancy or a stillborn child is entitled to maternity leave for six weeks after the miscarriage or stillbirth... Notification must be given at least four weeks before the employee intends to commence maternity leave... The payment of maternity

benefits will be... subject to the provisions of the *Unemployment Insurance Act*, 1996... An employer must grant an employee, during each annual leave cycle... three days paid [family responsibility] leave which the employee is entitled to take—(a) when the employee's child is born; (b) when the employee's child is sick or (c) in the event of death of [family member]. (*Basic Conditions of Employment Act*, pp.14,15)

234. **2.12.6.4** Reproductive rights must be guaranteed and reproductive health services must promote people's right to privacy and dignity. Every woman must have the right to choose whether or not to have an early termination of pregnancy.

235. Women and men will be provided with services which enable them to achieve optimal reproductive and sexual health. (*White Paper for the Transformation of the Health System in South Africa*, 8.6)

236. Recognising the values of human dignity, the achievement of equality, security of the person, non-racialism and non-sexism, and the advancement of human rights and freedoms which underlie a democratic South Africa; Recognising that both women and men have the right to be informed of and have access to safe, effective, affordable, and acceptable methods of fertility regulation of their choice... 2. (1) A pregnancy may be terminated--(a) upon request of a woman during the first 12 weeks of the gestation period of her pregnancy; (b) from the 13th up to the 20th week of the gestation period id a medical practitioner, after consultation with the pregnant woman, is of the opinion that--(i) the continued pregnancy would pose a risk of injury to the woman's physical or mental health; or (ii) there exists a substantial risk that the fetus would suffer from a severe physical or mental abnormality; or (iii) the pregnancy resulted from rape or incest; or (iv) the continued pregnancy would significantly alter the social or economic circumstances of the woman; or (c) after the 20th week of the gestation period is a medical practitioner, after consultation with another medical practitioner or a registered midwife, is of the opinion that the continued pregnancy--(i) would endanger the woman's life; (ii) would result in a severe malformation of the fetus; or (iii) would pose risk of injury to the fetus... 5 (2) Notwithstanding any other law or the common law... no consent other than that of the pregnant woman shall be required for the termination of a pregnancy. (*Choice of Termination of Pregnancy Act*, No. 92 of 1996)

237. Regulations passed in 1997 [for] Choice of Termination of Pregnancy Act, 1996. Name of Regulation: Regulations on information required from a practitioner terminating a pregnancy. Brief Description: Make provision for information to be recorded by a medical practitioner or registered midwife who terminates pregnancy, the manner of recording such information, the training course to be undergone by a registered midwife, etc. Implications: Provide uniform manner of recording the necessary information and ensure that patients receive high standard of medical care. (*Annual Report*, Department of Health, 1997, p.85)

238. **2.12.10.3** Redistribution of personnel will be achieved through more appropriate training, through incentives to work in underserviced areas, through limiting openings for private practice in overserviced areas, and through contractual obligations for those

receiving subsidised training... **2.12.10.4** Strenuous efforts must be made... to attract health workers in private practice back into the public sector, at least on a sessional basis.

239. The gap in medical staff requirements would best be filled through substantial increases in the number of doctors employed on a full-time basis in public facilities... A policy requiring new medical and other health professional graduates to spend a defined period working in the public sector prior to being allowed to enter private practice... will be implemented through the introduction of a two year period of limited registration after completion of the internship... Despite the strong preference for full-time medical staff, it remains likely that a substantial proportion of the additional medical staff requirements will be made up by attracting increased numbers of part-time medical staff to do sessional work in public PHC facilities... There will be many areas in the country where there will need to be some reliance on the use of services of GPs practicing in their own rooms. (*Towards a National Health System*, pp.26,28,31)

240. In order to ensure that medical doctors are available to the public sectors in the required numbers, recently passed legislation which makes provision for community service, will be used. Community service will be initiated in July 1998, when it will become compulsory for all newly qualified doctors... A total of 272 Cuban doctors have been deployed in eight provinces... To date [December 1997] a total of 20 doctors [were] recruited under [an agreement with CIM] Centrum Fur Internationale Migration und Entwcklung... [of the] European Union. (*Annual Report*, Department of Health, 1997, pp.10-11)

241. **2.12.10.5** One of the most important parts of the RDP in the health sector will be the complete transformation of health worker training. This must involve... developing new training programmes to reorientate existing personnel and to train new categories and auxiliary workers... **2.12.10.2** There must be a programme of retraining and reorientating all existing health workers to the Primary Health Care approach. The aim is to train 25 per cent of district health personnel by the end of 1995, and 50 per cent by the end of 1997.

242. A national audit of trained health personnel and their distribution has been undertaken and an audit of all training institutions is underway... All education and training programmes will be co-ordinated, reviewed and rationalised to meet the health needs of the country. (*National Human Resource Development Policy*, pp.1,4)
The current supply of professional nurses should be used to address the identified PHCN... In some areas, it may... necessary to transfer nurses from hospital positions to the PHC level... The second priority is to undertake rapid and carefully planned investments in PHCN training. Nurse training (including the training of PHC nurses) is allocated an average real growth of 5,1% per year. (*Restructuring the National Health System for Universal Primary Health Care*, pp.25,42)

243. **2.12.11.3** Essential drugs must be provided in all PHC facilities. An essential drugs list must be established to reduce the current wasteful expenditure on inappropriate drugs.

244. The (Essential Drugs List) will consist of medicines critically required for use in the public sector for the prevention and management of 90-95% of the common and important conditions in the country... EDL medicines will be available at all district hospitals, public providers and accredited private providers. (*Towards a National Health System*, p.35)

245. The registrar shall ensure than such an application in respect of medicine which appears on the latest Essential Drugs List or medicine which does not appear thereon nit which, in the opinion of the Minister, is essential to national health is subject to such procedures as may be prescribed in order to expedite the registration... The minister may prescribe conditions for the supply of more affordable medicines in certain circumstances so as to protect the health of the public, and in particular may--... (b) prescribe the conditions on which any medicine which is identical in composition, meets the same quality of standard and is intended to have the same proprietary name as that of another medicine already registered in the Republic... may be imported... The Minister shall, after consultation with the pharmaceutical industry and other stakeholders, prescribe a code of ethics relating to the marketing policies of pharmaceutical companies. (*Medicines and Related Substances Control Amendment Act*, 1997, pp.6-7)

246. The Standard Treatment Guidelines and Essential Drugs List (EDL), published in 1996, for primary care has undergone a revision...The [EDL] list has been distributed to 1218 medical interns and 300 pharmacist interns. At a hospital level, the first draft of the [EDL] of the most prevalent diseases, treatment guidelines for these conditions and the relevant medicines, has been compiled. The first draft has been distributed to 220 hospitals, 8 medical schools and al the provincial Departments of Health. (*Annual Report*, Department of Health, 1997, p.52)

247. **2.13.2** The RDP aims to transform the existing social welfare policies, programmes and delivery systems so as to ensure basic welfare rights are provided to all South Africans, prioritising those who have been historically disadvantaged... **2.13.3** Social welfare includes the right to basic needs such as shelter, food, health care, work opportunities, income security and all those aspects that promote the physical, social and emotional wellbeing of all people in our society, with special provision made for those who are unable to provide for themselves because of specific problems... **2.13.13** Social security measures must initially focus on the needs of those who have been historically disadvantaged, such as domestic workers, agricultural workers, seasonal workers, workers who are disabled, women, the homeless, and families in rural and informal settlements. **2.13.6** There must be a comprehensive review of all the policies and legislation regulating social welfare and social security. In particular the *National Welfare Act of 1978*, the *Social Work Act of 1978*, and *Acts* dealing with child and family welfare must be changed. New umbrella legislation which provides the framework for a development-oriented social welfare system based on the principles of equality, equity, access, user involvement and empowerment, and public accountability must be developed. **2.13.11** Social assistance in the form of cash or in-kind benefits should be given to those most at risk (such social assistance could take the form of work opportunities in public works programmes; the provision of food, clothing, and health care needs to those in need; cash in the form of disability grants, foster care grants, maintenance grants, or grants for veterans according to predetermined criteria).

248. The national goals of the proposed strategy are: To facilitate the provision of appropriate developmental social welfare services to all South Africans, especially those living in poverty, those who are vulnerable and those who have special needs... Poverty coincides with racial, gender and geographic or spatial determinants, and these will be taken into account in the targeting of programmes... In view of the widespread rural poverty, a rural development strategy will be developed by the Department of Welfare in consultation with all the relevant role-players, which will increase the access of rural people to developmental social welfare programmes... Participation at the community level will be given particular attention. A multi-pronged approach will be used to involve civil society in legislative processes. Any process to develop legislation will include a comprehensive communication and empowerment strategy... There will be universal access to an integrated and sustainable social security system. Every South African should have a minimum income, sufficient to meet basic subsistence needs, and should not have to live below minimum acceptable standards. (*Draft White Paper for Social Welfare*, pp.14,18,62,80) We will ensure fair and equitable access to social welfare, especially for those who have rights to pensions, but have so far not obtained access to the system. (*Rural Development Strategy*, p.6)

249. The new *Constitution* and other policy frameworks have necessitated the alignment of legislation with the principles and values enshrined in them. Two *Acts* were passed in the field of welfare during 1997, namely: a) *The Not-for-Profit Organisations Act*, 1997 (Act No. 71 of 1997); and b) *The Welfare Laws Amendment Act*, 1997 (Act No. 106 of 1997). Both *Acts* are key elements of welfare's efforts to promote self-reliance, fight poverty and build partnerships. The *Not-for-Profit Organisations (NPO) Act, 1997* which will come into operation during July 1998, replaces parts of the *Fund-raising Act, 1978*. The *NPO Act* lays the foundation for a strong NPO sector and will build a constructive relationship between the government and the sector. The *Welfare Laws Amendment Act, 1997*, parts of which came into operation on 1 April 1998, provides primarily for the introduction of the Child Support Grant and the phasing-out of the maintenance grant over a period of three years. The new grant focuses on children under the age of 7 years and will be paid to a primary caregiver at the level of R100 per child per month. (*Annual Report*, Department of Welfare, 1998, p.7)

250. In view of fiscal constraints, it is not possible for the welfare function to grow in real terms in the medium term. (*Draft White Paper for Social Welfare*, p.90)

251. **2.13.4** The goals of a developmental social welfare programme (include)... the empowerment of individuals, families and communities to participate in the process of deciding on the range of needs and problems to be addressed through local, provincial and national initiatives... **2.13.14** Social welfare rights and the distribution of benefits must be guided by the principles of user empowerment and participation through community- and worker-based citizens-rights education programmes.

252. The community development approach, philosophy, process, methods and skills will be used in strategies at local level to meet needs... Developmental social welfare strategies will be devised to ensure that all people have adequate economic and social protection, and

have access to welfare programmes which will promote development and enhance social functioning. (*Draft White Paper for Social Welfare*, pp.24,90)

253. Government implemented the Child Support Grant, from 1 April 1998; a data clean-up of the social security system to eliminate fraud and corruption, ghost recipients of social grants; and establishing a national security system... In the past year there has been an intense focus on the country's social security programme with policy positions being debated and delivery issues coming under close scrutiny. Social security is arguably the government's biggest and most effective poverty alleviation programme and all efforts are being made to establish it as an efficient and well-targeted mechanism for reaching the poor and vulnerable. Despite certain problem areas, a number of important steps were taken in the past year to improve service delivery to nearly 3 million South Africans in poor households who receive various social grants. The Public Service Commission (PSC) has also made recommendations on a model for social security which will be finalised with the provincial departments which will clarify national-provincial relations. A major clean-up of the data on our social pension system (SOCPEN) is under way and has already yielded savings... The Department of Welfare has developed the Flagship Programme as part of its anti-poverty strategy. R50 million has been invested in approximately 1140 anti-poverty projects benefitting 1376 women and 1291 children. (*Annual Report*, Department of Welfare, 1998, pp.9,30-31,34)

254. **2.13.12** The RDP aims to establish a national coordinating body with representation of workers, community members, the social welfare sector, the private sector, government, and other appropriate organisations to review existing legislation, policies and procedures and to monitor the implementation of a transformed social security system. **2.13.7.4** The planning, coordination and evaluation of social services must take place with community and inter-sectoral involvement... **2.13.19** Inter-sectoral units on areas such as mental health, child care, women, and juvenile justice must be developed to plan and implement integrated strategies aimed at improving services to these target groups. In addition, the relationship between social welfare, health, community development and labour institutions and related sectors must be improved.

255. Appropriate intersectoral governmental mechanisms will be established in consultation with the relevant departments. The national Department of Welfare will participate in intersectoral structures set up by other Government departments. Relevant non-governmental role-players will also be involved as the need arises... A task group representative of Government and civil society will be established immediately to address the reorientation, rationalisation and restructuring of the formal welfare sector... the terms of reference of the task group will be defined in consultation with the roleplayers. Appropriate, legitimate, transparent and effective governance mechanisms will be developed at local, district, provincial and national levels to build and consolidate the partnership between Government and all stakeholders in civil society... A representative mechanism will be set up at national level to ensure inclusivity and transparency in establishing legislative needs and to guide and co-ordinate drafting processes in accordance with accepted values and principles... New models: The creation of a small unit, consisting of people knowledgeable about both social security and community and social development,

and including stakeholders outside of Government, which will identify areas in emerging RDP public works programmes in which social security beneficiaries can take up work or service opportunities. An important task will be to identify for the RDP the groups of people who should be absorbed into public works programmes (p.82).

An intersectoral commission will be established... to educate policy-makers and the public regarding the needs of families for social support, and to consider realistic trade-offs. The commission will also be invited to explore the following: Linking the receipt of grants to community service; converting from grants per number of children to family allowance; procedures to improve the payment of maintenance by defaulting parents, and to enforce the payment of maintenance for families where parents are separated or divorced, in collaboration with the Department of Justice; issuing a proclamation to the effect that new grants to families will be temporary awards whose continuity will be conditional on the findings of the commission. (*Draft White Paper for Social Welfare*, pp.40,44,60)

256. The National Interim Consultative Committee on Developmental Social Services (NICC) was the first welfare governance structure to be appointed by the Minister for Welfare and Population Development for an interim period of one year. This was in response to the need by the stakeholders for a legitimate, participatory governance structure to promote consultation on major policy issues. The NICC submitted a report, "Introducing Democratic Governance in the Developmental Welfare Sector," in August 1997. The most important recommendation was that the permanent structure should be a statutory body. The NICC's first term of office ended on 15 August 1997. The second phase of the NICC's work--from 15 February 1998 to 30 June 1999--will involve the drafting of a National Welfare Bill to legislate for a permanent government structure. The Minister reappointed members who will represent the following constituencies: national government, provincial government, religious organisations, statutory bodies, professional bodies, consumers, funders, service providers, the NGO sector, National Welfare Social Services and Development Forum and training institutions. (*Annual Report*, Department of Welfare, 1998, pp.9-10)

257. **2.13.10** The national social security system must be designed to meet the needs of workers in both formal and informal sectors, and of the unemployed, through: social insurance which includes compulsory private contributory pension schemes or provident funds for all workers, and state social pensions; linking contributory pension/provident funds and non-contributory schemes, as well as the transfer of contributory pensions; and criteria which entitle workers to retire between the ages of 60 and 65, or to a social pension at 60.

258. The government will advocate that all people in formal employment belong to a compulsory retirement scheme. Public education programmes will be provided to promote retirement planning... Social assistance grants will continue to be provided in order to support elderly people who qualify for such benefits. The development of a savings scheme will be explored in order to encourage individuals to take responsibility for their own retirement as well as to alleviate the pressure on the social grants system. (*Draft White Paper for Social Welfare*, p.86)

259. **2.3.17** The rights of children must be protected and measures must be taken to ensure that community-based and workplace care centres are provided for children in need of alternate care. The RDP must ensure that immediate steps are taken to remove all children from prisons and police cells. Alternate detention centres with proper health facilities, counselling and other support services must be provided for children. Special programmes protecting homeless children, especially those on the streets, must be put into place.

260. A national early childhood development strategy will be devised as part of an intersectoral programme in collaboration with other Government departments, civil society and the private sector... In view of the fragmentation of efforts to address the needs of children in trouble with the law with Government departments and between NGOs, consensus is being sought on a holistic and integrated response... Vulnerable children will be prevented from becoming street children; street children will be reconciled with their families and communities; and if the latter is impossible, alternative ways to reintegrate street children into society will be explored and made use of. (*Draft White Paper for Social Welfare*, pp.102,108)

261. Transforming our child and youth care system. In 1995 when young people awaiting trial were released from prisons, the child and youth care system (which functions mainly within the welfare sector but is shared by Justice, Education, Correctional Services and SAPS) was unable to respond with appropriate resources and programmes. This situation together with South Africa's commitment to the implementation of the United Nations Convention on the Rights of the Child, resulted in an Inter-Ministerial Committee on Young People at Risk (IMC) being established by the Cabinet to design a new system and manage the crisis in the interim. In 1996 the IMC set up six pilot projects to test aspects of a new child and youth care system and to develop policy guidelines. Four of the projects have been finalised... The National Plan of Action for Children (NPA) is a programme which strives to protect children in difficult circumstances. Within the NPA, the Department of Welfare is responsible for the implementation of the International Convention on the Rights of the Child. There are several categories of children who are classified as being difficult circumstances, including those at risk of abuse or neglect. Children of divorcing parents and children undergoing adoption. In the past year, a number of initiatives have been taken to realise Welfare's objectives in these areas... The *Child Care Amendment Act* (Act 96 of 1996) took effect on 1 April 1998. In terms of this *Act*, several measures will come into operation to improve provided to children at risk. They include the establishment of a National Child Protection Register. All incidents where ill-treatment or deliberate injury to children are suspected will have to be reported to the Director-General of Welfare. Street shelters will have to be registered. An Action Plan to Prevent and Combat the Commercial Sexual Exploitation of Children was developed to implement the Agenda of Action approved by 122 Governments during the Stockholm World Congress in 1996. A Task Team was established to investigate a National Register for Convicted Sexual Offenders Against Children. The first report of this Task Team has been submitted to the Minister for Welfare and Population Development. (*Annual Report*, Department of Welfare, 1998, p.14)

262. **2.13.18** The existing pool of social service workers and their conditions of service must be reviewed. The present number of social workers (approximately 7 500) is inadequate and their training is often inappropriate. Many social workers must be reorientated and retrained within a developmental approach to social welfare. The national, provincial, and local social welfare departments must have both specialised and generic social service personnel at management, middle-management and operational levels. The curricula of social welfare and community development educational institutions must be reviewed. Within a five-year period a minimum of another 3 000 community development workers must be trained to work within provincial and local government structures to aid the process of prioritisation of community needs and allocation of resources. Social service managers must be trained with due regard to the need for affirmative action.

263. A five year action plan will be developed to eliminate inequity between employees along lines of race, rank, gender and disablement... An appropriately trained pool of personnel at all levels, which includes both generic and specialised services, will be developed... Training programmes will also be specifically designed to reorient existing personnel towards development approaches... The low salaries of social welfare personnel in both the public and voluntary welfare sectors is an issue that must be urgently addressed... Volunteer programmes will be developed by Government and its non-governmental partners. The appropriate and effective utilisation of volunteers in developmental social welfare services is critical. (*Draft White Paper for Social Welfare*, p.54)

264. **3.3.11.1** We must foster... a culture of teaching and learning... **3.3.11.2** The democratic government must enable all children to go to school for at least 10 years... The government must phase in compulsory education as soon as possible. To achieve this objective we must rebuild and expand our schools... We must ensure that no class exceeds 40 students by the end of the decade... **3.3.11.6** ... all schools and existing facilities are to be used to full capacity by the start of 1995 for both compulsory and non-compulsory learning... **3.3.11.7** Farm schools and community schools must be progressively incorporated into the ordinary school system, and additional schools must be provided in commercial farming areas.

265. The government is committed to the goal of providing access to general education for all children from a reception year up to Grade 9 (Standard 7), funded by the state at an acceptable level of quality, and to achieve this goal in the shortest possible time... The implementation of the reception year will take place over a period of years... Attendance in the reception or pre-school year should not be mandatory except in areas where capacity exists... The phasing-in of the state-supported reception year must be done in a manner which accords priority to those areas of greatest need...
ABET programmes can make more cost-effective use of available educational facilities. (*White Paper on Education and Training*, pp.31,73,75)

266. Subject to this *Act* and any applicable provincial law, every parent must cause every learner for whom he or she is responsible to attend a school from the first school day of the year in which such learner reaches the age of seven years until the last school day of the year in which such learner reaches the age of fifteen years or the ninth grade, whichever occurs first. (2) The Minister must... determine the ages of compulsory

attendance at school for learners with special education needs. (3) Every Member of the Executive Council [MEC] must ensure that there are enough school places so that every child who lives in his or her province can attend school as required. (*South Africa Schools Act*, Chapter 2, 3)

267. [I]n fulfilling their obligation to raise supplementary resources, governing bodies are not required to charge school fees. Whether or not to charge school fees is a matter for the parents of the school... At the parents' general meeting, any resolution which proposes fee payment must include the amount of fees to be charged, and ... equitable criteria and procedures for the total, partial or conditional exemption of parents who are unable to pay... the fees. (*Norms and Standards for School Funding*, 50,51)

268. A governing body of a public school must take all reasonable measures within its means to supplement the resources supplied by the State in order to improve the quality of education provided by the school... The school fund, all proceeds thereof and the assets (acquired by a public school on or after the commencement of this *Act*) must be used only for educational purposes at, or in connection with such school, or another public school determined by the governing body, unless otherwise agreed between the Head of Department and the governing body of the school... The following categories will be applicable for purposes of exemption of a parent from payment of such school fees—a. if the combined annual gross income of the parents is less than ten times the annual school fees per learner, the parent qualifies for full exemption; if the combined annual gross income of the parents is less than thirty times but more than ten times the annual school fees per learner, the parent qualifies for partial exemption; and if the combined annual gross income of a parents is more than thirty times the annual school fees per learner, the parent does not qualify for exemption. Any person who has the responsibility of a parent of a learner placed in a foster home, foster care or place of safety is exempted from payment of any school fees. (*South African Schools Act*, 3)

269. **3.1.4** Special attention must be given to (women and youth) in the planning and implementation of human resources development policies and strategies... **3.3.6** Within all education and training programmes special attention must be given to the special interests of girls and women... adult basic education and training programmes should give special emphasis to women trapped in the rural areas. Campaigns and information should also open up a wider range of learning opportunities and choices for women, which in turn should lead to a wider range of income-generating forms of employment. Girls and women should be encouraged to pursue non-traditional subjects such as maths and science... special steps must be taken to give full recognition and value to the work and skills that are traditionally associated with women... **4.3.14** Educational opportunities in the rural areas lag far behind those in the cities.

270. The Minister of Education proposes to appoint a Gender Equity Task Team... to investigate and advise the Department of Education on the establishment of a permanent Gender Equity Unit... If girls have been systematically discouraged from selecting subject combinations that emphasise mathematics and science, then achieving equitable education

requires that new ways be found to encourage more girls to select the subjects. (*White Paper on Education and Training*, pp.46,74)

271. [National education policy] shall be directed towards... achieving equitable education opportunities and the redress of past inequality in education provision, including the promotion of gender equality and the advancement of the status of women. (*National Education Policy Act*, 4)

272. The major rural education issues facing national and provincial governments are how to improve access to education, improve its quality and establish effective democratic structures for educational governance. To redress past neglect of rural education, there must be positive discrimination in favour of rural areas. (*Rural Development Strategy*, p.37) Under apartheid, Africans living in rural areas were denied educational opportunities to an even greater extent than those in urban areas. Most rural schools are poorly resourced with buildings, equipment, and books and without electricity and running water... The needs are immense. Government is committed to increase the level and availability of formal education in rural areas, and supply training and assistance to the new district and rural councils. The major rural education issues facing national and provincial governments are how to improve access to education, improve its quality and establish effective democratic structures for school management. To redress past neglect of rural education, there must be positive discrimination in favour of rural areas. ...The *South African Schools Act*... determines, in line with the *Constitution*, the right to basic education. The obligation to provide sufficient places in public schools lies with the provinces... Public spending on education will, as far as possible, be weighted to favour the poor and historically deprived schools. Most rural community schools and farm schools will fall into this category... Linked to this has been the allocation of provincial education funds for transport assistance to children in remote areas, to improve their access to schools. The Departments of Education and Health co-manage the Primary School Nutrition Programme to address the question of hunger in primary school children. The programme has been largely rural and has increased pupil registration and attendance at school. (*Rural Development Framework*, pp.61-62)

273. **3.3.4** Democratic school governance structures must be set up which involve democratically-elected parent and teacher representatives, as well as providing for student participation at a consultative level.

274. The governance of a public school is vested in its governing body... The following categories of persons must be represented on the governing body of a public school, in each case by a member or members of such category--parents who are not employed at the school; educators at the school; members of staff at the school who are not educators; and learners in the eighth grade or higher at the school. The principal must be a member... Parents must comprise the majority of members of a governing body who have voting rights. (*South African Schools Act*, pp.12,16)
. The National Department of Education (NDET) has produced a user-friendly guide for newly elected members of a School Governing Body (SGB) called *First Steps*. (*The Building has Begun!*, p.30)

275. Out of funds appropriated for this purpose by the provincial legislature, the Head of Department must establish a programme to—(a) provide introductory training for newly elected governing bodies to enable them to perform their functions; and (b) provide continuing training to governing bodies to promote effective performance of their functions...
Subject to this *Act*, the membership of the governing body of an ordinary public school comprises – (a) elected members; (b) the principal; (c) co-opted members. Elected members of the governing body shall comprise a member or members of the following categories: (a) Parents of learners at the school; (b) educators at the school; (c) members of staff who are not educators; and (d) learners in the eighth grade or higher at the school... A governing body must from amongst its members, elect office-bearers, who must include at least a chairperson, a treasurer and a secretary. (*South African Schools Act*, 23,29.1)

276. Almost all of the 30 000 public schools have now elected governing bodies. (*The Building has Begun!*, p.30)

277. **3.3.7** An integrated qualifications framework. By establishing a national qualifications framework which integrates all elements of the education and training system, we must enable learners to progress to higher levels from any starting point... The system must enable assessment and recognition of prior learning skills acquired through experience... **3.3.5.6** (The education and training bureaucracy must be reorganised... through the establishment of) a statutory South African Qualifications Authority with the responsibility for accreditation, certification and maintenance of national standards.

278. The Ministers of Education and Labour have established an Inter-Ministerial Working group to develop their common interests in an integrated approach to education and training and a National Qualification Framework, and to clarify their respective competencies with regard to training... The Inter-Ministerial Working Group of the Ministries of Education and Labour has prepared draft legislation for the creation of a National Qualifications Framework... The South African Qualifications Authority (SAQA)... will be brought into existence through legislation as a parastatal body, in the shortest possible time after the *NQF Act* has been passed. SAQA will be charged with developing the National Qualification Framework, on a fully consultative basis, for the Minister's approval. (*White Paper on Education and Training*, pp.16,26)

279. Since the inaugural meeting of SAQA, held 2-4 August 1996, the following has been achieved in overseeing the development of the NQF as envisaged in Section 5(1)(a)(1) of the *Act*: Consensus has been reached in SAQA about the conceptual framework needed to proceed with the development and implementation of the NQF. This includes the establishment of National Standards Bodies (NSBs) and Education, Training and Quality Assurance Bodies (ETQAs). (*Annual Report*, National Department of Education, 1997, p.76)

280. **3.3.8** We must expand early childhood educare by supporting an increase in private and public funding; institutionalising it within the ministry and provincial departments, and raising national awareness of the importance of such programmes. The democratic

government also bears the ultimate responsibility for training, upgrading and setting national standards for educare providers...

281. The national and provincial Departments of Education need to establish formal inter-departmental committees on ECD (Early Childhood Development) with their counterparts in the Departments of Health and of Welfare and Population Development, and link these with RDP human resource development planning at national and provincial levels... The new Directorate of Early Childhood Development and Lower Primary Education, acting through the appropriate National Curriculum Committee, will... be responsible for coordinating the reshaping of curriculum frameworks and related advice on teaching methodology... The centre of gravity for professional innovation, and the major responsibility for provision, will not lie with government departments but with non-government, community-based and private providers, resource and training agencies. (*White Paper on Education and Training*, pp.33-34)

282. The White Paper on Education and Training identified Early Childhood Development (ECD) as a priority which needed urgent attention... The CEM and HEDCOM approved a national Early Childhood Development pilot project which was launched in 1996 and will be run over a period of three years. (*Annual Report*, National Department of Education, 1997, p.41)

283. **3.3.6** Adult basic education and training programmes should give special emphasis to women trapped in the rural areas... **3.3.9.1** Special provision must be made for ABE (Adult Basic Education) within the future national ministry and government departments at all levels... **3.3.9.2** The provision of ABE must be expanded by building a partnership of all employer, labour, local and provincial government, community and funding agencies... **3.3.9.3** ABE must be centrally included in all reconstruction projects, and particularly programmes for the unemployed. Micro enterprises must also be given assistance with respect to ABE...

284. The main organisational programme of the national ABET programme will be the building of partnerships of all constituencies with a vital interest in the ABET enterprise... The partnerships are expected to undertake planning, arrange public advocacy, sponsor research and development, and mobilise financial resources for the programme. (*White Paper on Education and Training*, p.31)

285. A draft ABET policy document has served as the basis for wide consultation since 1995. In April 1997 a workshop was held where the policy was adopted by all stakeholders. The policy was since ratified by HEDCOM in October 1997 and by CEM late in December 1997... An ABET curriculum development process has been set in motion and a SAQA recognised qualification is expected or will be possible by 1999. (*Annual Report*, National Department of Education, 1997, pp.45,46)

286. **3.3.10** The RDP must redress (the learning needs of children and adults with physical or other disabilities and impairments) by establishing appropriate institutional structures and inter-sectoral groups, mounting a national advocacy campaign to raise awareness of the

issue, ensuring that existing facilities are optimally used, and developing new programmes as needed.

287. Provision of (Education Support Services and services to learners with special education needs) is a matter for provincial departments... The Ministry of Education favours the early appointment of a National Commission on Special Needs in Education and Training... The Department of Education will propose to the Heads of Education Departments Committee that an investigation into the holistic and integrative concept of ESS be undertaken. (*White Paper on Education and Training*, pp.28-29)

288. The National Commission on Special Needs in Education presented its final report to the Minister of Education in November 1997. (*Annual Report*, National Department of Education, 1997, p.53)

289. **3.3.11.8** we must find points of entry to permit reconstruction (of the existing curriculum) to start in 1994. Major stakeholders must reach agreement through the National Education and Training Forum on the management of curriculum and examinations in the transition period. We must establish institutes for curriculum development at national and provincial levels... **3.3.11.3** ... we must align the structure, curricula and certification with the new national qualifications system... **3.3.11.5** The new programmes, curricula and teaching approaches for the first four years of school must take into account the language, learning and developmental needs of young children... **3.3.11.9** Curriculum development must... pay special attention to (the areas of science, mathematics, technology, arts and culture).

290. Important developmental and coordination work at the national level has been done by the Curriculum Technical Sub-Committee of the National Education and Training Forum... Considerable interest has been expressed in the concept of a National Institute of Curriculum Development (NICD). In the light of the progress which has been made in establishing new National Curriculum Committees and a representative Coordinating Committee for the School Curriculum, the Department of Education will invite the Heads of Education Departments Committee and the main stakeholders and roleplayers in education and training to participate in a study of alternative forms such an Institute could take, and the ways in which it could function... The Ministry of Education will give support to a new intervention starting in 1995 to "recover" science and mathematics students and upgrade both their knowledge and attitudes to these subjects. (*White Paper on Education and Training*, pp.27,31)

291. A new national curriculum based on the principles of outcomes-based education was introduced in all Grade 1 classes in January 1998... A gradual and systematic phasing in of this new curriculum in all other grades within a defined period has been planned. (*The Building has Begun!*, p.30)

292. **3.3.11.4** Education from the present Standard 8 up to the present Standard 10 must be redesigned and incorporated into an integrated post-compulsory phase of learning, co-ordinated at national level and result in a Further Education Certificate (or National

Higher Certificate). This will integrate post-compulsory schooling with training... **3.3.12.2**
A balanced and flexible curriculum leading to the National Higher Certificate must be
developed for all learners in a variety of learning contexts: students learning within formal
institutions, workers in industry, out-of-school youth, and adults learning in community
learning centres.

293. The Ministry of Education is of the view that a National Commission on Further
Education is needed to undertake the research, consultation and planning required to set
this level of learning on an energetic growth path... The level of state subsidisation of
senior secondary education will depend most obviously on the level of per capita
expenditure that is allocated to the general education sector in the compulsory phase and
the priority government attaches to sustaining good quality schooling in the post-
compulsory phase. The levels of state subsidy will also be related to the extent to which
students and their families can be expected to contribute to the cost of provision, quite
apart from whatever voluntary contributions they might make. (*White Paper on Education
and Training*, pp.32,78)
Programmes and services provided by youth and community colleges shall be expanded
and shall develop specific initiatives which address the needs of out-of-school young women
and men... These shall include pre-employment training, vocational training and skills
development. It shall also include remedial courses. (*National Youth Policy*, 8.21)

294. The need to re-organise Further Education and Training... led to the Minister's
appointment of a National Committee on Further Education in late 1996. (*Annual Report*,
National Department of Education, 1996, p.38)
Policy work leading to legislation and implementation plans will continue, and in many
respects be completed during 1998. (*Annual Report*, National Department of Education,
1997, p.40)

295. **3.3.13.2** ... the new democratic government will consult all significant stakeholders
with a view to appointing a representative and expert higher education commission to
investigate and report urgently on the role of the higher education sector in national
reconstruction and development; the structure of the system; access/selection and
exclusion; the role of open learning and distance education; institutional governance and
the governance system as a whole; capacity-building and affirmative action in academic and
administrative appointments; the resource base for higher education, and the system of
student finance.

296. The government has approved the Minister of Education's proposal to appoint a
National Commission on Higher Education, and the commission has been appointed and
begun its work. (*White Paper on Education and Training*, p.33)

297. The Council on Higher Education is hereby established as a juristic person... [and
must] promote quality assurance in higher education... advise the Minister on any aspect
of education at the request of the Minister [including advice on the]... structure of the
higher education system; the planning of the higher education system; a mechanism for the
allocation of public funds; student financial aid; governance of higher education and the

Notes

higher education system... The council of a public higher education institution must provide appropriate measures for the redress of past inequalities and may not unfairly discriminate in any way. (*Higher Education Act*, 2.5,4.27)

298. The *Higher Education White Paper* and *Act* establish for the first time the policy and legislative framework for the creation of a single co-ordinated system of Higher Education. A key aspect is the establishment of the Council on Higher Education, which will advise the Minister on any aspect of higher education and which will be responsible for quality assurance through its Higher Education Quality Committee. (*Annual Report*, National Department of Education, 1997, p.31)

299. Consistent with the objectives of education and training within the National Youth Policy... information technology centres should be established in rural and remote areas as support facilities for distance education learners. The Departments of Education and Arts and Culture, Science and Technology shall, in liaison with groups such as CSIR, co-operate to investigate ways in which information technology centres can be created to support distance education and training. (*National Youth Policy*, 8.9.2)

300. **3.3.14.2** The reconstruction of education and training requires an overhaul of teacher/educator/trainer training and the industrial relations system in line with other sectors... **3.3.14.4** A transparent, participatory and equitable process to review salaries and conditions of service will be established. It will guarantee a living wage to the worst-paid teachers. It will also establish appropriate career paths, introduce criteria for the recognition and grading of teachers and trainers, and promote professional development within the proposed national qualifications framework.

301. The Technical Committee on Norms and Standards was set up by the National Department of Education to review norms and standards for teacher education, training and development. The recommendations in the technical committee's report define credits which will be pre-requisites for professional education. (*Norms and Standards*, p.51)

302. The Minister of Education... requires appropriate advice on all aspects of teacher education policy... The Committee for Teacher Education Policy will continue to provide this advisory function... The Ministry believes that the most direct way of raising the quality of learning and teaching is through a comprehensive reform and re-direction of in-service education for teachers. (*White Paper on Education and Training*, p.30)

303. Notwithstanding anything to the contrary contained in any law but subject to the provisions of this section, the *Labour Relations Act* or any collective agreement concluded by the Education Labour Relations Council, the Minister shall determine the salaries and other conditions of service of educators... [subject to the] concurrence of the Minister of Finance... The salary and other conditions of service of an educator may not be adversely affected by a transfer under this section without the consent in writing of that educator... The South African Council of Educators, which was established in terms of a collective agreement reached in the Education Labour Relations Council, shall be deemed to be established in terms of this *Act*... [Among the council's aims are:] promote professional

development of educators; establish a code of professional ethics; establish a fair and equitable enquiry procedure. (*Employment of Educators Act*, 4.1,8.1,28.1)

304. **3.3.15.1** The RDP proposes a substantially restructured and expanded training system... **3.3.15.4** Education and training for skills development must be modular and outcome-based; must recognise prior learning and experience; must develop transferable and portable skills; must have common standards, and must be integrated within the national qualifications and accreditation system. Training programmes and schooling after Standard 7 should form part of an integrated system. Training for self-employment is essential and must be offered.

305. The Ministry will give full attention to the substantial volume of research and development work which has already been done in connection with the National Training Board's National Training Strategy Initiative. (*White Paper on Education and Training*, p.32)

306. Curriculum 2005 has been introduced at the beginning of 1998. The blending of a conventional senior secondary school (STD 8, 9 and 10) with technically rich, job orientated subjects (in Grades 10, 11 and 12) ensures that further education be capable of producing transferable skills with a SAQA recognised Further Training Certificate. (*Annual Report*, National Department of Education, 1997, p.37)

307. **3.4.3** The RDP arts and culture policies aim to... ensure that resources and facilities for both the production and the appreciation of arts and culture are made available and accessible to all (priority must be given to those people and communities previously denied access to these resources)... **3.4.6** Ultimately government is responsible for the provision of cultural amenities for each community. As an immediate measure, established community arts centres should be subsidised by government. In the longer term, the Ministry of Arts and Culture should work with local and regional government and community structures to form community arts centres throughout the country... **3.4.9** Nationally and within each region, democratic Arts Councils will be established as statutory bodies. Allocations to such bodies will be made by the government, operating within its policy framework.

308. While it is the goal of the Ministry to ensure adequate public subsidies for the arts, culture and heritage, the policy outlined in this document is located within the reality of existing budgets and the requirements for fiscal discipline... Eventually, as... more funds are accessed from Treasury through the ongoing efforts of the Ministry, the admittedly limited resources for the arts will be spread more widely... The Ministry intends to develop the concept of multifunctional, multidisciplinary community arts centres through a number of pilot projects... These centres will serve two of the Ministry's most important principles i.e. providing access and redressing imbalances. The Ministry recognises that it cannot achieve this ambitious vision by itself. The Ministry will seek to develop relationships with the private sector, provincial and local authorities around the country, the international community, and various local communities themselves... It is proposed to establish the new National Arts Council (NAC) as a statutory body. The Council will seek to bring equity to the arts and culture dispensation. The National Arts Council would receive a

parliamentary grant through the Department... The principal task of the NAC will be to distribute public funds to artists, cultural institutions, NGOs and CBOs. (*White Paper on Arts, Culture and Heritage*, p.8,21,24,28,29)

309. DACST aims, by providing necessary infrastructure in disadvantaged communities, to contribute to the stabilisation of youth and children. To this end, the nine provincial governments identified locations for 43 community arts centres for either refurbishment or construction, to be funded from the R50 million allocated to DACST from the RDP Fund. (*Annual Report*, Department of Arts, Culture, Science and Technology, 1997, p.89) Two of the 43 projects were subsequently canceled, and the 41 projects left were classified as follows: 21 arts centres, 14 libraries, 2 museums and 4 theatres distributed in all 9 provinces... To date R22 million has been spend. 15 of the 41 projects have been completed by October 1998. (*Department of Arts, Culture, Science and Technology RDP Monthly Report*, October 1998, p.6)

310. **3.4.3** The RDP arts and culture policies aim to... conserve, promote and revitalise our national cultural heritage so it is accessible to all communities... **3.4.7** With local and provincial government, the Ministry should establish libraries, museums, galleries, monuments and historical sites. These should reflect the many different strands of South African culture. Each community should have these facilities located within reach.

311. It is proposed to establish the new National Heritage Council (NHC) as a statutory body. The Council will seek to bring equity to heritage promotion and conservation. The National Heritage Council will receive a parliamentary grant through the Department... The Ministry and the NHC will establish a national initiative to facilitate and empower the development of living heritage projects in provinces and local communities... The strategy will be to facilitate the development of a structure and environment in which projects can be initiated by communities themselves. There is hereby established a juristic person known as the National Heritage Council to Co-ordinate the management of the national heritage, the affairs, common to it, and the divisions and agencies associated with it... There is hereby established the South African Heritage Agency, under the authority of the SAHA Council as provided for in this *Act*... The SAHA... must endeavour to ensure that any community or body of persons with a cultural interest in any heritage resource has reasonable access to such heritage resource. (*National Heritage Act*, pp.9,18,20,31)

312. DACST currently funds three national libraries: The state library in Pretoria, the South African library in Cape town and the South African Library for the Blind in Grahamstown... The department currently provide funding for the Declared Cultural Institutions... There are some 400 publicly funded museums comprising small municipal institutions, provincial museums services and large nationally funded museums which attract more than half a million visitors a year. (*White Paper on Arts, Culture and Heritage*, pp.29,33)
Some 30 buildings, building complexes and sites were declared national monuments in the course of the year [1997]. The most prominent were the Passive Resistance site in Durban, the house of Steve Biko and Florisbad... The National Monument Council received R5 800

000 from the department for the 1997/98 financial year. (*Annual Report*, DACST, 1997, p.63)

313. **3.4.3** The RDP arts and culture policies aim to... place arts education firmly within the national education curricula as well as in non-formal education structures;... and cooperate with educational bodies and the media in eradicating illiteracy, and in promoting a reading and learning culture... Arts education should be an integral part of the national school curricula at primary, secondary and tertiary level, as well as in non-formal education. Urgent attention must be given to the creation of relevant arts curricula, teacher training, and provision of facilities for the arts within all schools.

314. Art, culture and heritage education which redresses past cultural biases and stereotypes, as well as the imbalance in the provision of resources shall be addressed by encouraging its location in educational structures at all levels of learning. To this end the Ministry will be represented in all appropriate national arts, culture, and heritage education policy, curriculum and accreditation structures... The Ministry [DACST] will actively promote the constitutional right of every learner in the General Education and Training Phase to access equitable, appropriate lifelong education and training in the arts, culture and heritage to develop individual talent and skills through the transformation of arts education within the formal school system... Community libraries and resource centres have exceptionally important role to play as facilitators of lifelong learning, and should be linked to arts, community and education centres... Crucial to the growth and sustainability of the arts, is the development of skilled human resources. This would include educating and training arts and culture practitioners... educators... administrators, curators and managers. (*White Paper on Arts, Culture and Heritage*, p.25-27, 29)

315. Since the success of the department's [DACST] representation on the Learning Area Committees established by the Department of Education, DACST has been involved in relevant structures related to the process of promoting arts education, e.g. the National Standards Body which will contribute to the National Qualifications Framework. (*Annual Report*, DACST, 1997, p.46)

316. **3.4.3** The RDP arts and culture policies aim to... link culture firmly to areas of national priority such as health, housing, tourism, etc., to ensure that culture is entrenched as a fundamental component of development.

317. The *Urban Development Strategy* and the *Rural Development Strategy* provide the socio-political context within which our policies will function... Implementing the policies in this draft *White Paper* will therefore involve co-operation of many government departments... The Department will explore creative inter-departmental co-operation in seeking to unlock potential public resources and expertise for the arts. (*White Paper on Arts, Culture and Heritage*, pp.13,30)

318. In 1997 DACST embarked on a number of initiatives intended to enhance the economic and social benefits of arts and culture. At the heart of these was the Cultural Industries Growth Strategy (CIGS)... The CIGS process is designed: to produce an

economic analysis of the cultural industries and to provide data to inform strategic decision-making; to establish and support stakeholder for a in each sector to pool the resources of stakeholders in identifying and initiating growth and development strategies in each sector; to identify impediments to growth; to explore linkages between cultural industries and the macro-economic framework (*GEAR*). (*Annual Report*, DACST, 1997, p.84)

319. **3.4.3** The RDP arts and culture policies aim to... establish and implement a language policy that encourages and supports, financially and otherwise, the utilisation of all the languages of South Africa... **3.4.10** The Pan-South African Language Institute proposed in the Interim Constitution must be constituted as a matter of urgency.

320. The development of previously marginalised languages is regarded as a prerequisite for meaningful multilingualism and real language equality. The role of the Pan South African Language Board, as delineated in the *Pan South African Language Board Act #59 of 1995*, is noted. (*White Paper on Arts, Culture and Heritage*, p.26)

321. The Multilingualism Campaign will be launched in 1998. The campaign will promote the benefits of multilingualism and will encourage the public service and society to view multilingualism as an asset... The Department, in consultation with the Pan South African Language Board, has started the process of amending the *Pan South African Language Board Act*. (*Annual Report*, DACST, 1997, p.27)

322. **3.4.5** Existing publicly funded and parastatal culture and arts structures, such as the Performing Arts Councils, the National Gallery, museums, libraries, archives and monuments must be democratised. Commissions to investigate the organisation, funding, policies and future roles of such structures must be established as a matter of urgency. These commissions should report within six months of their appointment, and complete the tasks of transformation within two years.

323. The Performing Arts Councils. Their transformation has already begun, with the appointment of representative boards, the rightsizing of their infrastructure and opening of their facilities to a broader spectrum of arts practitioners... The national government will no longer take primary responsibility for funding the PACs and their activities. Provinces and the local municipalities in which they are located should play a more active funding role since it is their inhabitants who benefit most from the presence of the PACs... The PACs will receive declining subsidies from central government as transfer payments over the next three years... A proportion of funding freed from this streamlining process will be channelled by the National Arts Council for distribution to a wider variety of artists, cultural groups and art disciplines... The Department will carry out a review of the Declared Cultural Institutions as one of its most immediate tasks... In the interim, state-funded museums have been encouraged to redirect their outputs to new activities which reflect the overall goals of the Government. (*White Paper on Arts, Culture and Heritage*, pp.22-24,34)

324. **3.4.11** The government will encourage and facilitate cultural exchange between the people of South Africa and the rest of the world.

325. The imperative of the Ministry's policies for international relations is to maximise opportunities for South African arts, culture and heritage practitioners and institutions to interact with the rest of the world... Particular attention will be given to liaison with other Southern African countries. (*White Paper on Arts, Culture and Heritage*, p.39)

326. Since January 1997, DACST has assisted approximately 70 arts and culture groups, individuals and institutions or bodies to participate in international cultural events... While the official cultural policy previously favoured relations with Europe and North America, relations over the past year have been broadened to encompass the rest of Africa, South America and Asia. (*Annual Report*, DACST, 1997, p.50)

327. **3.4.12** A statutory national body should be created to encourage the development of a healthy, vibrant and diverse local South African film and audio-visual industry, reflecting the realities of all the people of South Africa. This body should work to give the majority of South African viewers and audio-visual practitioners access to audio-visual communications.

328. The *Film Development Strategy*, after a process of consultation, was launched in November 1996. The National Film and Video Foundation (NFVF)–a statutory body which will operate at arms length from government--is to be established following the passing of the National Film and Video Foundation Bill by Parliament in the last quarter of 1997. The NFVF aims to promote the development of an indigenous film industry that caters for all language and cultural groups while providing entertainment, education and information. (*Annual Report*, DACST, 1997, p.55)

329. There is hereby established a juristic person known as the National Film and Video Foundation... [the objects of which include] (a) to develop and promote film and video industry ; (b) to provide, and encourage the provision opportunities for persons, especially from disadvantaged communities, to get involved in the film industry; (c) to encourage the development and distribution of local film and video products; (d) to support the nurturing and development of and access to the film and video industry; (e) in respect of the film and video industry. (*National Film and Video Foundation Act*, 1997, p.2)

330. **3.4.15** The framework will make provision for tax incentives and rebates to encourage investment in arts and culture.

331. Given the absence of specific arts related tax incentives for the private sector, government has to find other means of encouraging private sector involvement in the arts. (*White Paper on Arts, Culture and Heritage*, p.31)

332. **3.5.3** Sport and recreation should cut across all developmental programmes, and be accessible and affordable for all South Africans, including those in rural areas, the young and the elderly.

333. With regard to physical resources the Department accepts that provincial and local authorities should... ensure that rural areas are not excluded from the overall facilities plans. (*Getting the Nation to Play*, p.56)

334. Several facilities will be erected in the areas of tribal authorities for the first time. (*Annual Report*, National Department of Sport, 1996, p.23)

335. **3.5.4** Particular attention must be paid to the provision of facilities at schools and in communities where there are large concentrations of unemployed youth. Sport and recreation are an integral and important part of education and youth programmes. In developing such programmes it should be recognised that sport is played at different levels of competence and that there are different specific needs at different levels.

336. Out-of-school sport: The basic unit of delivery is the club i.e. a single-sport local body, run by and for its members... The Department of Sport and Recreation shall restrict its future activities and the financing of programmes and activities to national programmes of which the content deals primarily with physical recreation... The Department of Sport and Recreation shall... endeavour to encourage the private sector, provincial departments and local authorities to utilise recreational programmes for out-of-school and after-school youths as a tool towards leading South Africa's marginalised youth and latchkey children towards positive lifestyle choices and quality of life experiences. (*Getting the Nation to Play*, pp.23,63,68)
The Department of Welfare shall work with the National Youth Commission to develop the concept of a multi-purpose youth centre further and to establish a pilot programme. In all cases, a multi-purpose youth center...shall be based on identified needs whilst maximizing the use of existing resources...The National Youth Policy has two central objectives in regards to sport and recreation: to broaden the participation of young men and women in a wide range of sporting and recreational pursuits; and to promote excellence in sports by young people at national and international levels... The Departments of Education and Sports and Recreation, in association with the Unites Schools Sports Association of South Africa, shall take responsibility for ensuring these [school-based] facilities and programmes are developed wherever possible... [T]he Department of Education will investigate ways in which school facilities can be used by the local community for sport and recreation after school hours; and the Department of Public Works, Defense, and Public Enterprises and the National Parks Board will investigate the use of state owned facilities, including parks. (*National Youth Policy*, 8)

337. The business plan for the construction/upgrading of 126 basic sports/recreation facilities from the R50 million granted to the DSR for this purpose was approved on 19/01/1996. Seventy six contracts were signed during 1996 and construction of these facilities has commenced. Several facilities will be erected in the areas of tribal authorities for the first time. A sketch plan for nine indoor sports/recreation centres–one per Province–to be constructed at a cost of +R4 million each in the various Provinces from a further R50 million allocated by the former RDP office, was prepared by the Department of Public Works. (*Annual Report*, National Department of Sport, 1996, p.23)

338. **3.5.5** A sports policy... should include issues such as the establishment of an independent national sports controlling agency for the control of drugs in sport, as well as a national sports academy to undertake and coordinate training programmes concerning coaching, refereeing, umpiring and sports management.

339. Amongst the components of the (National Leisure and Sports Academy) will be the National Coaching and Accreditation Institute which would offer coaching, refereeing and administration modules... It is recommended that the Department of Sport and Recreation in association with the Sports Movement, establish: A Drug Testing and Education unit which: will co-ordinate sample testing; and develop education programme around drug abuse. (*Getting the Nation to Play*, pp.59-60)

340. Several discussions and investigations took place during 1996 regarding the establishment of a national sports academy. Through the academy, the DSR wants to ensure that athletes are exposed to the latest technology in sport and sports science and medicine in order to improve their preparation and performance. NOCSA is the lead agent for the National Academy on behalf of the Department. A feasibility study is underway to determine costings for the project. (*Annual Report*, National Department of Sport, 1996, p.19)

341. To develop a code of ethics for sport and recreation in South Africa... The DSR is aware, however, of the potential for negative practices in sport, e.g. Substance abuse, exploitation, violence, etc... The DSR will provide an ethical framework that encompasses fair play, anti-doping legislation, codes of conduct, tobacco and alcohol sponsorships, the environment and player rights. (*Getting the Nation to Play*, p.21)

342. There is hereby established a corporate body to be known as the South African Institute for Drug-Free Sport... The objectives of the Institute are—(a) to promote participation in sport, free from the use of prohibited substances or methods intended to artificially enhance performance, thereby rendering impermissible doping practices which are contrary to the principles of fair play and medical ethics, in a manner consistent with protecting the health and well-being of competitors, and the rights of all persons who take part in sports; (b) to encourage the development of programmes for the education of the community in general, and the sporting community in particular, in respect of the dangers of doping in sport;... (f) to encourage the development and maintenance of a sport drug testing laboratory... (*South African Institute for Drug-Free Sport Act*, p.5)

343. **3.6.3** The national youth service programme must better educate, develop, train and empower youth, and enable them to participate in the reconstruction of society through involvement in service projects in the community such as literacy, welfare, and improving infrastructure. All development and job creation programmes such as a national public works programme must address the problem of youth alienation and unemployment... **3.6.1** Care must be taken to ensure that the programme does not displace or substitute workers in permanent employment... **3.6.4** A national institution must coordinate the programme in consultation with other sectors... **3.6.5** Appropriate government departments must more forcefully represent youth interests, including through the allocation of

resources to organisations involved in youth work. An autonomous National Youth Council should be given support in coordinating youth activities, lobbying for the rights of young people, and representing South Africa internationally. A review of legislation affecting youth and the implementation of youth service programmes must also be carried out.

344. The Government will consider establishing special programmes aimed at addressing the needs of young people, in particular, to address the backlog in education and training, job creation and recreation. (*White Paper on Reconstruction and Development*, p.41)
Job creation:... Women and youth require special targeting. (*Public Works towards the 21st Century*, p.5)
The National Youth Service will provide new life, work and educational opportunities to those young men and women who are no longer at school and who are unemployed... [and will] link community service and internships to career-oriented studies; be linked to the national strategy for economic growth; tap into public and private sector, as well as civil society resources; give special emphasis to rural development projects... For those young men and women who are not students and who are unemployed, specific Youth Career Guidance Centers shall be established. These centres should be community-based organisations supported by government, the private sector and the local community. (*National Youth Policy*, 8.1.4)
The approach of the welfare departments will be to develop a strategy for... advocating within Government and society a comprehensive youth policy to meet the needs of the youth... Interdepartmental and intersectoral co-operation, in particular co-ordination with youth commissions and other stakeholders, will ensure a holistic approach to youth development. (*Draft White Paper for Social Welfare*, p.112)

345. There is hereby established a commission, to be known as the National Youth Commission, with the powers and duties conferred on or assigned to it by or under this *Act* or any other law... [the objects of the commission include:] (a) to co-ordinate and develop an integrated national youth policy; (b) to develop an integrated national youth development plan that utilises available resources and expertise for the development of the youth and which shall be integrated with the Reconstruction and Development Programme... (e) to implement measures to redress the imbalances of the past relating to the various forms of disadvantage suffered by the youth generally or specific groups or categories of persons among the youth;... (h) to co-ordinate the activities of the various provincial government institutions involve din youth matters... In addition to any other duties or functions assigned or entrusted by this *Act* or any other law—a) the Commission shall—prioritise national youth issues and initiate youth programmes in accordance with the national youth policy;... monitor and review the policies and practices of -(aa) organs of state at any level; (bb) statutory bodies or functionaries; (cc) public bodies and authorities with regard to youth matters, and may make any recommendations that the Commission deems necessary... (xi) evaluate any *Act* of Parliament or any other law in force at the commencement of this *Act* or any other law proposed by Parliament or any other legislature after the commencement of this *Act*, affecting or likely to affect the implementation of the integrated national youth policy and make recommendations to Parliament or such other legislature with regard thereto; (xiii) recommend to Parliament the adoption of new legislation which would promote the implementation of an integrated

national youth policy; (xiv) monitor and review the compliance with international conventions, international covenants and international charters. (*National Youth Commission Act 1996*, 2.1,2.2,8)

346. The National Youth Commission is a statutory body of government established through legislation passed by parliament, the *National Youth Commission Act* 19 of 1996. The Commission is constituted of five full-time members, five part-time members and nine commissioners nominated by premiers of each province... The Commission was appointed by President R.N. Mandela on South African Youth Day, June 16 1996... To date the NYC has held a National Youth Summit in Cape Town attended by 200 delegates from major youth, political and community organisations participating (June 1997), Provincial Youth Summits involving 1400 young people and representatives, over 3000 young women and men participated in 35 Youth Hearings held in rural and urban settings across the country. Three major publications have been produced, namely the *National Youth Policy* (9 December 1997), the *National Clearing House for Youth Employment and Entrepreneurship* (12 June 1998), and finally the *Green Paper on National Youth Service* (October 1998). (*National Youth Commission Pamphlet*)

347. **3.6.6** The democratic government must support the International Convention on the Rights of the Child, and the supporting Plan of Action. It must work to protect the lives of children, to promote the full development of their human potential, and to make them aware of their needs, rights and opportunities. The needs of children must be paramount throughout all programmes aimed at meeting basic needs and socio-economic upliftment.

348. Parliament ratified the Convention on the Rights of the Child in June 1995... With the ratification of the Convention, legislation in South Africa will have to be reviewed and revised to conform with these provisions... The (Interministerial Steering Committee of the Cabinet Committee established to develop a national programme for children) has also advised against a separate programme for children and that the goals for children will be adopted as goals of the RDP. (*Rural Development Strategy*, p.34)

349. The rights of children are largely protected by the latest two Welfare legislations, namely the *Not-For-Profit Organisations Act* and the *Welfare Amendment Act* (1997). The NPA is a programme designed to protect children in difficult situations. The Department of Welfare is responsible for the implementation of the International Convention on the rights of children. (*Annual Report*, Department of Welfare, 1998, p.14)

350. **4.2.1** The fundamental principles of our economic policy are democracy, participation and development. We are convinced that neither a commandist central planning system nor an unfettered free market system can provide adequate solutions to the problems confronting us. Reconstruction and development will be achieved through the leading and enabling role of the state, a thriving private sector, and active involvement by all sectors of civil society... **4.2.5** In restructuring the public sector to carry out national goals, the balance of evidence will guide will guide the decision for or against various economic policy measures. The democratic government must therefore consider: increasing the public sector in strategic areas through, for example, nationalisation, purchasing a shareholding

in companies, establishing new public corporations or joint ventures with the private sector; and reducing the public sector in certain areas in ways that enhance efficiency, advance affirmative action and empower the historically disadvantaged, while ensuring the protection of both consumers and the rights and employment of workers... **4.4.4.3** The processes of commercialisation and privatisation of parastatals must be reviewed, to the extent that such processes are not in the public interest. This will require the elaboration of more appropriate business plans, and publication of those plans for open debate. The democratic government will reverse privatisation programmes that are contrary to the public interest.

351. Restructuring of state assets is not driven by ideology. We shall privatise where necessary. But we shall also set up new state enterprises where market imperfections and failures play themselves out to undermine social programmes. (*Address* by President Nelson Mandela to Parliament, 6 February 1998)
The privatisation of state-owned enterprises is one of several vehicles the government has proposed as a means to driving this vision. Privatisation has been adopted as a government policy and the Ministry of Public Enterprises entrusted with the mandate to co-ordinate and manage the process. This challenging under-taking has the potential to radically transform the socio-economic landscape of our country. Among the challenges, our tasks are: (a) ensuring that the state enterprises are run more efficiently and profitably (b) allowing for a broader-based participation in the mainstream economy. (http://www.ope.pwv.gov.za/html/overview.htm)

352. The RDP Fund will benefit from proceeds from the sale of state assets. Government recognises that the location and composition of state assets may not be optimal and has begun an audit to assess whether resources could be released through more efficient usage. (*White Paper on Reconstruction and Development*, 2.3.4)

353. Objectives of Restructuring. The initiative to restructure State Assets is part of the process of implementing the Government has concretised some of these objectives in its so-called 'six pack' programme namely: belt tightening; reprioritisation of state expenditure; restructuring of state assets and enterprises; restructuring of the public service; building new inter-governmental relations; developing an internal monitoring capacity for the above programmes... The main objectives of restructuring are... increase economic growth and employment, meeting basic needs, redeployment of assets for growth, infrastructural development by mobilising and redirecting private sector capital, reduce state debt, enhance competitiveness and efficiency of state enterprises, finance growth and requirements for competitiveness and develop human resources... Organised labour in general and employees of the relevant public enterprises should participate in policy formulation processes... Historically disadvantaged groups. The capacity of the historically disadvantaged communities to participate and benefit fully in the restructuring programmes should be ascertained and enhanced. Participation and transparency. All key stakeholders should be full participants in the policy-making process, Boards of Directors and other appropriate decision-making structures at an agreed level. (*National Framework Agreement*, 4,5.3,5.5,5.6)

354. Within the context of government policy and in accordance with the procedures agreed in the National Framework Agreement with organised labour, the process of restructuring state assets is now proceeding... The nature of restructuring, as outlined in the framework agreement, may involve the total sale of the asset, a partial sale to strategic equity partners or the sale of the asset with government retaining a strategic interest. (*Growth, Employment and Redistribution*, 7.2)

355. Strategic Equity Partners for Telkom South Africa's signing of the agreement for the sale of 30% stake in Telkom on March 1997. The consortium–Thintana Communication– which cost R5,7 billion represented the single biggest inflow of capital ever into South Africa since 1994, and is made up of Telkom Malaysia and SBC of USA. (*Annual Report*, Department of Communications, 1996/97)

356. A water services authority—(a) may perform the function of a water services provider itself; and (b) may—(i) enter into a written contract with a water services provider; or (ii) form a joint venture with another water services institution, to provide water services [following a public disclosure of intent to do so and of other interests and any rate of return on investment]... (2) A water services authority may only enter into a contract with a private sector water services provider after it has considered all known public sector water services providers which are willing and able to perform the relevant functions. (*Water Services Act*, 1997, pp.13)

357. **4.2.2** Our central goal for reconstruction and development is to create a strong, dynamic and balanced economy which will: eliminate the poverty, low wages and extreme inequalities in wages and wealth generated by the apartheid system, meet basic needs, and thus ensure that every South African has a decent living standard and economic security; address economic imbalances and structural problems in industry, trade, commerce, mining, agriculture, finance and labour markets; address economic imbalances and uneven development within and between South Africa's regions; ensure that no one suffers discrimination in hiring, promotion or training on the basis of race or gender; develop the human resource capacity of all South Africans so the economy achieves high skills and wages; democratise the economy and empower the historically oppressed, particularly the workers and their organisations, by encouraging broader participation in decisions about the economy in both the private and public sector; create productive employment opportunities at a living wage for all South Africans; develop a prosperous and balanced regional economy in Southern Africa based on the principle of equity and mutual benefit, and integrate into the world economy in a manner that sustains a viable and efficient domestic manufacturing capacity and increases our potential to export manufactured products.

358. Points of Departure. Sustained growth on a higher plane requires a transformation towards a competitive outward-oriented economy. The strategy developed below attains a growth rate of 6 percent per annum and job creation of 400 000 per annum by the year 2000, concentrating capacity building on meeting the demands of international competitiveness. Several inter-related developments are called for: accelerated growth of non-gold exports; a brisk expansion in private sector capital formation; an acceleration in

public sector investment; an improvement in the employment intensity of investment and output growth; and an increase in infrastructural development and service delivery making intensive use of labour-based techniques. The expansion envisaged in the above aggregates is substantial and entails a major transformation in the environment and behaviour of both the private and the public sectors. This must include: a competitive platform for a powerful expansion by the tradable goods sector; a stable environment for confidence and a profitable surge in private investment; a restructured public sector to increase the efficiency of both capital expenditure and service delivery; new sectoral and regional emphases in industrial and infrastructural development; greater labour market flexibility; and enhanced human resource development... An Integrated Strategy. The core elements of the integrated strategy are: a renewed focus on budget reform to strengthen the redistributive thrust of expenditure; a faster fiscal deficit reduction programme to contain debt service obligations, counter inflation and free resources for investment; an exchange rate policy to keep the real effective rate stable at a competitive level; consistent monetary policy to prevent a resurgence of inflation; a further step in the gradual relaxation of exchange controls; a reduction in tariffs to contain input prices and facilitate industrial restructuring, compensating partially for the exchange rate depreciation; tax incentives to stimulate new investment in competitive and labour absorbing projects; speeding up the restructuring of state assets to optimise investment resources; an expansionary infrastructure programme to address service deficiencies and backlogs; an appropriately structured flexibility within the collective bargaining system; a strengthened levy system to fund training on a scale commensurate with needs; an expansion of trade and investment flows in Southern Africa; and a commitment to the implementation of stable and coordinated policies. (*Growth, Employment and Redistribution*, 1.3,1.4)

359. **4.2.9** All of our policies must aim to alleviate inequalities in incomes and wealth and expand productive opportunities. Critical programmes in this area include urban and rural development, industrial strategy, support for small and micro enterprise (including small-scale farming), job creation, land reform and other programmes discussed in earlier chapters. The democratic government must also create laws and institutions to end discrimination in hiring, promotion and training.

360. With regard to the challenge around redistribution, the past years have seen the introduction and extension of policies aimed at more equity in access to social services. These have important redistributive effects, and in the case of education and training, land reform and urban development, will also have favourable consequences for economic growth in the longer term. There has been some redistribution of wage income over the past two decades, partly as a result of union pressure. A continuation and possible acceleration of this process has been made possible by increases in productivity. Improvements in education, skills, labour effort and management are now crucial for wage increases and are increasingly being addressed in industrial negotiations. (*Growth, Employment and Redistribution*, Appendix 1)

361. **4.4.1** A five per cent growth rate and the creation of 300 000 to 500 000 non-agricultural jobs per annum can be achieved within five years.

362. The strategy developed below attains a growth rate of 6 percent per annum and job creation of 400 000 per annum by the year 2000, concentrating capacity building on meeting the demands of international competitiveness. (*Growth, Employment and Redistribution*, 1.3)

363. **4.2.7** We can only achieve our economic objectives if we establish transparent, participatory and accountable policy-making procedures in both the public and private sectors. The democratic government, the trade union movement, business associations and the relevant organisations of civil society must cooperate in formulating economic policy. The democratic government must review the inherited economic departments and agencies to streamline policy-making and implementation and to define appropriate relationships with forums and the various tiers of government... **4.4.5.2** The democratic government must work together with organised labour and business in the National Economic Forum (NEF) to ensure coordination between macro-economic policies and trade, industrial and technology strategy. If necessary, it must restructure the NEF to ensure appropriate participation and powers... **4.4.5.1** The RDP must work with existing forums, such as the NEF, the National Electricity Forum and the National Housing Forum, and must develop a more coherent and representative system on a regional and sectoral basis. These forums must continue to build consensus around industrial and trade policy. In particular, they must: address the needs of industrial sectors forced to adjust and the question of how to share the costs of adjustment; identify new economic sites of competitive advantage; develop aspects of industrial and trade policy, and deal with problems of extending infrastructure and meeting basic needs.

364. The RDP will be implemented by the line Departments of National Government, by Provincial and Local Government, and by parastatals, but through the widest possible consultation with and participation of the citizenry of South Africa. Structured consultation processes at all levels of Government will be introduced to ensure participation in policy-making and planning, as well as project implementation. The empowerment of institutions of civil society is a fundamental aim of Government's approach to building national consensus. Through this process Government aims to draw on the creative energy of our communities. To facilitate effective involvement, Government will introduce programmes that will enhance the capacity of community organisations... The RDP envisages a social partnership and Government should therefore provide services and support to all sectors, especially organised labour, the civics, business, women's groups and the churches. Moreover, Government has a duty in terms of the RDP to encourage independent organisation where it does not exist, such as rural areas... The social partnership envisaged by the RDP does not, however, imply that mass organisations do not retain the right to their own interpretation of–and their own goals for–the RDP. It does imply that their is agreement to find solution to constraints which will emerge in the RDP's implementation... Thus a series of agreements or accords will be negotiated to facilitate the full participation of civil society, together with Government, in order to find ways to take down the barriers which emerge during the course of the RDP. (*White Paper on Reconstruction and Development*, 7.1.1,7.6.7,7.6.8)
TOWARDS A NATIONAL SOCIAL AGREEMENT. A strong tradition of collective bargaining characterises the South African industrial and social environment. Sectoral and regional agreements are likely to contribute to structuring future growth and development.

There is an important role also for a broad national agreement, to create an environment for rapid growth, a brisk investment trend and accelerated delivery of public services based on equity and universal access. The challenge facing the government and its social partners is to ensure that a national agreement underpins rapid growth, job creation, and development. The immediate objective of the agreement would be to ensure that the recent depreciation of the currency does not translate into a vicious circle of wage and price increases leading to instability in the financial markets and a decline in competitive advantage. For this reason it is important that wage and salary increases do not rise more than productivity growth. It is equally important that price restraint should be maintained, facilitated through an effective competition policy and continued trade liberalisation. In the longer term, a broad social agreement might address a wider range of issues related to economic restructuring, income distribution and social policies. Orderly collective bargaining between organised labour and employers must remain the foundation of industrial relations. (*Growth, Employment and Redistribution*, 9)

365. The recent acceptance of tri-partite institutions which combine representatives from business, labour and government, has made possible the achievement of advanced agreements on labour relations, productivity programmes and investment planning. (*Support Measures for the Enhancement of the International Competitiveness of South Africa's Industrial Sector*, p.32)

366. **4.2.10** Our economic policies require human resource development on a massive scale. Improved training and education are fundamental to higher employment, the introduction of more advanced technologies, and reduced inequalities. Higher labour productivity will be the result of new attitudes towards work in the context of overall economic reconstruction and development.

367. Enhancing productivity. The Department of Labour has embarked on the development of a new human resource development strategy, in partnership with all major stakeholders, which is planned to culminate in new legislation in 1997. Central to this strategy is a new financing mechanism and governance framework which aims to increase the aggregate level of effective investment in training. Towards this end the government is investigating the feasibility of introducing a mandatory levy on payroll. The matter is currently under negotiation with the social partners represented in NEDLAC. The strategy includes the following: establishment of a tripartite national coordinating council, responsible for giving strategic direction to human resource development and for building an energetic coherent national system; restructuring of industry training boards to facilitate best practice training, under industrial management; strengthening of the levy-based industrial training financing mechanism; appropriately focused funding of training for emergent enterprises and the unemployed; an overhaul of the guidance, training, placement and labour market information services of the Department; and development of an information and planning capacity to support the national training strategy. In addition, there will be deliberate campaigns to enrich human resource development programmes within government departments and agencies, aimed at effective service delivery. Management training initiatives are already underway in several key departments. Government recognises that it has an important role to play in financing education and

training activities aimed at the unemployed and the small business sector and in enhancing the quality of technical and vocational education and training. Sustained improvements in the quality of general schooling are also largely the responsibility of the fiscus. Industrial training must remain mainly the responsibility of employers. Government seeks to facilitate the development of financing mechanisms that will enjoy broad support from both the business sector and organised labour. (*Growth, Employment and Redistribution*, 8.4)

368. **4.3.4** Macro-economic policies must take into consideration their effect upon the geographic distribution of economic activity. Additional strategies must address the excessive growth of the largest urban centres, the skewed distribution of population within rural areas, the role of small and medium-sized towns, and the future of declining towns and regions, and the apartheid dumping grounds.

369. The success of government's strategy for "growth, employment and redistribution" (*GEAR*) is dependent on government's maintenance of a sound fiscal and macro-economic framework. The *GEAR* strategy is an economic reform programme directed towards: a competitive fast-growing economy that creates sufficient jobs for all job seekers; a redistribution of income opportunities in favour of the poor; a society capable of ensuring that sound health, education and other services are available to all; and an environment in which homes are safe and places of work are productive. These principles form the macro-economic framework within which the *Rural Development Framework* is drafted. Rural development will contribute to this policy by: diversified job creation through local economic development, including the growth of small and medium scale enterprises; redistributing government expenditure to formerly deprived areas; an expansionary infrastructure programme to address service deficiencies and backlogs, at the same time delivering infrastructure and essential services cost-effectively; social and sectoral policy development in many fields, particularly education and health services, and through widening access to resources in order to improve household and national productivity. (*Rural Development Framework*, p.7)

370. The country's largest cities are not excessively large by international standards, and the rates of growth of the various tiers also appear to be normal. Hence there appears to be little reason to favour policies which may artificially induce or restrain growth in a particular centre, region or tier. (*Urban Development Strategy*, p.9)

371. **4.3.6** The incentives for decentralisation introduced under apartheid frequently proved excessively discretionary and open to misuse. Still, in many areas simply eliminating them would cause severe job losses. For this reason, the democratic government must establish clear-cut guidelines and procedures for reviewing decentralisation incentives. Where communities and workers can certify that the subsidies are being utilised in a sustainable, non-exploitative manner, the democratic government must maintain the incentives. Otherwise, it must redirect subsidies to ventures that promote linkages within the local economy.

372. Appendix 1. Although the Regional Industrial Development Programme (RIDP) is under review, it was expanded in 1993 to include a simplified scheme applicable to smaller enterprises. Past attempts through the Regional Industrial Development Programme to encourage decentralisation of industry to the former homelands have failed, as have most of these programmes internationally... The new RIDP seeks to promote development on the basis of regional resource endowment and comparative advantage. It is expected to lead to greater concentration of industrial activity at established urban centres, and is therefore not a mechanism for rural development. (*Rural Development Strategy*, pp.9,16)

The legacy of decentralisation and deconcentration policies has left these cities and towns with industrial zones and townships far away from town centres... Costly and uneconomic subsidies will be phased out... Public investment at all levels will be expected to relate to the economic or functional base and potential of an area (*Urban Development Strategy*, pp.13-22).

Before its reformulation in 1991, the Regional Industrial Development Programme (RIDP) sought to subsidise industrial development in or near the borders of the crowded former homelands. However, the policy failed both to reduce economic disparities between regions and to stimulate economic linkages. The newly formulated strategy of the Department of Trade and Industry seeks to promote development on the basis of regional resource endowment, comparative advantage and demonstrated economic viability. It will include a package of incentives, including investment incentives, depreciation allowances and development finance, as well as other assistance such as training and information. In an effort to identify bankable projects, the DTI has been analysing regional comparative advantage as part of its Regional Industrial Location Strategy and it will provide such information to prospective investors. It has also been carrying out analyses of industrial clusters, some of which are based on agro-industrial linkages: forestry products, including pulp and paper as well as timber industries; footwear; food processing and beverages; and textiles. Previously the National Economic Forum carried out studies into tourism, sugar and fruit juice production, among other things. In appropriate locations, all of these, and many others;, could provide the basis for local economic development. If local authorities wish to attract industries, they will need information on the assistance available from the RIDP or the DTI's Centre for Small Business Promotion. Local authorities should also consider complementary investment in facilities to improve living conditions in order to raise the social wage. (*Rural Development Framework*, p.35)

Industrial incentives: Government is... promoting more rapid industrial development. Tax incentives have been introduced for new investments in manufacturing plant, equipment and buildings, and a tax holiday is now available to new industrial projects for a period of time determined by regional location, job creation and industrial priority. Closely related to these measures are 12 industrial priority investigations and regional industrial location studies, and a comprehensive review of competition policy. The simplified Regional Industrial Development Programme has been adapted as a grant programme tailored to the needs of small and medium-sized firms. (*Medium Term Budget Policy Statement*, 1997, p.16)

373. Regional initiatives include Lubombo Agriculture and Tourism SDIs, the Fish River SDIs in the Eastern Cape based on proposals for a large port at Coega. Within the SDIs are some 20 or more mega-projects involving more than R500 000 investments each of which are in progress or will be nearing implementation during 1998. At the beginning of

1998, 390 projects to the value of R77 billion were at different stages of planning or development with the potential to create some 60,000 jobs. (*Government's Report to the Nation – 1998*, p.15)
Close on to 400 projects relating to SDIs have attracted investments to the tune of about R77 billion (Fish River SDI = R4,617,686,275 fixed capital, Wild Coast SDI = R451,000,000 fixed capital and Maputo SDI = R7,221,144,000 fixed capital). (*DTI Budget Vote*, 15 May 1998)

374. **4.3.5** In order to foster the growth of local economies, broadly representative institutions must be established to address local economic development needs. Their purpose would be to formulate strategies to address job creation and community development (for example, leveraging private sector funds for community development, investment strategies, training, small business and agricultural development, etc.). If necessary, the democratic government must provide some subsidies as a catalyst for job-creation programmes controlled by communities and/or workers, and target appropriate job creation and development programmes in the most neglected and impoverished areas of our country. Ultimately, all such projects should sustain themselves.

375. Some of the important [LED] options are market development, small and medium scale enterprise development, small-scale agriculture–especially after land reform–tourism, and labour-based infrastructure development... [LED] can be promoted through deliberate capacity building so that individuals take control of their own destinies, and with the injection of outside financial support. However, with little overall support available compared to need, communities will have to manage with as little as possible, and target it well. (*Rural Development Strategy*, pp.2,16)
As a matter of urgency, government is resolved to establish a policy framework for Local Economic Development (LED); promote the concept of LED at national, provincial and, most importantly, at local government level; establish fiscal and regulatory mechanisms to support LED; assist relevant stakeholders in urban and rural areas to initiate LED ventures--effectively as pilot projects–and thereby gain experience in the utilisation of LED techniques. (*Urban Development Strategy*, p.33)

376. **4.3.8** The RDP aims to improve the quality of rural life. This must entail a dramatic land reform programme to transfer land from the inefficient, debt-ridden, ecologically-damaging and white-dominated large farm sector to all those who wish to produce incomes through farming in a more sustainable agricultural system. It also entails access to affordable services, and the promotion of non-agricultural activities. In the "homelands," where most rural people live, social services and infrastructure remain poorly developed, and this must be remedied... **4.3.11** Rural communities need practical access to health, education, support for entrepreneurship (including agriculture), financial services, welfare, and police and the courts. The objective of rural development policy must be to coordinate the activities of the relevant democratic government agents, and to pass much of the control of democratic government-funded services to the rural people for whom they are intended, within the framework of national and provincial policy in each sector.

377. **4.3.11** Rural communities need practical access to... financial services... The objective of rural development policy must be to coordinate the activities of the relevant democratic government agents, and to pass much of the control of democratic government-funded services to the rural people for whom they are intended, within the framework of national and provincial policy in each sector. This will require fundamental changes to institutions and processes.

378. **4.3.11** Rural communities need practical access to health, education, support for entrepreneurship (including agriculture), financial services, welfare, and police and the courts... **4.4.7.11** To better serve micro enterprise, the democratic government must double the existing number of local service centres and satellites. These satellites must enable the democratic government to provide for rural women involved in small, micro and medium-sized enterprises. All training programmes for micro enterprise must provide appropriate child care.

379. By the year 2020, South Africa must have: more diverse agriculture, with farms of many sizes providing incomes (or part incomes) to many more people; an "economy of participation" that allows local residents to produce and to sell competitively, small and irregular amounts of produce and other wares into both local and regional markets; periodic markets organised in rings which allow for the operation of economies of scale and low unit costs on market days; more diverse commercial and service sectors in country towns and the countryside, and greater integration between towns and the rural areas, especially on market days; much greater access for rural people to government support and information and to commercial services, with a more logical spatial network of towns, services, roads and transport systems serving both market traders and customers; close availability of water, sanitation and fuel sources, giving everyone more time for economic productivity and better health; local government structures to which everyone has easy access and within which women play an equal and active role; close links of local government with civil society and business through which are expressed the needs and priorities of different groups of rural people; dignity, safety, and security of access for all, especially women, to useful employment, housing, and land, with people able to exercise control over their society, community and personal lives, and to invest in the future; fewer, healthier, safe, well-nourished children with access to well resourced schools; a healthy and productive environment capable of sustaining the many agricultural, social and cultural activities on which the country depends; fewer poor people in the rural areas of South Africa. (*Rural Development Framework*, p.1)

380. The main strategy is to create a national network of local service centres (LSCs) where a variety of services can be accessed. The LSCs in rural areas will receive subsidisation, and *some* activities in all LSCs may be subsidised to assist with targeting... The LSCs will mostly assist entrepreneurs in obtaining access to hard skills training, for which they must pay, and will provide on-site 'hand-holding' to developing businesses for sustained periods. (*Rural Development Strategy*, p.17)
The Department of Trade and Industry has set up new structures of support for emerging business. These include a national network of Local Business Service Centres (LBSCs) operated by local NGOs, the Khula Enterprise Finance Company for financial services,

and the Ntsika Enterprise Promotion Agency (NEPA) which will provide entrepreneurial training... LBSCs will be accredited NGOs. The LBSCs in rural areas will be subsidised by government. Some activities in all LBSCs may be subsidised to help single out deserving clients... Within NEPA, the Business Development Services (BuDS) unit has been set up to assist the establishment of Local Business Service Centres Any organisation, such as an NGO, can apply for accreditation to BuDS. BuDS will provide advice, the provision of some resources to build capacity, with role models, new ideas and good practices... Khula will also work with NGOs and banks to provide financial services at local level, providing local capital and some coverage of initial operating costs. (*Rural Development Framework*, pp.35-36)

381. Rural local authorities must work to encourage the development of local financial services, but never through subsidising them, for they must be financially viable to be sustainable... [The Department of Trade and Industry encourages] development of a state guarantee scheme for agricultural finance, in place of direct state credit for farmers. (*Rural Development Strategy*, pp.11,17,18)
Government has taken a number of measures to restructure rural financial markets with the objective of building, from bottom up, a system of financial services that provides... broader access for all. Simultaneously, as part of wider macro-economic reforms, subsidies on interest rates have been removed. The Strauss Commission which examined all aspects of rural finance, made recommendations for further improvements to rural financial markets including the new role for the Land Bank... (*Policy Document on Agriculture*, p.3)
Rural women's access to finance: For the first time rural women have access to financial services through the transformed Land Bank. Rural women will be able to lend as much as R25 000 from the Land Bank for agricultural production. Through building up a track record, lenders will be able to extend their loans to as much as R18 000 on a no-collateral basis. (*Ministry of Agriculture Press Release on Rural Women's Access to Finance*, 26 March 1998)

382. **4.3.13** Generally, the democratic government must support capacity-building in the District Councils, Local Councils, and voluntary community structures such as local development forums. To advise communities of their options, it must train a cadre of Community Development Officers. Their training must include sensitivity to gender issues. The Community Development Officers must work for the District Councils. Wherever possible, they must come from the areas they serve.

383. To facilitate effective involvement, Government will introduce programmes that will enhance the capacity of community organisations... Government must therefore provide resources in an open and transparent manner and in compliance with clear and explicit criteria to mass organisations to ensure that they are able to develop or maintain the ability to effectively participate as negotiation partners of Government. (*White Paper on Reconstruction and Development*, 7.1.1, 7.6.8)
There are various training programmes available through different government departments, but access is limited compared to the large demand. Community and local government structures will need to obtain the services of non-governmental organisations and the private sector for capacity building, and should obtain funding for this from donor

funds, including the National Development Agency which is being set up specifically for this purpose... The Minister responsible for the RDP does not intend that his Office should act as a gatekeeper for donor funds to CBOs or NGOs, nor to recommend to donors which NGOs they should support. Given the international trend amongst donors to increase support to NGOs rather than governments it is unlikely that total donor funds to the NGO sector will decline significantly. NGOs are not the responsibility of government... CBOs such as civics, community development forums and trusts are less widespread in rural than urban areas, but nevertheless more numerous than is often realised. They will need to mobilise to maintain pressure on local government for the delivery of services, and also to maintain pressure on people to pay for services... There is no doubt that CBOs must be involved in steering projects from start to finish, and that they require capacity building to become more proficient at this role. However, whether their members should be the ones to build the project itself, and be paid to do it with state funds is a separate question. Under Treasury rules it not easy for government departments to subcontract services or projects to community bodies, and such rules cannot be changed quickly. Further, it is not easy for CBOs to show technical and managerial competence. (*Rural Development Strategy*, pp.3,28)

Those who stress good governance and transparency and argue for participation, see a role for NGOs in rural development greater than as mere deliverers of services. They seek to involve NGOs and CBOs in the policy dialogue and in decision making. In this connection, the strengthening of NGOs and CBOs as separate, specialist institutions is important. Partnerships with these organisations will maximise the benefit of rural development initiatives for local communities... It is the responsibility of government to provide an environment in which those that can prove themselves can flourish, in competition with other non-statutory organisations. Donors should be encouraged to fund NGOs and CBOs independently and in their own right. CBOS such as civics, community development forums and trusts are less widespread in rural than urban areas, but nevertheless more numerous than is often realised. They are needed to pressure local government to deliver services to their members, as well as to encourage their members to pay for services where this is necessary. CBOS seek state support for capacity building in order to organise their membership; to represent them more adequately; to be involved in service delivery and as project managers and as implementers. There is no doubt that CBOs must be involved in steering projects from start to finish, and that they require capacity building to become more proficient for this purpose. However, whether members should be paid with state funds to implement projects for their members is a separate question. Under Treasury rules it is not possible to enter into government contracts for works and services (valued at more than a small sum) without a public tender process. NGOs and CBOs may not have the technical and managerial experience (eg., in road building or housing construction) to compete successfully in such a process... The National Development Agency is being set up specifically to allow CBOs to obtain funding for skills training. CBOs should ensure that NGOs, who are funded to support them, have a commitment to build CBO leadership, not just to lobby for them... Service NGOs in rural areas have a good record of supporting CBOs. However, many have found difficulty in moving from advocacy to development implementation... The paucity of state experience in rural development in South Africa leads to the expectation that NGOs will continue to assist government with capacity building, training and experimentation for some years. At the same time, it will be essential for them to maintain their independence, if they are both to complement state services and to provide an alternative. (*Rural Development Framework*, pp.63-65)

384. **4.3.14** Educational opportunities in the rural areas lag far behind those in the cities. Human resource development forms a key component in building the rural economy. It must include the opening up and reorganisation of agricultural schools to meet the needs of the majority. Training and retraining of new and existing extension workers, community development officers and officials dealing with land reform is critical to the success of our rural development and land reform programme. These training and retraining programmes must be designed within the first 18 months of the RDP.

385. Under apartheid, Africans living in rural areas were denied educational opportunities to an even greater extent than those in urban areas. Most rural schools are poorly resourced with buildings, equipment, and books and without electricity and running water... The needs are immense... Government is committed to increase the level and availability of formal education in rural areas, and supply training and assistance to the new district and rural councils. The major rural education issues facing national and provincial governments are how to improve access to education, improve its quality and establish effective democratic structures for school management. To redress past neglect of rural education, there must be positive discrimination in favour of rural areas... The *South African Schools Act*... determines, in line with the *Constitution*, the right to basic education. The obligation to provide sufficient places in public schools lies with the provinces... Public spending on education will, as far as possible, be weighted to favour the poor and historically deprived schools. Most rural community schools and farm schools will fall into this category... Linked to this has been the allocation of provincial education funds for transport assistance to children in remote areas, to improve their access to schools. The Departments of Education and Health co-manage the Primary School Nutrition Programme to address the question of hunger in primary school children. The programme has been largely rural and has increased pupil registration and attendance at school. (*Rural Development Framework*, pp.61-62)

386. Agricultural extension bridges the gap between available technology and farmers' practices through the provision of technical advice, information and training... For many small-scale and resource-poor farmers, public extension represents the main source of information on improved technology and also provides access to other opportunities for agricultural progress through links to training, research sources... and markets... Agricultural improvement in SA, especially among small-scale and resource-poor farmers... requires a major effort to improve the quality of extension services available to farmers. This effort will consist of, among other things, (a) the review of the nature of demand for extension services and a reassessment of current training extensionists will be initiated; (b) initiatives to improve the linkage between research institutions and field level extensionists, with researchers becoming more involved in the upgrading of extensionist knowledge. (*Policy Document on Agriculture*, pp.41-42)

387. **4.4.2** Objectives of industry, trade and commerce policy. **4.4.2.1** The key goals of our industrial strategy are a substantial increase in net national investment, especially in manufacturing, job creation and the meeting of basic needs. Through the prudent implementation of macro-economic policies such as monetary policies, and in particular such instruments as interest rates and an increase in public sector investment, gross investment in industry will increase. In general, our objective is to enhance our technological capacity to ensure that as part of the restructuring of industry, South Africa emerges as a significant exporter of manufactured goods. The industrialisation strategy aims at the promotion of a more balanced pattern of industrial development, capable of overcoming the acute over-concentration of industrial activities in certain metropolitan centres of the country. **4.4.2.2** Trade and industrial policy must respond to the demands of reconstruction and development. In particular, industrial expansion should follow from the extension of infrastructure to urban, peri-urban and rural constituencies. Some of this new demand will be met by utilising the considerable excess capacity that exists within industry. That should lower unit costs, raise productivity and foster innovation, providing a new impetus for international competitiveness. **4.4.2.3** While trade policy must introduce instruments to promote exports of manufactured goods in general, industrial policy must support and strengthen those internationally competitive industries that emerge on the basis of stronger internal linkages, meeting the needs of reconstruction and raising capacity utilisation.

388. [T]rade and industrial policies aim to promote an outward-oriented industrial economy, integrated into the regional and global environment and fully responsive to market trends and opportunities... Based on the foundations which have been laid over the past two years, trade and industrial policies will seek to enhance the competitive capacity and employment absorption of manufacturing, alongside continued promotion of tourism as an export sector and appropriate growth-oriented policies in other sectors... Stronger growth of more labour-intensive components of industry, facilitated by shifts in industrial policy, is vital... The unreliability of raw materials exports in the 1980s persuaded policy-makers that the central thrust of trade and industrial policy had to be the pursuit of employment-creating international competitiveness. This entails a shift away from demand-side interventions, such as tariffs and subsidies, which raised prices received by producers, to supply-side measures designed to lower unit costs and expedite progress up the value chain. (*Growth, Employment and Redistribution*, 2.3, 5.2, 8.2, Appendix 1)

389. **4.4.2.5** Policy must address the constraints on those segments of manufacturing that fall outside of bulk steel, metals and chemical production. The adjustments following from the recent GATT agreement require a balance between promoting efficiency and reducing and sharing out the painful impact of adjustment among various parties concerned.

390. Closely related are the twelve industrial priority industry investigations as well as the regional industrial locations studies. These major initiatives are intended to identify mechanisms to enhance the competitiveness of selected industrial sub-sectors. While the clusters may be eligible for the proposed tax holiday, specific interventions will also be considered where necessary. These studies involve constant interaction with both owners and workers. (*Growth, Employment and Redistribution*, 5.3)

391. Industrial Development Finance Incentives: South Africa has a very well developed financial sector which provides business and industrial financing. In addition a number of specialised institutions have been established to provide finance for industrial development. The Industrial Development Corporation (IDC) operates nationally, offering an extensive range of, financing facilities for small, medium and large scale industries to assist entrepreneurs in the establishment and expansion of economically viable manufacturing concerns in SA. The most general form of financing is by means of medium to long term low interest rates but in certain cases the IDC may also take equity in industrial enterprises... The IDC also offers specific financing facilities such as: (a) Low interest rate scheme for the promotion of exports to promote investment directed at exports, and the scheme is available to industrialists/groups with the total assets (fixed plus current assets) of approximately R1 million or more at a time of the application. (http://www.dti.pwv.gov.za/dtiwww/Invguide.htm)

392. **4.4.6.2** The RDP will introduce strict anti-trust legislation to create a more competitive and dynamic business environment. The central objectives of such legislation are to systematically discourage the system of pyramids where they lead to over-concentration of economic power and interlocking directorships, to abolish numerous anti-competitive practices such as market domination and abuse, and to prevent the exploitation of consumers. Existing state institutions and regulations concerned with competition policy must be reviewed in accordance with the new anti-trust policy. The democratic government should establish a commission to review the structure of control and competition in the economy and develop efficient and democratic solutions. It must review existing policy and institutions with the aim of creating more widely spread control and more effective competition. To that end, it must consider changes in regulation or management in addition to anti-trust measures.

393. The review of competition policy which is presently under way will be reflected in strengthened new legislation. The main objectives of competition policy are to encourage competition among firms, protect consumers and downstream firms from restrictive practices, and to open up new opportunities for investment... Corporate governance and asset restructuring. Government has prepared a protocol on corporate governance of all state entities which ensures decisive leadership by government and includes the following:... appropriate regulatory policies, aimed at ensuring that pricing policies are fair and fully recover operating costs, while also promoting competition or protecting consumers against monopolistic practices... It is equally important that price restraint should be maintained, facilitated through an effective competition policy and continued trade liberalisation. (*Growth, Employment and Redistribution*, 5.3,7.2,9)

394. To Provide for the establishment of the Competition Commission responsible for the investigation, control and adjudication of restrictive practices, abuse of dominant position and mergers and for the establishment of a Competition Appeal Court and for matters connected therewith... The purpose of this *Act* is to promote and maintain competition in South Africa in order to: promote the efficiency, adaptability, and development of the economy; provide consumers with competitive prices and product choices; ensure that

small and medium-sized enterprises have an equitable opportunity to participate in the economy. (*Competition Act*, 2.5.6-9)

395. **4.4.3.2** A democratic South Africa must rapidly restructure the relationships with neighbouring African countries, who import about 20 per cent of our exports. More balanced and less exploitative trade patterns will result in more mutually beneficial outcomes. That will strengthen the Southern African region in its relations with emerging global trading blocs, as discussed in the section on Southern African Regional Policy below.

396. The core elements of the integrated strategy are... an expansion of trade and investment flows in Southern Africa... A further key element of the strategy is the gradual integration of the economies of Southern Africa through the trade and investment protocols of SADC... Another critical policy thrust has been the expansion of market access through preferential trade arrangements with industrial countries and pursuit of regional economic integration. The following developments deserve specific mention:... the signing of bilateral trade treaties with several African countries and rapidly growing trade with neighbors has seen exports from within the Southern African Customs Union area to the rest of the Southern African region quadruple. (*Growth, Employment and Redistribution*, 1.4,
5.3, Appendix 1)

397. Article 2 (Objectives) of the Protocol on Trade in the Southern African Development Community (SADC Region) advances that the objectives of the Protocol are (1) to further liberalise intra-regional trade in goods and services on the basis of fair, mutually equitable and beneficial trade arrangements, complemented by Protocols in other areas; (2) to contribute towards the improvement of the climate for domestic, cross-border and foreign investment; and (3) to establish a Free Trade Area in the SADC Region. Ongoing negotiations between RSA and SADC states on the proposed Free Trade Agreement in SADC member states towards a more non-reciprocal market access accompanied by investment flows. Launch of SDIs, e.g. Lubombo (capital = R177,048,544) and Maputo Corridor (R7,221,144,000) with maximum job prospects of 160 and 359 respectively are major steps in this direction. (*DTI Budget Vote*, 15 May 1998)

398. **4.4.3.3** Tariff reductions on imports form both a GATT requirement and a strategic instrument for trade policy. Presently, they are subject to negotiation within the National Economic Forum. The government must develop democratic and consistent procedures for revising tariffs and export incentives. It must simplify the tariff structure and begin a process of reducing protection in ways that minimise disruption to employment and to sensitive socio-economic areas. National agencies concerned with international trade and tariffs must be sensitive to the interests of the Southern African region as a whole. **4.4.3.4** We must develop more cost-effective incentives schemes, designed to improve performance and not just the volume of exports. Trade policy strategies to promote exports must consider ways to reduce the bias against small and medium-sized exporters. They should facilitate the provision of short-term export finance to small business. Any duplication

between the trade-promotion arms of the Department of Trade and Industry and the private-sector South African Foreign Trade Organisation should be eliminated.

399. The core elements of the integrated strategy are:... a reduction in tariffs to contain input prices and facilitate industrial restructuring, compensating partially for the exchange rate depreciation... While long-term survival strategies have had to be developed for certain sensitive sectors, general progress towards an outward-oriented stance is reflected in a number of achievements: replacement of former quantitative restrictions with tariffs; rationalisation of the tariff structure by almost halving the number of tariff lines; abolition of import surcharges, completed in October 1995; phasing down of tariffs, begun in 1995, by on average one-third over five years; and phasing out of the general export incentive scheme, to be completed by the end of 1997. (*Growth, Employment and Redistribution*, 1.4,5.1)

400. South Africa uses import tariff protection selectively to encourage domestic industrial development. In the case of... products manufactured in SA, import tariffs already exist. Manufacturers of products not presently subject to an import tariff can apply for the imposition of a protective tariff... Factors such as the industry's contribution to the economy, export potential, local content, value added in the production process and the industry's growth and export potential are important considerations for the granting of protection... Provision also exists for the rebate/refund of the import tariff on raw materials/components used in the manufacturing, processing, finishing or packing of goods for export. The rebate/refund duties in such cases is subject to permit but permits are readily granted in an endeavour to boost South Africa's export performance. (*Industrial Investment Incentives*)

401. **4.4.6.3** The domination of business activities by white business and the exclusion of black people from the mainstream of economic activity are causes for great concern for the reconstruction and development process. A central objective of the RDP is to deracialise business ownership and control completely, through focused policies of black economic empowerment. These policies must aim to make it easier for black people to gain access to capital for business development. The democratic government must ensure that no discrimination occurs in financial institutions. State and parastatal institutions will also provide capital for the attainment of black economic empowerment objectives. The democratic government must also introduce tendering-out procedures which facilitate black economic empowerment. Special emphasis must also be placed on training, upgrading and real participation in ownership.

402. Government will explore the need and scope for an appropriate co-ordinating mechanism to ensure that foreign joint-venture initiatives give due attention to black partners. (*White Paper on National Strategy for the Development and Promotion of Small Business in South Africa*, 4.10)

403. **4.4.6.4** The democratic government must develop policies to ensure that foreign investment creates as much employment, technological capacity and real knowledge transfer as possible, allowing greater participation by workers in decision-making.

404. Several developments are needed for South Africa to attract a more substantial volume of foreign direct investment: an overall macroeconomic environment conducive to growth and an expanding domestic and regional market; gradual removal of exchange controls; improved domestic savings and stead reductions in the fiscal deficit; a tax regime favourable to foreign investment; restructuring of state assets so as to create opportunities for equity investment in public corporations by foreign partners; improved labour market flexibility and increased training for a more skilled work force; and reduced crime and improved social stability. (*Growth, Employment and Redistribution*, Appendix 12)

405. The Departments of Foreign Affairs and Trade and Industry have increased their cooperation, resulting in better utilisation of resources. This is already contributing to the effective promotion of SA's economic interests at home and abroad. Since 1994, a total of R32 billion in new direct foreign investment has entered SA. (*Ministry of Foreign Affairs Budget Vote*, 7 May 1998)

406. **4.4.7.1** Small businesses, particularly those owned and operated by black entrepreneurs, must form an integral part of the national economy and economic policy. Micro producers should develop from a set of marginalised survival strategies into dynamic small enterprises that can provide a decent living for both employees and entrepreneurs. Policies to that end must focus on women, who are represented disproportionately in this sector, especially in the rural areas. **4.4.7.2** Government agencies must provide infrastructure and skills to raise incomes and create healthier working conditions in small businesses. They must protect the rights of workers, both family members and others, and provide training in productive and managerial skills. **4.4.7.4** In the context of a supportive industrial strategy, all levels of the democratic government--central, regional and local--must where possible foster new, dynamic relationships between large, small and micro enterprises in ways that do not harm the interests of labour. As discussed in the chapter, 'Implementing the RDP,' the government must require financial institutions to lend a rising share of their assets to black-owned enterprise. All levels of the state should also, as far as possible, support joint marketing strategies and technological development within the small-scale sector. **4.4.7.5** The democratic government must rationalise and restructure existing parastatals to support small enterprise as far as their underlying purposes allow. It should reorganise the SBDC and reform the lending criteria of other agencies such as the IDC and the development corporations so that they incorporate small and micro enterprise in their plans as far as feasible, and end corruption and nepotism in their lending programmes. **4.4.7.7** All levels of the democratic government must review their procurement policies to ensure that, where costs permit, they support small-scale enterprise. In particular, we must explore new policies on the procurement of furniture and school uniforms, which micro producers might supply. Procurement regulations must, however, require appropriate labour standards for suppliers. **4.4.7.10** The development of social and economic infrastructure, including pre-schools, water supplies, roads and electrification, will go a long way to improving productivity. Infrastructural programmes must therefore take the implications for micro enterprise into account.

407. The promotion of small, medium and micro enterprises (SMMEs) is a key element in the Government's strategy for employment creation and income generation... various programmes and institutions have been established to give effect to the strategy, including: the Small Business Centre attached to the Department of Trade and Industry; Ntsika Enterprise Promotion Agency to provide non-financial assistance; Khula Enterprise Finance Limited for wholesale loans; Khula Credit Guarantee Limited for loan guarantees; a pre-shipment export finance guarantee facility to expand access to working capital; and the Competitiveness Fund for consultancy advice on technology and marketing. The Simplified Regional Industrial Development Programme will be continued in a modified form as a grant programme tailored to the needs of small and medium-sized firms. (*Growth, Employment and Redistribution*, 5.4)

Financial services are needed, not only by employers and small scale business people, but also by farm workers, the landless, pensioners and small holders. Financial services need to be readily available to make a real difference to people and economic development. In 1996, the Presidential Commission on Rural Financial Services proposed that the Land Bank retain its primary purpose of providing both wholesale and retail finance for land purchase (an important adjunct to the land reforms) and for agricultural production. The bank will be required also to provide project financing and to increase its lending to small-scale farmers, and it will be required to adopt a "best practice ethic" for lending. Some of its lending will be at province level and through development corporations. Some will be through agency agreements with the Post Office. There are also proposals to promote a third tier of banking through NGOs, credit unions and other retail organisations. The Land Bank is one of five National Development Finance Institutions (NDFIs), which will have complementary functions. Finance and support services for rural non-farm enterprises will be available through Khula enterprise Finance Limited, an NDFI set up by the DTI. Both the Land Bank and Khula will on-lend to local intermediaries. Major attempts are being made to extend the outreach and accessibility of financial institutions and entrepreneurs who have not previously had access to formal financing systems. Banks, post offices and a variety of non-government organisations are likely to become part of a broad web of financial institutions falling within a regulatory framework still to be established. The framework will promote the growth of pluralism, including, for instance, less formal organisations, such as saving clubs and stokvels, which will remain important to entrepreneurs who are starting out in business. (*Rural Development Framework*, p.36)

408. The National Small Business Council is hereby established as a juristic person... The functions of the Council are to—(a) represent and promote the interests of small business, with emphasis on those entities contemplated in the National Small Business Support Strategy; and (b) advise the national, provincial, and local spheres of government on social and economic policy that promotes the development of small business. (*National Small Business Act*, 2)

409. Initiatives aimed at supporting small and medium-sized business development are gathering momentum. The *National Small Business Act* was passed in November 1996, providing for the establishment of Ntsika Enterprise Promotion Agency and a National Small Business Council. The Khula Enterprise Finance Corporation is operational, and has initiated a credit guarantee scheme and a capacity building project targeted at retail financial intermediaries. (*Medium Term Budget Policy Statement*, 1997, p.16)

410. ...as of January 1998, only 633 indemnities have been granted by Khula's Credit Guarantee scheme, indicating a lack of activity in areas government has prioritised need. (*Financial Access for SMMEs: Towards a Comprehensive Strategy*, p.2)

411. ...local governments could lock in low interest rates for capital and operating expenditures for a limited time period, to qualifying SMMEs, if the loan is matched with some other income-generation programme--procurement of goods and services, for instance, by local government--which local SMMEs can tap into provided they have access to affordable finance. In such a case, a government loan at below-market interest rates should be clearly disclosed to the borrower and to the public at large, and the interest subsidy should be explicitly phased out after an appropriate period so that the investment in the SMME becomes sustainable on its own terms. (*Financial Access for SMMEs: Towards a Comprehensive Strategy*, p.21)

412. Procurement Policy in the Ministry of Public Enterprise: parastatals are to contract with the government on job creation and black economic empowerment initiatives. Part of the core business can be sourced from the historically disadvantaged through structured empowerment schemes... The National Empowerment Fund is to be used as a potential source of establishing new businesses/jobs through Employment Ownership Schemes... Sub-contracting as part of service provision to emerging business by parastatals is to be involved in the Spatial Development Initiatives. Possible incentives could be introduced for progressive parastatals, e.g. tax rebates. (*Ministry of Public Enterprise Parliamentary Media Briefing*, 7 July 1998)
Different Public Enterprises are at different levels of development in terms of black small business development. Black Business Empowerment (BEE) in the Public Enterprise: ESKOM has adopted a policy framework in respect of small business development. In 1997, ESKOM spent approximately R286 million on SMMEs and also secured future coal supplies from small black-owned coal mining firms. (*Public Enterprise Ministry Budget Vote*, 22 May 1998)

413. The selection of contract strategies, the packaging of contract and the employment of affirmative procurement practices can tip the scales in favor of the local economy. In particular, Affirmative Procurement which seeks to engage the participation of small, medium and micro enterprises is to a large extent self targeting towards local enterprises. (*Green Paper on Public Sector Procurement Reform in South Africa*, pp.117-18)

414. **4.4.7.8** A specific programme must be established to ensure government support for women entrepreneurs. It must be easily accessible and include skills training and access to credit... **4.4.7.11** To better serve micro enterprise, the democratic government must double the existing number of local service centres and satellites. These satellites must enable the democratic government to provide for rural women involved in small, micro and medium-sized enterprises. All training programmes for micro enterprise must provide appropriate child care.

415. The following areas and/or target groups seem particularly relevant, with emphasis furthermore on enterprises owned or controlled by entrepreneurs from formerly disadvantaged communities:... start-up and expanding enterprises owned by women and, in particular, women with children... Special attention has to be given to the planning and physical infrastructure needs of women entrepreneurs. (*White Paper on National Strategy for the Development and Promotion of Small Business in South Africa*, 3.5.4,4.6.3)

416. Women living in the rural areas often have neither industrial nor commercial jobs, nor land on which to support themselves... A newly established Sub-directorate: Women's Land Rights within the Department of Land Affairs has been tasked to develop policy guidelines to facilitate women participation in land reform... The policy is in line with the Ministry's commitment to the Beijing Platform to... take legislative and administrative measures to give women and men equal rights to economic resources including access to... credit facilities... and appropriate supporting technology... The Departments of Agriculture and Land Affairs are examining how to address the discrimination encountered by women who try to borrow money from private institutions. Implementation of the recommendations by the Strauss Commission regarding Rural Finance should also assist... In terms of training, the Department of Welfare plans to encourage community development programmes to promote... micro-enterprises, small business... for women so as to address widespread rural poverty. It recognises the need for access to credit and skills training if such programmes are to succeed. (*Convention for the Elimination of all Forms of Discrimination against Women, First South African Report*, 14)

417. **4.4.7.11** To better serve micro enterprise, the democratic government must double the existing number of local service centres and satellites.

418. One of the most important instruments to spread support for small enterprises at local level is the envisaged nation-wide network of Local Service Centres (or, more appropriately, called Business Service Centres). (*White Paper on National Strategy for the Development and Promotion of Small Business in South Africa*, 5.8)

419. During the 1996/97 budget year, the DTI fundamentally transformed the institutional support base for small, medium and micro enterprises (SMME) by, among others, creating and providing financial support to Ntsika Enterprise Promotion Agency... Ntsika was established as a wholesale agency with a mandate to address non-financial support services... A total of R18m was spent in implementing the following interventions... (a) LBSC Programme was launched to create... a network of SMME service providers that will develop... effective delivery of support to all SMMEs; (b) 15 LBSC were fully accredited and funds amounting to R675 000 disbursed; (c) 12 LBSC were partially accredited and funds amounting to R300 000 were disbursed. (*Annual Report*, Department of Trade and Industry, 1996/97, pp.81-83)

420. **4.4.8.4** A greater share of government initiatives which facilitate technological development, knowledge acquisition and training must directly benefit small and micro enterprise... **4.4.8.6** Appropriate technology for small and medium-sized enterprises must be purchased where necessary and applicable from other developing countries. **4.4.8.7**

Scientific research should link up with technological advance in industry, commerce and services and in small and micro production. In particular, there must be research into appropriate and sustainable technologies for the rural areas.

421. Over the past few years a number of institutions have started to focus on the technology needs of small enterprises, with the CSIR the most important parastatal. The DTI's Support Programme for Industrial Innovation can also be used for this purpose, as could research sponsored by the Foundation for Research Development and more proactive work by the National Productivity Institute. In fact, time seems ripe for a well propagated, multi-year programme, spearheaded by the CSIR, involving all relevant bodies, both public and private, to systematically address... needs in the field of appropriate technology. (*White Paper on National Strategy for the Development and Promotion of Small Business in South Africa*, 4.9)

422. A major effort will be made to operationalise and implement the policies outlined in the *White Paper* on small business promotion. The relevant legislation is under consideration and various programmes and institutions have been established to give effect to the strategy, including:... the Competitiveness Fund for consultancy advice on technology and marketing. (*Growth, Employment and Redistribution*, 5.4)

423. Supporting Technology Enhancement in Industry. A pilot Technopreneur Programme was launched in 7 colleges around the country. A further 20 colleges have committed to implementing the project in 1997. The objective of the programme is to facilitate technology and entrepreneurial skills transfer and development. The following have been achieved: (a) 160 entrepreneurs were trained; (b) 112 small businesses were started; (c) 29 small businesses revived, (d) 104 jobs were created. (*Annual Report*, Department of Trade and Industry, 1996/97, p.83)
Technology: Technology and Human Resources in Industry Programme (THRIP) of the Department of Trade and Industry allocated R21 million and contributed to 207 projects involving 110 companies and 1 000 students of which 29% were black and 27% women... The Support Programme for Industrial Innovation has over the last 4 years cost R43,2 million and has generated some 1 800 jobs, R87,5 million in exports and enterprises that have provided R117 million in tax. (*Department of Trade and Industry Budget Vote*, 15 May 1998)

424. 4.4.8.5 Girls and women should be encouraged to obtain technical and scientific skills. The Ministry of Education must establish targets in the study of science and technology in educational institutions it subsidies. Research in the science and technology arena by the democratic government, parastatals and educational institutions must cater equally to the needs of women in this area.

425. Equity through Redress... Programmes need to redress the inequalities which have excluded black women and men from the mainstream of South African society... Awarding of grants will be based on... gender targets. (*White Paper on Science and Technology*, 9.3,9.4) There are... developments in this direction... such as the Technology and Human Resources for Industry Programme (THRIP) which comprises a partnership between higher education

institutions, business, industry and government... The Ministry of Education therefore supports, among others, the following measure: prioritising access of black and women students to masters, doctoral and postdoctoral programmes, and designing a human resource development plan for higher education. (*Education White Paper*, 2.88,2.91)

Based on the overwhelming support received in response to the *Green Paper for the Introduction of Technology Education* across the general education system, DACST will assist the Department of Education in developing technology programme for schools. (*White Paper on Science and Technology*, 9.7)

426. **4.4.8.6** New legislation must ensure that agreements to import foreign technology include a commitment to educate and train local labour to use, maintain and extend technology... The democratic government must limit excessive payment of royalties and license fees.

427. Both technology transfer and human resource development are crucial to the advancement and development of local industry. South Africa's policies ought to ensure that the country enjoys the maximum benefit of foreign participation by incorporating a requirement for technology transfer and human resource development as integral conditions for foreign tenders. (*Green Paper on Public Sector Procurement Reform in South Africa*, p.97)

428. **4.4.8.8** The democratic government must redirect military/strategic production to civilian production. Policies should encourage former employees to develop spin-offs.

429. Defence Research. The defence sector in general is a repository of considerable skills in instrumentation, control and advanced materials handling. Extending or converting these skills to civil use could broaden our industrial skills base considerably... The defence R&D effort will be a forum for technology assessment, rather than the first stage in large scale production of weapons... The central issue in the defence technology debate in South Africa has recently been whether sufficient spin-off can occur for the Defence Research and Development budget to have a positive effect on high technology development in the civilian sector... The view that defence technology should be phased out in favour of civilian technology, or converted into it, is not tenable. (*White Paper on Science and Technology*, 8.2.5)

430. DENEL: It will after years of profits, make its first loss since incorporation as a private company in 1992. Redeployment of company resources towards commercial sector in pursuit of company strategy to reduce dependence on military business. Whereas a revenue of R3 billion and net profit after tax of R82 million were recorded in 1996/97, reduced revenue and losses are expected for the 1997/98 period. Key challenges for 1998/99 and beyond include inter alia: increase commercial (non-military) sales to over 50% of the total revenue. (*Denel: Current State-Owned Enterprises Undergoing Privatisation*, @http://ope.pwv.gov.za/html/denel.htm)

431. DTI bilateral work programmes with other line departments and parastatals: DTI contributed to the strengthening of South Africa's arms control system and participated in the National Conventional Arms Control Committee. Bilateral work with the Department of Defence has focused on developing strategies to raise the competitiveness of defence-related industries. (*Annual Report*, Department of Trade and Industry, 1996/97, pp.79-80)

432. **4.4.8.9** The democratic government must develop extensive institutional support and enhance government capacities to ensure successful research foresight. Because science and technology play a crucial role in the RDP, a strong coordinating agency in government must maintain on-going consultation with key stakeholders.

433. Visions and Goals... stakeholders, especially those who were formerly marginalised, are part of a more inclusive and consultative approach to policy decision-making and resource allocation for science and technology activities. (*White Paper on Science and Technology*, Preamble).
The technology transfer programme of the Department of Trade and Industry, which serves to police and advise on licensing and royalty agreements, will be converted into an agency dedicated to facilitating access by firms to needed technologies. (*Growth, Employment and Redistribution*, 5.3)

434. **4.4.9.1** Distribution patterns have been severely distorted by apartheid and in the last two decades by particular investment patterns. Problems have emerged, including the biased location of distribution outlets, a distorted relationship between property investment and shopping malls, and excessive concentration of ownership, particularly in the link with the large conglomerates and racial composition. **4.4.9.2** These issues must be addressed in order to achieve more geographically balanced and accessible distribution, lowered costs of distribution, modernised linkages between production and distribution, and greater participation by black people in the distribution chain.

435. **4.5.1.2** The minerals in the ground belong to all South Africans, including future generations. Moreover, the current system of mineral rights prevents the optimal development of mining and the appropriate use of urban land. We must seek the return of private mineral rights to the democratic government, in line with the rest of the world. This must be done in full consultation with all stakeholders.

436. Business Climate. Points of departure: i) The policy shall endorse free-market principles and shall allow government intervention only to the extent of meeting the aims of the policy... Resource Management... Policy proposals – views expressed: v) Mineral rights must be returned to the State (publicly owned) and a system of State (Crown) held mineral rights, which are leased to companies, be introduced.
viii) The existing system of public and private ownership of mineral rights should be retained. (*Discussion Document on a Minerals and Mining Policy for South Africa*, 1.1,3.1.4)
As articulated in its macroeconomic strategy, Government has committed itself to a continuing process of economic liberalisation, thus strengthening the competitive capacity of the economy, fiscal and tariff reform and bureaucratic deregulation. These are essential

steps toward enhancing the country's competitiveness, attracting foreign direct and portfolio investment and creating a climate conducive to business expansion. The mining industry among other will benefit in the long term from these developments... Government will create a stable macro-environment that supports economic development at national, provincial, and local levels and in which business, subject to appropriate regulation, can operate profitably, be internationally competitive and satisfy their shareholders' and employees' expectations. In this way Government will encourage investment in mining as in other industries. Consideration should be given to using tax measures to improve access to mineral rights... Government's long-term objective is for all mineral rights to rest in the State for the benefit of and on behalf of all the people in South Africa; State-owned mineral rights will not be alienated; Government will promote minerals development by applying the "use-it or lose it"/"use-it and keep-it" principle... The right to prospect and to mine for all minerals will vest in the State... provision will be made for: a. guaranteeing the continuation of current prospecting and mining operations in accordance with the "use-it and keep-it" principle. (*White Paper: A Mineral and Mining Policy for South Africa*, 1.2.3.2, 1.3.6)

437. SA currently pursues a dual system of mineral rights in which ownership is distributed between the state which holds 1/3, and private ownership 2/3. While the government recognises the constitutional constraints of changing the current mineral rights system, it does not accept the system of dual state and private ownership of minerals. Government's long-term objective is for all mineral rights to vest in the state, but as a transitional measure a new system for all minerals is proposed, the main aspect being that the right to prospect and mine for all minerals will vest in the state. (*Appropriation Bill, Debate on Vote No 24: Minerals and Energy*, p.2)

438. **4.5.1.5** Our RDP must attempt to increase the level of mineral beneficiation through appropriate incentives and disincentives in order to increase employment and add more value to our natural resources before export. Moreover, this policy should provide more appropriate inputs for manufacturing in South Africa.

439. Minerals Beneficiation. Points of departure: i) The aim of the policy shall be to develop South Africa's mineral wealth to its full potential and to the maximum benefit of the entire population. (*Discussion Document on a Minerals and Mining Policy for South Africa*, 11.1)
Government will encourage municipalities to capitalise on the comparative advantage associated with mineral activity in their area of jurisdiction and will support mutually beneficial partnership between the mining industry and municipalities.
The tax system should encourage the adding of value to raw materials... The aim of the policy will be to develop South Africa's mineral wealth to its full potential and to the maximum benefit of the entire population. Government, therefore, will promote the establishment of secondary and tertiary mineral-based industries aimed at adding maximum value to raw materials... Beneficiation projects should be initiated on the basis of market forces and decisions taken by individual companies pursuing well-considered business objectives... to promote mineral beneficiation, efficient supply-side measures will be

introduced, such as lower royalty rates for projects that include beneficiation. (*White Paper: A Mineral and Mining Policy for South Africa*, 1.2.3.2, 1.5)

440. **4.5.1.6** A democratic government must consider mechanisms to encourage companies to sell to local industries at prices that will enhance their international competitiveness.

441. Minerals Marketing. Point of departure: The policy shall endorse free market principles and shall allow government intervention only to the extent of meeting the aims of the policy. (*Discussion Document on a Minerals and Mining Policy for South Africa*, 12.1) Government will seek to create an enabling environment for municipalities to maximize the positive role the mining sector can play in promoting Local Economic Development and Integrated Development Planning... Mineral marketing will be based on market principles. Government's role will be supportive, and intervention will generally be limited to addressing market failures... All measures which restrict the sale of South African minerals on foreign markets will be opposed. (*White Paper: A Mineral and Mining Policy for South Africa*, 1.1.4, 1.6)

442. **4.5.1.8** Democratisation of the mining sector must involve new laws to build workplace democracy for miners by requiring employers to negotiate the organisation of work with their employees and their unions. Programmes must be established to allow financial participation by workers in mining companies in a meaningful way (including measures to influence the policies of financial institutions, especially insurance companies and pension funds, that hold significant stakes in the mining sector and in which our people have substantial investments). And anti-trust legislation and other measures must be implemented to permit the monitoring and appropriate control of mining, mineral processing and marketing.

443. Access and Ownership. Point of departure: To ensure equal opportunity and non-discrimination in respect of access, ownership and employment in the mineral industry. Background information and perceptions: iii) The racial ownership patterns which grew in the diamond and later gold mining industries, provide the origins of today's situation wherein significant control of the major mining houses lies in the hands of a small group of exclusively white shareholders. Issues and arguments: vii) There is much to be gained by creating among mining and other employees an understanding of the opportunities for share acquisition through the stock exchange... x) There is a need to democratise the mining industry, both in terms of its ownership and in terms of worker participation in decision making. Mechanisms need to be developed to allow workers to take ownership stakes in mining companies and influence their policies... Policy proposals--views expressed: ii) Investigate measures to increase black ownership and participation in the mining industry... vii) The evolution of a better spread of ownership should take place through natural business activities and not through Government intervention... viii) The State should take a constructive interventionist role in altering the patterns of ownership in the industry and promoting black ownership at all levels... ix) Measures to dilute control of the mining industry by a minority of shareholders and increase participation by a wider spread of citizens through steps such as effective employee share ownership schemes and management and worker buy-outs should be investigated... x) To allow workers to take

ownership stakes in companies the following mechanisms should be investigated: Using retirement funds that have significant investments in the mining industry to entitle workers to nominate directors to the conglomerates that administer the mines; Changing the *Companies Act* and tax laws to make employee share ownership plans a real option for mineworkers and their retirement funds to take control of certain mines through leveraged buy-outs; Setting up trust institutions to allow mineworkers, on a collective basis to accumulate equity stakes in the mining industry. This process should be encouraged and facilitated by the Government as part of its programme of black empowerment. (*Discussion Document on a Minerals and Mining Policy for South Africa*, 2.3,2.4).
Government will:... v) address past racial inequities by ensuring that those previously excluded from participating in the mining industry gain access to mineral resources or benefit from the exploitation thereof... vi) Take on reasonable legislative and other measures to foster conditions conducive to mining which will enable entrepreneurs to gain access to mineral resources on an equitable basis... Government will continuously promote a wider spread of ownership and seek to facilitate acceleration of the changes that are already underway... Government will encourage real worker participation in the management of all mines. (*White Paper: A Mineral and Mining Policy for South Africa*, 1.3.2,2.4)

444. The government together with business and the employees in the mining industry, set up... the Gold Crisis Committee (GCC). The purpose of setting up the committee was to see if we could stem the tide of job losses by reviewing proposed retrenchment notices submitted by the industry to the committee, and recommending other alternatives. The formation of GCC is possibly the first of its kind anywhere in the world where the government, business and labour sit together in an attempt to find common solutions to a shared problem. (*Appropriation Bill, Debate on Vote No 24: Minerals and Energy*, p.1)

445. 4.5.1.9 The RDP must put into place mechanisms to ensure orderly down-scaling of our mines so as to minimise the suffering of workers and their families. Measures should include the reskilling and training of workers for other forms of employment.

446. Downscaling. Point of departure: The aim of the policy shall be to ameliorate the social consequences of sizable downscaling and mine closure... Issues and arguments: ii) Companies believe the government has a socio-economic obligation to assist in alleviating the consequences of sizeable downscaling or closure through a combination of counselling, training and other initiatives targeted at the retrenchees and their dependents and other measures aimed at stimulating the demand for labour... Policy proposals–views expressed: v) Government has a socio-economic obligation to assist in alleviating the consequences of downscaling and closure. (*Discussion Document on a Minerals and Mining Policy for South Africa*, 8.1,8.3,8.4)
Government will endeavour to ameliorate the social consequences of sizeable downscaling and mine closure... Government has an obligation to assist employers, employees, industry suppliers and mine-linked communities in anticipating and managing the consequences of large-scale job losses. (*White Paper: A Mineral and Mining Policy for South Africa*, 3.6.4)

447. Preliminary estimates show that through the GCC, we have saved up to 42% of the jobs that were threatened. Various GCC task teams have been formed to continue to explore possible solutions to the gold crisis. (*Appropriation Bill, Debate on Vote No 24: Minerals and Energy*, pp.1-2)

448. **4.5.1.10** The RDP envisages a new set of minimum standards for the mining industry that ensure fair wages and employment conditions for all workers and a health and safety system that recognises the special hazards related to mining.
4.5.1.11 In future all workers must have the right to live at or near their place of work in decent accommodation and shall have full control over their after-tax salaries. In addition, the mining companies must take some responsibility for the education, training and social needs of miners and their families as an integral part of labour policy on the mines.

449. Mining Safety and Health. Point of departure: The policy shall provide for enforcing safe and healthy working conditions at all mines. Background information and perceptions: i) The recommendations of the Leon Commission of inquiry into safety and health in the mining industry and the report of the Parliamentary Mineral and Energy Portfolio Committee have been accepted in principle by the Cabinet... Human Resources Development. Point of departure: To encourage and support education, training and technological development in the mineral industry. Background information and perceptions: iii) To meet current and future operational requirements, the mineral industry will need to deploy well educated and trained workers, technologists, managers and scientists. Housing and Living Conditions. Point of departure: To provide an acceptable standard of housing and living conditions for mineworkers, by providing a range of flexible low-cost housing options... Industrial Relations and Employment Conditions. Point of departure: To create a productive and non-adversarial approach to industrial relations and set new minimum standards for work in mining. (*Discussion Document on a Minerals and Mining Policy for South Africa*, 9,10.1,10.2,10.4)

450. The owner of every mine that is being worked must
ensure, as far as reasonably practicable, that the mine is designed, constructed and equipped to provide conditions for safe operation and a healthy working environment with a communication system--and equipment--necessary to achieve those conditions... Employees must not be made to pay for health and safety training... Every mine with 20 or more employees must have a health and safety representative for each shift at each designated workplace in the mine... [A manager must] provide health and safety representatives with the facilities, assistance and training necessary to enable them to function effectively... A Mine Health and Safety Council is hereby established to advise the Minister on health and safety at mines. (*Mine Health And Safety Act*, 2,10,25,26,30,41)

451. Mine health and safety: On the 30 June (1997) the Ministry launched the Tripartite Mine Health and Safety Council which advises the Minister on health and safety issues in the mining industry. *Mine Health and Safety Act*: had come into operation on 15 January 1997 with the application of section 56(3) being suspended pending an agreement between labour and business on the reversal of onus. The agreement was reached and section 86(3) was deleted through an amendment... and this means that the reversal of onus of proof is

replaced by a system of administrative fines, applicable to employers. The *Act* is of paramount importance... it has ushered in a new era... to the area of health and safety in the mines. Compared with the 1996 figures, a decrease of about 10% in fatal mine accidents has been achieved. The Ministry's target is to improve this by 30% in the period between 1998-2001. (*Appropriation Bill, Debate on Vote No 24: Minerals and Energy*, p.3)

452. **4.5.1.12** Existing legislation must be strengthened to ensure that our environment is protected. Before a new mine can be established there must be a comprehensive environmental impact study.

453. Environmental Management. Point of departure: The policy shall provide for the maintenance of balanced and responsible standards with regard to the interface between mining and the environment that are based on local needs and requirements, but also take due cognisance of international practices. (*Discussion Document on a Minerals and Mining Policy for South Africa*, 5.1)

454. A major step forward in the achievement of sound environmental management in South Africa was taken under the *Environmental Conservation Act* (Act 73 of 1989) in September 1997 to make environmental impact assessment compulsory for a wide range of developmental activities. (*Annual Report*, Department of Environmental Affairs and Tourism, 1998, p.46)

455. Mining companies are required by the law to make financial provision for mining related environmental rehabilitation. (*Green Paper on the Mineral Policy of South Africa*, 1.2).
Mining activities impact on the environment to varying degree. Three important areas identify themselves for policy and regulation, namely (a) the environmental impact of exploration, (b) the environmental impact over the life of a mine including mine closure and financial assurances for site rehabilitation, and (c) maintaining rehabilitation measures where mining activity has ceased. (*White Paper: Minerals and Mining Policy for South Africa*, 4.1)

456. **4.5.1.13** In the spirit of mutual cooperation, the RDP should extend across our borders by using our considerable expertise in mineral exploration and exploitation to rehabilitate and develop the mineral potential of our neighbours. In this regard a special facility should be created to promote investment in the sub-continent.

457. Regionalisation and Internationalisation. Point of departure: To encourage international cooperation with emphasis on Southern Africa, and to base such cooperation on the principle of mutual benefit... Policy proposals–views expressed... The feasibility of creating a special facility for South African outward investment into the region, currently restricted by exchange control, should be prioritised. (*Discussion Document on a Minerals and Mining Policy for South Africa*, 14.1,14.4)
South African-based mining companies wish to see a speeding-up in the comprehensive dismantling of foreign exchange controls... The nature of international mineral markets and of South Africa's mineral resources must be taken into consideration when promoting

investment, including the effect of increased supplies on prices... Government will participate in the co-ordination of the policies of southern African countries so that the region can benefit optimally from its mineral wealth by taking specific steps to: a. remove barriers to the movement of labor, capital, goods and services... c. encourage cross-border mineral processing... d. foster regional cooperation in technology development... f. disseminate investment and exploration of information among member countries. (*White Paper: A Mineral and Mining Policy for South Africa*, 1.1.3.1,5.4)

458. **4.5.1.14** The government must consider ways and means to encourage small-scale mining and enhance opportunities for participation by our people through support, including financial and technical aid and access to mineral rights. However, standards in respect of the environment, health and safety and other working conditions must be maintained.

459. Small Scale Mining and Mineral Development. Point of departure: The government shall encourage and facilitate the development of the small exploration and mining sectors and of mining activities in underdeveloped regions and shall provide assistance to this effect based on sound business principles. (*Discussion Document on a Minerals and Mining Policy for South Africa*, 6.1)
Government will encourage and facilitate the sustainable development of small-scale mining in order to ensure the optimal exploitation of smaller mineral deposits and to enable this sector to make a positive contribution to the national, provincial and local economy... Information on mineral rights and mineral deposits available for development will be made accessible, particularly for the benefit of small-scale miners... All spheres of government and development agencies will work towards coordinating their activities in respect of the promotion of small-scale mining activities... Health and safety standards will be maintained in small-scale mining operations. (*White Paper: A Mineral and Mining Policy for South Africa*, 1.4.2, 1.4.4.1)

460. **4.5.2.2** The RDP aims to create a restructured agricultural sector that spreads the ownership base, encourages small-scale agriculture, further develops the commercial sector and increases production and employment. Agriculture should be oriented to the provision of affordable food to meet the basic needs of the population and towards household food security. The pursuit of national food self-sufficiency proves too expensive and will not meet these aims. Moreover, it could undermine trade with neighbouring countries better able to produce foodstuffs. **4.5.2.3** The present commercial agricultural sector will remain an important provider of food and fibre, jobs and foreign exchange. The RDP must provide a framework for improving its performance by removing unnecessary controls and levies as well as unsustainable subsidies. **4.5.2.4** Support services provided by the democratic government, including marketing, finance and access to cooperatives, must concentrate on small and resource-poor farmers, especially women.

461. Agricultural production systems and practices will be organised in such a manner as to improve national as well as household food security... The government should therefore support the full spectrum of production systems and practices, from urban food gardens and small-scale production for household income and food security to large-scale

production systems which can add considerably to national food security. (*White Paper on Agriculture*, 2.2)

462. **4.5.2.5** Comprehensive measures should be introduced to improve the living and working conditions of farm workers. All labour legislation must be extended to farm workers, with specific provisions relating to their circumstances.

463. Agricultural production practices and systems should favour the use of labour wherever it is economically justified... (To optimise the utilisation of labour in agriculture) will require, amongst others, effective labour organisations, good labour relations, the appropriate training of farm workers and finding a balance between labour and mechanisation by means of appropriate technology. (*White Paper on Agriculture*, 2.5)

464. Sections 1 and 2 (Chapter 1) of the *Labour Relations Act*, 1995 extend its application to farm workers.

465. [B]alanced with the rights of the owner or person in charge, an occupier shall have the right— (a) to security of tenure... (*Extension of Security of Tenure Act*, p.6)

466. Farm worker Incentive Scheme: 11 197 farm worker dwellings were connected (electrified) during 1997 bringing the total farm worker connections to 81 355 since 1992. (*Ministry of Public Enterprise Budget Vote*, 22 May 1998)
The Rural Housing Loan Fund (RHLF), set up as a section 21 company with a revolving fund sourced from a DM50 million German government grant... Loans totalling R36 million had been made by the RHLF by the end of October 1997. The average loan to the end-user by non-traditional lenders accessing finance from the RHLF is around R3 000 and assists people in developing a recognised credit history. (*Annual Report*, Department of Housing, 1997, pp.25,26)
Because farm workers and their families often live on isolated homesteads, on land owned by others, special attention must be given to their rights. It is necessary to ensure that land owners do not infringe or undermine the basic rights of workers as set out in the Bill of Rights, e.g. human dignity, freedom and security, servitude and forced labour. Farm workers and their families, living on the land of others, are entitled to equal access to government services and to subsidies and grants, such as the national housing subsidy, to which their low income entitles them. Farm workers must also be covered by legislation on occupational health and accident insurance, not only for physical accidents connected with the use of machinery, but also those resulting form the misuse, or unsafe storage, of toxic agricultural chemicals. As labour tenants are a specific category of rural dwellers who are particularly vulnerable, with specific land needs, the *Land Reform (Labour Tenants) Act* (3 of 1996) provides for the protection of their rights and for the acquisition of land for labour tenants who will be able to access the Settlement/Land Acquisition Grant for this purpose. The Extension of Tenure Security Bill aims to provide security of tenure for vulnerable occupiers of rural and peri-urban land. It provides for government actively to promote and support long term security for vulnerable occupiers, protecting them against unfair eviction, and regulating the relationship between land owners and occupiers. (*Rural Development Framework*, p.59)

467. **4.5.2.6** Efficient, labour-intensive and sustainable methods of farming must be researched and promoted. To this end, extension workers should be trained and retrained and the agricultural education and research institutions restructured. The RDP must support effective drought management by providing agro-meteorological advice to farmers rather than subsidising losses, which in the past encouraged environmentally destructive farming methods.

468. Drought will be recognised as a normal phenomenon in the agricultural sector and it will be accommodated as such in farming and agricultural financing systems... The Government should not support measures that soften the negative impact on farm incomes caused by poor risk management as this will cause farmers to use high-risk methods which could endanger resource conservation... It is of the utmost importance that ways should be found to optimise the utilisation of labour in agriculture... Mechanisation does not always increase farm profits and economic viability. Labour is a relatively freely available production resource which can be fully utilised in the production system, provided that better training is given. (*White Paper on Agriculture*, 2.3,2.5)

469. **4.5.2.7** Increased attention must be paid to additional processing and value-adding activities derived from agriculture. This is linked to modernising marketing and exporting activities, and to the considerable potential for supplying a growing tourist industry.

470. The addition of value close to the point of production promotes income generation and development in that area, and should be encouraged wherever it is economically justified. The promotion of local farm services and the local processing of farm products will enhance the rural economy, increase the viability of farm production and reduce rural poverty. (*White Paper on Agriculture*, 2.6)
Agricultural research needs to focus beyond biological potential but must include value-added processing technologies. Given South Africa's export-oriented growth strategy, agricultural research can play a major role in opening new opportunities through research in non-traditional crops. It can lead to improved technology which will enable us to exploit our comparative and competitive advantages... The research system must therefore pay attention to trade related product development which ranges from product improvement, to increasing durability. (*Policy Document on Agriculture*, p.37)

471. The government would like to see a strong ARC, which continuously seeks ways of increasing productivity in agriculture. It is therefore interested in transformation of the organisation in a manner that will ensure excellent service and sustainability. To this end a new Board... appointed in 1997 has already began focusing on the development of a strategic vision for the institution... Public funding will increasingly prioritise the needs of small-scale resource-poor farmers and hence will among others focus on the following areas: (a) integrated farming systems, (b) land care and water management and (c) environmental issues. (*Policy Document on Agriculture*, pp.39-41)

472. **4.5.3.3** The administration of fisheries should be transferred from the Department of Environmental Affairs to a Department of Agriculture, Forestry and Fisheries. The Sea Fisheries Advisory Committee and the Quota Board should be retained, but their

membership and functions should be revised. For inshore fisheries and monitoring of catches, there should be greater community involvement in enforcement. For offshore resources, consideration must be given to establishing a regional 'Coastguard' involving the Southern African Development Community countries.

473. This document sets out the main policy principles that the Department of Environmental Affairs and Tourism of the Government of South Africa will endeavour to implement through its marine fisheries management institutions... Two measures are proposed for urgent implementation: the establishment of a Commerical Public Company to which quotas are allocated and which in turn rent them to fishers who do not have quotas; the establishment of an Implementation Committee of finite life. (*A Marine Fisheries Policy for South Africa*, 1,4.6.1)

474. **4.5.3.6** The RDP promotes the tightening of regulations governing land use in sensitive areas.

475. Objective 48: Fragile ecosystems. To ensure the sound management of fragile ecosystems, including monitoring, rehabilitation, and *in situ* conservation to preserve biodiversity. (*Green Paper for Environmental Policy for South Africa*, p.46)

476. The Department of Water Affairs and Forestry is developing a National Forestry Action Programme (NFAP) as a framework within which to implement South Africa's new forestry policy as described in the *White Paper* published in February 1996. The NFAP will, among other things, be characterised by ensuring strategies that the forestry sector is fully integrated into a wider resource management strategies emphasising linkages with land use planning and integrated catchment management. (*National Forestry Action Programme, Discussion Document 1*)

477. **4.5.4.3** With respect to the local mass market, education, access to facilities and the support of black entrepreneurship are critical.

478. Key objectives:... to promote domestic tourism amongst all South Africans... to provide appropriate tourism education, training, awareness and capacity building programmes, especially aimed at previously neglected groups... Marketing and promotion: Domestic marketing should be a provincial responsibility. The following policies and initiatives should apply:... facilitate the provision of facilities (including transportation) that would encourage domestic travel by the previously neglected. (*White Paper on Development and Promotion of Tourism in South Africa*, 4.4,5.11)

479. While the tourism industry has tremendous potential to create jobs, the Government recognises that appropriate skills and experience are necessary to facilitate employment growth as well as international competitiveness. The main principles governing tourism educational approach are, among others, (a) make training more accessible to the previously neglected groups; (b) encourage capacity building... and address specific needs of SMMEs and emerging entrepreneurs. (*White Paper on the Development and Promotion of Tourism in South Africa*, 5.2)

480. **4.5.4.3** In addition, promotion of ecotourism and enhancement of South Africa's unique cultural and political heritage must be prioritised.

481. Responsible tourism: Responsible tourism implies tourism industry responsibility to the environment through the promotion of balanced and sustainable tourism and focus on the development of environmentally based tourism activities (e.g. game-viewing and driving)... It implies the responsibility to respect, invest in and develop local cultures and protect them from over-commercialisation and over-exploitation. (*White Paper on Development and Promotion of Tourism in South Africa*, 3.4)

482. The President launched Robben Island Museum and unveiled a National Monuments Council Plague commemorating the declaration of Robben Island. (*Annual Report*, Department of Arts, Culture, Science and Technology, 1997, p.61)

483. **4.5.4.4** Community involvement in tourism projects must be encouraged, stressing partnerships with other agencies and initiation and ownership of enterprises. Communities must be given access to finance, management skills, upgrading of tourist service skills, language proficiency and connections with marketing infrastructure. Training institutions should be located in areas accessible to local communities to prevent leakage of skills from the area. This could be combined with other extension services and development training programmes at regional and local level.

484. This White Paper proposes **Responsible Tourism** as the key guiding principle for tourism development. Responsible tourism means responsibility of government and business to involve the local communities that are in close proximity to the tourism plant and attractions through the development of meaningful economic linkages (e.g. the supply of agricultural produce, etc.) It implies the responsibility to respect, invest in and develop local culture and protect them from over-commercialisation and over-exploitation... (Responsible tourism) also implies the responsibility of local communities to become actively involved in the tourism industry, to practice sustainable development and to ensure the safety and security of the visitors. Tourism education and training is one of the pillars of the development of a new responsible tourism in South Africa. One of the main principles governing the approach to education and training is to ensure that training is accessible to the previously neglected groups in the society in terms of appropriateness, affordability, location, costs and language of instruction. (*White Paper on Development and Promotion of Tourism in South Africa*, 3.4,5.2)

485. **4.5.5.5** A coordinated, mutually-beneficial policy within the region could offer some of the world's greatest natural and recreational tourist attractions.

486. South Africa is committed to working with other countries in Southern Africa in developing its tourism industry. South Africa will collaborate with regional tourism organisations such as SADC and RETOSA in the development of tourism in Southern Africa. Appropriate bilateral relations will also be established with neighbour countries. A number of areas of cooperation should be actively encouraged: (i) environmental conservation and development of related products such as trans-border protected areas (ii)

international marketing, e.g. joint international marketing campaigns with SADC countries, etc. (*White Paper on the Development and Promotion of Tourism in South Africa*, 5.13)

487. **4.5.4.7** Full and transparent environmental impact assessments should be conducted for all major tourism projects.

488. Key elements of responsible tourism are, among others, (a) avoid waste and over-consumption; (b) involve the local community in planning and decision-making; (c) Assess environmental, social and economic impacts as a prerequisite to developing tourism... Environmental management:... Specific principles and policy guidelines for environmental management as it relates to the tourism industry are as follows:... encourage ongoing social and environmental audits of tourism projects conducted in an inexpensive, rapid and participatory way. (*White Paper on Development and Promotion of Tourism in South Africa*, 3.4,5.6)

489. A major step forward in the achievement of sound environmental management in South Africa was taken under the *Environmental Conservation Act* (Act 73 of 1989) in September 1997 to make environmental impact assessment compulsory for a wide range of developmental activities. (*Annual Report*, Department of Environmental Affairs and Tourism, 1998, p.46)

490. **4.6.5** In addition to meeting basic energy and lighting needs for households, specific attention must be paid to making electricity available to micro, small, medium-sized and agricultural enterprises in both urban and rural areas. The benefits of cheap electricity presently enjoyed by large corporations must be extended to all parts of the economy.

491. Recognise the supply of electricity for micro-enterprise as a crucial component for economic development of historically disadvantaged areas. (*South African Energy Policy Discussion Document*, p.207)

492. **4.6.7** The development of an advanced information network should play a crucial role in facilitating the provision of high-quality services to all the people of South Africa. It must provide a significant advantage to the business sector as it reduces costs and increases productivity, and serves as an integral part of financial services, the commodities market, trade and manufacturing. **4.6.8** The basic infrastructural network must remain within the public sector. Certain value-added services could be licensed within the framework of an overall telecommunications programme. An integrated system of groundline, microwave, fibre-optic and satellite communications must substantially enhance the overall system. **4.6.9** The RDP aims to bring telecommunications closer to all potential users. A telecommunications regulatory authority must be established, which should be separated from policy and operating activities.

493. The primary object of this *Act* is to provide for the regulation and telecommunication matters in the public interest, and for that purpose to—(a) promote the universal and affordable provision of telecommunications services; (b) promote the provision of a wide

range of telecommunication services in the interest of the economic growth and development of the Republic; (c) make progress toward the universal provision of telecommunication services,; (d) encourage investment and innovation in the telecommunications industry... (g) ensure that, in relation to the provision of telecommunication services the needs of the local communities and areas are duly taken into account; (h) ensure that the needs of disabled persons are taken into account in the provision of telecommunication services;... (j) ensure fair competition within the telecommunications industry... There is hereby established a juristic person to be known as the South African Telecommunications Regulatory Authority;... The Authority shall be independent and impartial in the performance of its functions... Telkom shall be deemed to be the holder of a license to provide public switched telecommunication services... with a period of validity of 25 years from the date of the commencement of this *Act*... (c) Any service of Telkom contemplated in this subsection may be provided by a wholly owned subsidiary of Telkom, without such subsidiary being required to hold a license in terms of this *Act*... The manner of determining fees and charges shall be prescribed only in respect of fields where no or insufficient competition exists. Provided that within 12 months after the date of commencement of this *Act*, the Minister shall determine such fees and charges in respect of Telkom, and such fees and charges shall be in force until the third anniversary of the date on which the Minister issued a license to Telkom. (*Telecommunications Act*, 2,5.1-3,36.1.a,45.2,58,59)

494. **4.6.12** A review of the current situation within all transportation systems must be undertaken in order to assess the capacity of these systems and how they could enhance the development of other sectors of the economy and contribute to the RDP. Particular attention must be paid to the regulatory structures of the transportation systems.

495. Introduction. Early in 1995 the Department of Transport embarked on a project to review and revisit transport policy and formulate new policy where it has become necessary to adjust to a changed environment. (*Green Paper on National Transport Policy*)

496. One of the goals of the government's transport policy is to support the goals of the RDP for meeting basic needs, growing the economy, developing human resources, and democratising decision making. Implementing, regulating and advisory bodies: Within the transport sector there exist various regulatory and advisory bodies, for example the National Transport Commission (NTC), an independent Regulating Committee for Airports Company and the ATNS Company, and Road Transportation Boards. Consideration will be given to the establishment of Maritime Safety Agency, an Aviation Safety Agency, and a Road Agency for the primary roads, to allow for more focused service provision in these three areas. The Transport Advisory Committee has been disbanded as it is felt that the very important input to the Minister and the Department of Transport from private sector interest groups would best be effected through direct representations. (*White Paper on National Transport Policy*)

497. **4.7.2** The democratic government must modify regulations and support innovative financial institutions and instruments which mobilise private domestic savings to help fund the RDP, while not reducing incentives for personal savings. The democratic government

must enhance accountability, access and transparency in the financial sector. In cooperation with other stakeholders, it must review both regulations and regulatory system to determine which aspects prove an unnecessary impediment to the RDP, and more generally to greater efficiency in the allocation of savings. Government must encourage the private sector to cooperate in extending financial services to those who presently do not have access to these services. The establishment of a smoothly functioning and inexpensive payments system, assuring safety of consumer deposits, must be considered a high priority. To improve flexibility in the legal environment, parliament should establish an oversight committee for the financial sector.

498. There are four objectives associated with *access to affordable finance* for SMMEs: to significantly increase the level of commercial and NGO lending (and financial services) to SMMEs at interest rates (and fees) not inflated by unreasonable risk perceptions, and to assure that credit beneficiaries are, increasingly, the direct recipients of transparent, appropriately-targeted subsidies; to improve the outreach and efficiency of both conventional and alternative financial institutions, especially in unserved rural areas; to stimulate the provision of start-up and small-scale equity products for SMMEs; and to expand the number of SMMEs listed on the Johannesburg Stock Exchange. (*Financial Access for SMMEs: Towards a Comprehensive Strategy*, p.4.)

499. **4.7.2** The democratic government must introduce measures to combat discrimination on the grounds of race, gender, location and other non-economic factors. The democratic government must, in consultation with financial institutions, establish prudent non-discriminatory lending criteria, especially in respect of creditworthiness and collateral; reform the laws on women and banking to ensure equality; forbid blanket bans on mortgage bonds to specific communities ('redlining'); require banks to give their reasons when turning down a loan application; establish community liaison boards; develop simpler forms for contracts and applications, and create an environment which reduces the risk profile of lending to small black-owned enterprises and requires banks to lend a rising share of their assets to small, black-owned enterprise. The law must also require that financial institutions disclose their loans by race and gender; their assets and liabilities by subregion and sector; their staff by race and gender; the location of their branches and defaults by neighbourhood. To enforce laws against discrimination, the democratic government must establish an ombuds for the financial sector. At the local level, ombuds structures must include community representatives. Where anti-discrimination measures do not generate enough credit for housing, small enterprise and other RDP programmes, the government must provide appropriate kinds of financial support. The democratic government should consider reapplying the *Usury Act* to small loans (in addition to loans above R6 000, as presently applies), and should enforce the *Act* more effectively.

500. Given the past and present regulatory and statutory discrimination in South Africa, it is essential that new policies, strategies and legislative actions by the State should be particularly sensitive to the removal of entrenched discriminatory mechanisms and conventions in respect of gender, race, religion, and creed. Government has particularly identified the need to support the role of women in the housing delivery process. (*Housing White Paper*, 4.4.6)

501. Disclosure and penalties. In order to ensure that there are penalties in place should banks and institutional investors not significantly increase the volume of investment in SMME, a variety of measures including new legislation modelled on the US *Community Investment Act* (CRA) could be introduced. The main objectives of such measures would be increasing the disclosure of who lends and to whom (in general terms while assuring client confidentiality), improving the monitoring of SMME financing, assessing penalties for non-performance and discriminatory behaviour and outcomes, and establishing a customer-driven complaints process. (*Financial Access for SMMEs*, 3.4.3)

502. While interest rate deregulation--in the form of a larger *Usury Act* exemption than the present R6 000, in the context of a general review and modernisation of the *Usury Act*--and changes to banking legislation could together increase the numbers of creditors willing to become active in SMME markets, international experience cautions against summarily lifting interest rate ceilings. In order to prudently liberalise interest rates, the following four conditions should prevail: 1) high levels of macroeconomic stability; 2) high levels of bank solvency; 3) high levels of competition and low barriers to entry in the financial sector; and 4) strong and capable supervisory institutions, and ability to intervene in the case of bank failure... Decisions on raising the *Usury Act* exemption will be made once the rest of the regulatory apparatus is in place. (*Financial Access for SMMEs*, p.22)

503. **4.7.4** The democratic government must establish a Housing Bank to ensure access to wholesale finance for housing projects and programmes. A Guarantee Fund will protect private sector funds from undue risk. Approximately half the Bank's funds will come from the government in the form of recurrent housing subsidies, in order to ensure affordable bonds.

504. The possibility of a "National Housing Bank" was raised in the Reconstruction and Development Programme. Following extensive investigations, including international expertise from a number of countries, it was concluded that an institution tasked with unlocking housing finance at the wholesale level at scale and on a sustainable basis, has become necessary. Given the nature of its envisaged activities the name "Bank" is believed not to be appropriate, and the proposed institution will rather be known as the National Housing Finance Corporation. The range of interventions identified to be necessary to mobilise credit are believed to require the efforts of a focused agency which will have to be seen to be transparently accountable and whose performance can be objectively measured in terms of effectiveness and efficiency... Various parastastals and no-Governmental organisation involved in the provision of housing credit, play an important role in the provision of credit and especially in developing innovative new approaches to such provision. The capacity of this sector, however, is currently relatively limited, and although Government intends to provide specific support in order to grow and expand this sector, focus will in the short-term also have to be on the major banks if the availability of credits is to be enhanced. The need for special purpose lending vehicles as pioneering and innovating institutions is, however, recognised and programmes to ensure the sustained growth and expansion of this sector are envisaged to be part of the mandate of the National Housing Finance Corporation. (*Housing White Paper*, 5.5.3,5.5.3.2)

505. **4.7.5** Community banks of various types have proven able to finance informal entrepreneurs, especially women. The democratic government must encourage community banking. It must reform regulations to foster the development of community banks while protecting customers. Where possible, government structures at all levels should conduct business with these institutions. The government must encourage the established banks and other financial institutions to help fund the community banks.

506. In order to create an enabling environment for a second tier of banking, it is necessary to review the *Mutual Banks Act*. Furthermore, it may prove necessary to consider a form of deposit insurance for special purpose institutions so as to assure public confidence at a time when many informal (and new, formal) financial institutions have struggled to survive. Introducing a system of deposit insurance would protect depositors, especially in smaller banks and savings and loan institutions. (*Financial Access for SMMEs*, p.20)

507. **4.7.6** Pension and provident funds should be made more accountable to their members, and insurance companies to contributors. The democratic government must change the law to ensure adequate representation for workers through the trade unions and compulsory contributions by employers, and move towards industry funds. It must also legislate a transformation of the boards of the Mutual Funds to make them more socially responsible. The RDP must embark on a review of financial institution legislation, regulation and supervision to ensure the protection of pension and provident funds and other forms of savings and investment.

508. Notwithstanding the rules of a fund, every fund shall have a board consisting of at least three members, one of whom may be elected by the members of the fund. The duties of a board shall be to... ensure that adequate and appropriate information is communicated to the members of the fund informing them of their rights, benefits and duties in terms of the rules of the fund... The object of the Adjudicator is to dispose a complaint by investigating the complaint making the order which a court of law may make... These amendments will contribute to members' protection and will also serve as an effective and economical mechanism to deal with complaints. (*Pension Funds Amendment Act*, pp.6,22)

509. **4.7.7** The *Interim Constitution* contains several mechanisms which ensure that the Reserve Bank is both insulated from partisan interference and accountable to the broader goals of development and maintenance of the currency. In addition, the law must change the *Act* governing the Reserve Bank to ensure a board of directors that can better serve society as a whole. The board must include representatives from the trade unions and civil society. In future, a stronger board of governors should emerge through the appointment of better-qualified individuals. The new constitutional requirement that the board of governors record its decisions, publicise them when feasible, and account to parliament should help in developing a more professional executive, with greater credibility to exercise its mandate than the present board of governors.

510. The primary object of the South African Reserve Bank is to protect the value of the currency in the interests of balanced and sustainable growth in the Republic. The South African Reserve Bank, in pursuit of its primary object, must perform its functions

independently and without fear, favour or prejudice, but there must be regular consultation between the Bank and the Cabinet member responsible for national financial matters. (*Constitution of the Republic of South Africa*, 224)

511. To amend the *South African Reserve Bank Act, 1989*, so as to redetermine the primary objective of the South African Reserve Bank; to further regulate the appointment of certain directors of the Bank... The Bank shall be managed by a board of fourteen directors consisting of- (a) a Governor, three Deputy Governors... and three other directors, which Governor, Deputy Governor and other directors shall be appointed by the Minister President of the Republic after consultation with the Minister and the Board; and (b) seven directors elected by the shareholders. (*South African Reserve Bank Amendment Act*, Introduction,3.1)

512. In terms of Section 32 of the *Reserve Bank Act*, the Bank must submit a monthly statement of its assets and liabilities and an annual report to Parliament. The Bank is therefore accountable to Parliament. The Governor of the Reserve Bank holds regular discussions with the Minister of Finance and appears before the parliamentary Standing Committee on Finance from time to time. (*Introduction to the South African Reserve Bank*, @http://www.resbank.co.za)

513. **4.7.8** The democratic government should immediately increase the resources available in the Reserve Bank and other appropriate agencies for combating illegal capital flight. Furthermore, the democratic government must enter into discussions with holders of wealth in an effort to persuade them of the harmful effects their actions are having on our economy.

514. Restriction on receiving of payments in the republic of South Africa:... In terms of the powers vested in it by Regulation 8, the Treasury hereby prescribes that, except with the permission of a bank authorised under Exchange Control Regulations to deal in foreign exchange, Republic currency may not be received in payment by any person in respect of goods exported by him from the Republic. (@http://www.resbank.co.za)

515. **4.8.3** The following rights of workers must be in the *Constitution*: the right to organise and join trade unions; the right to strike and picket on all economic and social matters, and the right to information from companies and the government. **4.8.4** The *Constitution* should not prohibit the conclusion of union security agreements, including closed and agency shops. The right to lock out should not be in the *Constitution*.

516. Everyone has the right, peacefully and unarmed, to assemble, to demonstrate, to picket and to present petitions... Everyone has the right to freedom of association... Everyone has the right to fair labour practices. Every worker has the right a) to form and join a trade union; b) to participate in the activities and programmes of a trade union; and c) to strike... (*Constitution of the Republic of South Africa*, 17,18,23)

517. An employer must display at the workplace where it can be read by employees a statement in the prescribed form of the employee's rights under this act in the official languages which are spoken at the workplace... Rights of Employees: Every employee has the right to—(a) make a complaint to a trade union representative, a trade union official or a labour inspector concerning any alleged failure of refusal by an employer to comply with this *Act*; (b) discuss his or her condition of employment with his or her fellow employees, his or her employer or any other person;... (d) refuse to agree to any term or condition of employment that is contrary to this *Act* or any sectoral determination. (*Basic Conditions of Employment Act*, pp.16,31)

518. **4.8.5** All workers should be entitled to a living wage and humane conditions of employment in a healthy and safe working environment. The interlocking elements of the RDP, in particular the promotion of collective bargaining, minimum wage regulation, affirmative action, education and training, technological development, and provision of services and social security, must all be combined to achieve a living wage for rural and urban workers and reduce wage differentials. The required levels of growth for the successful implementation of the RDP can only be achieved on the basis of living wage policies agreed upon by government, the labour movement and the private sector.

519. The core elements of this integrated package are:... a structured flexibility within the collective bargaining system to support a competitive and more labour-intensive growth path, including ... reduced minimum wage schedules for young trainees... The determination of minimum wages remains, in certain sectors of the economy, to protect the vulnerable and the weak. The approach will not be to set one minimum wage across the whole economy but to determine appropriate standards by sector and area. The determination of these minimum wages must follow proper hearings, investigations and consideration of relevant economic conditions, the potential for employment creation and the alleviation of poverty. (*Growth, Employment and Redistribution*, 8.1)

520. New legislation must address both the new standards and the procedures and institutions to make the standards effective. This *Green Paper* proposes a legislative model of "regulated flexibility." This is a policy approach that aims to balance the protection of minimum standards and the requirements of labour market flexibility. (*Green Paper: Policy Proposals for a New Employment Standards Statute*, 4)
In this strategy there are two broad thrusts relating to labour market policy. The first is the pursuit of regulated flexibility aimed in part at extending the protection and stability afforded by this regulatory framework to an increased numbers of workers. The second is the promotion of continued productivity improvements aimed at bolstering the development of skills across the full spectrum of the workforce in both the formal and non-formal sectors. These points of departure are the basis of Government's labour market policies and will be further elaborated in response to the report of the Comprehensive Labour Market Commission. The Government will pursue a policy of regulated flexibility in managing the labour market. This entails the regulation of the labour market in a manner that allows for flexible collective bargaining structures, variable application of employment standards and voice regulation. (*Growth, Employment and Redistribution*, 8.1)

521. The purpose of this *Act* if to advance economic development and social justice by fulfilling the primary objectives of this *Act* which are—to give effect to and regulate the right to fair labour practices conferred by section 23(1) of the *Constitution*. (*Basic Conditions of Employment Act*, p.7)

522. **4.8.7** Effective implementation of the RDP requires a system of collective bargaining at national, industrial and workplace level, giving workers a key say in industry decision-making and ensuring that unions are fully involved in designing and overseeing changes at workplace and industry levels. **4.8.8** Industrial bargaining forums or industrial councils must play an important role in the implementation of the RDP. Agreements negotiated in such forums should be extended through legislation to all workplaces in that industry.

523. The major development in the primary segment of the labour market over the past two years has been the new *Labour Relations Act*. This has four key features. It establishes a single industrial relations system for all employees, promotes collective bargaining by providing certain organisational rights for trade unions, establishes new procedures and institutions for resolution of disputes and provides for workplace forums to facilitate a shift from conflictual employer-employee relations towards joint problem-solving with employee participation. The reduced incidence of industrial unrest in recent years attests to the considerable progress made in this regard... The appropriate determination of wages is a critical component of the medium term macroeconomic strategy. It is a precondition for sustaining the competitive advantage of the currency depreciation, and it is the key to ensuring the maintenance of industrial competitiveness in the longer term. A sudden upsurge in nominal wage demands would either unleash a wage-price spiral that would soon erode any semblance of a real depreciation or force a severe tightening of monetary policy leading to higher interest rates and economic contraction. It is therefore important that wage and salary increases do not exceed average productivity growth... The Minister of Labour's discretion to extend or not to extend agreements should be broadened to permit the Minister to bring labour market considerations into play. Wage agreements must be sensitive to regional labour market conditions, the diversity of skills levels in firms of varying size, location or capital intensity and the need to foster training opportunities for new entrants to the labour market... The Department of Labour will encourage, through the mechanisms provided in the *Labour Relations Act*, the rationalisation of collective bargaining arrangements to meet the challenges of the new economic environment while recognising the diversity of the domestic labour market. (*Growth, Employment and Redistribution*, 8.1,8.3)

524. **4.8.9** Legislation must facilitate worker participation and decision-making in the world of work. Such legislation must include an obligation on employers to negotiate substantial changes concerning production matters or workplace organisation within a nationally negotiated framework, facilities for organisation and communication with workers on such matters, and the right of shop stewards to attend union meetings and training without loss of pay as well as to address workers.

525. General functions of workplace forum. A workplace forum a) must seek to promote the interests of all employees in the workplace, whether or not they are trade union members; b) must seek to enhance efficiency in the workplace, c) is entitled to be consulted by the employer, with a view to reaching consensus, about the matters referred to in section 84; and d) is entitled to participate in joint decision-making about the matters referred to in section 86:... (Joint decision-making...) disciplinary codes and procedures; rules relating to the proper regulation of the workplace in so far as they apply to conduct not related to the work performance of employees, measures designed to protect and advance persons disadvantaged by unfair discrimination; and changes by the employer or by employer-appointed representatives on trusts or boards of employer-controlled schemes, to the rules regulating social benefit schemes. (*Labour Relations Act*, 79,86)

526. **4.8.10** In addition to the reform of labour law, company and tax law must be amended to ensure that the rights of workers are protected and extended, for example in relation to workers' access to company information.

527. Disclosure of information. An employer must disclose to the workplace forum all relevant information that will allow the workplace forum to engage effectively in consultation and joint decision-making. (*Labour Relations Act*, 89)

528. **4.8.11** Instruments of government such as subsidies, taxes, tariffs, tenders etc. must all be utilised to encourage stakeholder participation in the RDP and promote worker rights, human resource development and job creation.

529. Industrial incentives: Government is... promoting more rapid industrial development. Tax incentives have been introduced for new investments in manufacturing plant, equipment and buildings, and a tax holiday is now available to new industrial projects for a period of time determined by regional location, job creation and industrial priority. (*Medium Term Budget Policy Statement*, 1997, p.16)
Employer incentives should be developed to encourage private sector employers to train and employ a young unemployed person. Such incentives may include wage subsidies or tax rebates. (*National Youth Policy*, 8.3.3)
Procurement policy in Public Enterprise Ministry: The Ministry is to recommend that the parastatals have to compact with the government on their job creation and black economic empowerment initiatives. Part of core business requirements can be sourced from the historically disadvantaged through... structured black empowerment schemes... Transparency in parastatal tendering and procurement processes, procedures and structures is to be a requirement. Deliberate, proactive programmes around core business are to be established by parastatals... cross-border and international investment initiatives. The National Empowerment Fund is to be used as a potential source of establishing new businesses and jobs through Employee Ownership Schemes. (*Ministry of Public Enterprise, Parliamentary Media Briefing*, 7 August 1998)

530. **4.8.13** Affirmative action measures must be used to end discrimination on the grounds of race and gender, and to address the disparity of power between workers and management, and between urban and rural areas.

531. Anti-discriminatory measures to protect individuals combined with measures to encourage institutional and cultural change by employing organisations; [and] accelerated training and promotion for individuals from historically disadvantaged groups in this context... with strong legal protection against discrimination and harassment. (*Employment and Occupational Equity: Policy Proposals*, p.30)

532. The *White Paper* is primarily focused on the field of human resource development management and targets three groups--black people, women and people with disabilities--who are identified in the Employment Equity Bill as having suffered most from unfair past discrimination... The objectives of the Public Service Affirmative Action policy are... to: 1. Enhance the capacities of the historically disadvantaged through the development and introduction of practical measures that support their advancement within the Public Service.. 2. Inculcate in the Public Service a culture which values diversity and support the affirmative action of those who have previously been unfairly disadvantaged. 3. Speed up the achievement and progressive improvement of the numeric targets set out in the *White Paper on the Transformation of the Public Service*... National departments and provincial administrations are required to develop their own policies which must incorporate a well-prepared and well-managed programme in line with this White Paper to ensure that affirmative action is firmly embedded in the management systems and practices of their organisation... Public Service affirmative action program must contain, as a minimum, the following: a. Numeric targets; b. Employee Profile; c. Affirmative Action survey; d. Management Practices Review, e. Performance Management; f. Affirmative Action plan; g. Responsibilities; h. Policy Statement. (*White Paper on Affirmative Action in the Public Sector*, 3)

533. "equal opportunity and fair treatment through the elimination of unfair discrimination; and... positive measures to redress the disadvantages in employment experienced by black people, women and people with disabilities, in order to ensure their equitable representation in all occupational categories and levels in the workforce." (*Employment Equity Act*, 1)

534. **4.8.14** Legislation must prohibit sexual harassment, and education programmes must be launched to make workers and employers aware about the issue and about how to lodge complaints.

535. Hate speech and sexual harassment are particular forms of harassment. No employer may subject applicants or employees to harassment in the workplace, or permit other employees to engage in harassing behaviour. (*Green Paper on Policy Proposals for a New Employment and Occupational Equity Statute*, 4.4)
No person may unfairly discriminate, directly/indirectly, against an employee, in any employment policy or practice, on one or more grounds, including race, gender, sex, pregnancy, marital status, etc. (*Labour Relations Act*, 2.6.3).

536. **4.8.15** The international labour conventions of the International Labour Organisation (ILO) concerning freedom of association, collective bargaining, workplace representation and other fundamental rights must be ratified by the South African government.

537. South Africa has recently ratified the "Convention on the Elimination of all Forms of Discrimination Against Women" of 1979... The *Basic Conditions of Employment Act* and the *Wage Act* do not comply with many international standards reflected in International Labour Organisation Conventions. These Conventions are indications of what government, employers and trade unions consider appropriate minimum international norms and standards. The proposals for new legislation are guided by these standards where they are appropriate for South Africa. (*Green Paper on Policy Proposals for a New Employment and Occupational Equity Statute*, 5.9,5.10)

538. Today we are active members of the International Labour Organisation and participate in appropriate forums at both the Africa and SADC levels. We have ratified the key international conventions including those related to freedom of association, the right to organise and to bargain collectively. (Minister of Labour Tito Mboweni *Budget Vote*, 23 April 1998)

539. **4.9.1** The democratic government must negotiate with neighbouring countries to forge an equitable and mutually beneficial programme of increasing cooperation, coordination and integration appropriate to the conditions of the region. In this context, the RDP must support the goals and ideals of African integration as laid out in the Lagos Plan of Action and the Abuja Declaration. **4.9.8** A democratic South African government should apply for membership in the SADC and possibly the PTA, and should support reforms in the SACU to enhance democracy and equity.

540. South Africa became a member of SADC in 1994, and has since been actively involved in the activities of the Community. (*Annual Report*, DACST, 1997, p.48)
South Africans are able to look back on 1998 and note how many of our foreign policy objectives were achieved and how successfully we pursued our foreign policy priorities. Here I would like to point to only a few, including: ... our continued leadership of SADC. (*Annual Address*, Minister Nzo, Department of Foreign Affairs, 1 October 1998)

541. Relations with southern Africa are a cornerstone of foreign policy. As SADC chair since 1996 South Africa co-operates with its neighbours for balanced regional development and regional stability... As OAU member, South Africa assisted the Zaire/Congo peace process and worked with the DRC and other war-ravaged countries for reconstruction. Legislation to curtail South African-based mercenary activites and a draft *White Paper on Peace-Support Operations* will be put before Parliament during 1998. (*The Building has Begun!*, p.33)

542. **4.9.3** A democratic government must develop policies in consultation with our neighbours to ensure more balanced trade... **4.9.4** Developing the capacity of our neighbours to export manufactured goods to South African markets requires the democratic government, in consultation with neighbouring states, to encourage and promote industrial development throughout the region. A democratic government must contribute towards the development of regional and industrial strategies for specific sub-sectors, such as mineral beneficiation, auto components and textiles.

543. The core elements of the integrated strategy are... an expansion of trade and investment flows in Southern Africa... A further key element of the strategy is the gradual integration of the economies of Southern Africa through the trade and investment protocols of SADC... Another critical policy thrust has been the expansion of market access through preferential trade arrangements with industrial countries and pursuit of regional economic integration. The following developments deserve specific mention:... the signing of bilateral trade treaties with several African countries and rapidly growing trade with neighbors has seen exports from within the Southern African Customs Union area to the rest of the Southern African region quadruple. (*Growth, Employment and Redistribution*, 1.4,5.3,Appendix 1)
Exports to Africa have grown by 70% in the three years 1995 to 1997 and imports by 58%. (*The Building has Begun!*, p.33)

544. Article 2 (Objectives) of the Protocol on Trade in the Southern African Development Community (SADC Region) advances that the objectives of the Protocol are (1) to further liberalize intra-regional trade in goods and services on the basis of fair, mutually equitable and beneficial trade arrangements, complemented by Protocols in other areas; (2) to contribute towards the improvement of the climate for domestic, cross-border and foreign investment; and (3) to establish a Free Trade Area in the SADC Region... Ongoing negotiations between RSA and SADC states on the proposed Free Trade Agreement in SADC member states towards a more non-reciprocal market access accompanied by investment flows. (*Department of Trade and Industry Budget Vote*, 15 May 1998)

545. **4.9.6** One element of regional policy, defended particularly in the call for a Southern African Social Charter by trade unions, is that minimum standards with regard to rights of workers to organise be established across the region as a whole. This will allow a process of greater integration to become one of levelling up rights and conditions of workers, rather than of levelling them down to the lowest prevailing standard.

546. **4.9.7** A democratic government should encourage technical and scientific cooperation with our neighbours to enhance the development of expertise in the region in areas such as agricultural research and development, environmental monitoring and protection, health and other research.

547. Regional cooperation:... South Africa will collaborate with regional tourism organisations such as SADC and RETOSA in the development of tourism in Southern Africa. Appropriate bilateral relations will also be established with neighbour countries. A number of areas of cooperation should be actively encouraged: (i) environmental conservation and development of related products such as trans-border protected areas (ii) international marketing, e.g. joint international marketing campaigns with SADC countries, etc. (*White Paper on Development and Promotion of Tourism in South Africa*, 5.13)
South Africa must adopt a proactive approach in international relations dealing with environmental issues. In doing so it should prioritise its engagements and relations according to the following hierarchy: immediate neighbours; SADCC region; African

continental; developing country; and global relations. (*Green Paper on Environmental Policy for South Africa*, p.53)

548. **5.2.1 The People shall govern.** The RDP vision is one of democratising power. Democracy is intimately linked to reconstruction and development. We will not be able to unleash the resources, neglected skills and stunted potential of our country and its people while minority domination of state and civil institutions persists. Without thoroughgoing democratisation, the whole effort to reconstruct and develop will lose momentum. Reconstruction and development require a population that is empowered through expanded rights, meaningful information and education, and an institutional network fostering representative, participatory and direct democracy.

549. Minority control and privilege in every aspect of our society are the main obstruction to developing an integrated programme which will unleash all the resources of our country and fundamentally change the way that policy is made and programmes are implemented. Above all, the people affected must participate in decision-making. Democratisation will begin to transform both the state and civil society. Democracy is not confined to periodic elections. It is, rather, an active process enabling everyone to contribute to reconstruction and development. (*White Paper on Reconstruction and Development*, 1.3.7)

550. Believing that South Africa belongs to all who live in it, united in our diversity... adopt this constitution as the supreme law of the republic so as to: Heal the divisions of the past and establish a society based on democratic values, social justice and fundamental human rights... Build a united and democratic South Africa. (*The Constitution of the Republic of South Africa*, Preamble)

551. **5.3.1** The new *Constitution* must reinforce the RDP, ensuring that equality of rights of citizens is not just formal, but substantive. The new *Constitution* should ensure that social, economic, environmental and peace rights are more fully embodied in the Bill of Rights.

552. 24(1) Everyone has the right a) to an environment that is not harmful to their health or well-being; and b) to have the environment protected... 26(1) Everyone has the right to have access to adequate housing... 27(1) Everyone has the right to have access to a) health care services, including reproductive health care; b) sufficient food and water; and c) social security, including, if they are unable to support themselves and their dependents, appropriate social assistance... 29(1) Everyone has the right a) to a basic education, including adult basic education; and b) to further education, which the state, through reasonable measures, must make progressively available and accessible. (*Constitution*, Chapter 2)

553. **5.2.10** Ensuring gender equity is another central component in the overall democratisation of our society. The RDP envisages special attention being paid to the empowerment of women in general, and of black, rural women in particular. There must be representation of women in all institutions, councils and commissions, and gender issues must be included in the terms of reference of these bodies... **5.3.2** The *Constitution* must

recognise the fundamental equality of men and women in marriage, employment and in society. There should be a continuous review of all legislation to ensure that this clause in the *Constitution* is not undermined. These principles must override customary law.

554. 9(1) Everyone is equal before the law and has the right to equal protection and benefit of the law. 9(2) Equality includes the full and equal enjoyment of all rights and freedoms. To promote the achievement of equality, legislative and other measures designed to protect or advance persons, or categories of persons, disadvantaged by unfair discrimination may be taken. 9(3) The state may not unfairly discriminate directly or indirectly against anyone on one or more grounds, including race, gender, sex, pregnancy, marital status, ethnic or social origin, colour, sexual orientation, age, disability, religion, conscience, belief, culture, language and birth. (*Constitution*, Chapter 2)

555. Women's needs. A staggering number of women suffer persistent humiliation and violence at the hands of the men in their midst... People must be encouraged to report such crimes and insist that the police act with urgency and integrity in all cases. As a great proportion of men continue to be employed in mines, industries and towns away from home, women are often the heads of household in rural areas... they are often also the sole breadwinner. With scant formal education or training, they have little chance of obtaining paid employment. Customary law provides wives with only secondary rights of access to land... As women are usually responsible for providing food for the household, they tend to use it for this purpose, which may also prevent them from growing crops for sale. Development efforts in rural areas must therefore begin with provision of support to women... Although numerous surveys have charted the most urgent needs of women, in the long run the most important is likely to be participation in local politics whereby they can directly influence the development process. To achieve such a breakthrough, women must be offered education and training, and information to help them contribute to community planning. Women's groups require encouragement and support on many fronts... Having a separate source of income is important for women who need funds with which to care for the family. Short-term welfare measures, whether in the form of a grant or a pension, or public works payments, are helpful... A precondition for better income-earning opportunities is the release from drudgery through the provision of essential infrastructure--water and energy--and a recognition of women's rights to land. Access to health care services, including reproductive health care, is a right under the *Constitution*, but a great deal has to be done to extend these facilities into the remote rural areas... As women traditionally have been oppressed by some aspects of customary law, it is essential that they are informed of changes in their position... They must hold the government to the commitments made at the Beijing Conference and when signing the International Convention for the Elimination of Discrimination Against Women in 1995. The realisation of these principles depend on fundamental changes in attitude towards the role of women and their contribution to society. (*Rural Development Framework*, pp.57-58)

556. The Commission [on Gender equality] shall be independent... (1) In order to achieve its object referred to in section 119 (3) of the *Constitution*, the Commission—a, shall monitor and evaluate practices and policies of—i. Organs of state at any level; ii. Statutory bodies or functionaries; iii. public bodies or authorities; and iv. private businesses,

enterprises, and institutions, in order to promote gender equality and may make any recommendations that the Commission deems necessary; b. shall develop, conduct or manage—i. information programmes; and ii. education programmes, to foster understanding of matters pertaining to the promotion of gender equality and the role and activities of the Commission;c. shall evaluate—i. any Act of Parliament; ii. any system of personal and family law or custom; iii. any system of indigenous law, customs or; iv any other law, in force at the commencement of this *Act* or any law proposed by Parliament or any other legislature after the commencement of this *Act*, affecting or likely to affect gender equality or the status of women and make recommendations to Parliament or such other legislature with regard thereto; d. may recommend to Parliament or any other legislature new legislation which would promote gender equality and the status of women;... h. shall monitor the compliance with international conventions, international covenants, and international charters, acceded to or ratified by the Republic, relating to the object of the Commission. (*Commission on Gender Equality Act*, 11)

557. **5.3.3** The *Constitution* should permit the regulation of the use of property when this is in the public interest. It should also guarantee a right to restitution for victims of forced removals.

558. 25(1) No one may be deprived of property except in terms of law of general application, and no law may permit arbitrary deprivation of property... 25(2) Property may be expropriated only in terms of law of general application a) for a public purpose or in the public interest; and b) subject to compensation, the amount of which and the time and manner of payment of which have either been agreed to by those affected or decided or approved by a court... 25(3) A person or community dispossessed of property after 19 June 1913 as a result of past racially discriminatory laws or practices is entitled, to the extent provided by an *Act* of Parliament, either to restitution of that property or to equitable redress... No provision of this section may impede the state from taking legislative and other measures to achieve land, water and related reform, in order to redress the result of past racial discrimination... (*Constitution*, Chapter 2)

559. **5.3.4** The *Constitution* should provide for sufficient central government powers so as to coordinate and implement the RDP effectively.

560. 85(1) The executive authority of the Republic is vested in the President. 85(2) The president exercises the executive authority, together with the other members of the Cabinet, by implementing national legislation except where the *Constitution* or an *Act* of Parliament provides otherwise; developing and implementing national policy; coordinating the functions of state departments and administrations; preparing and initiating legislation; and performing any other executive function provided for in the *Constitution* or in national legislation. (*Constitution*, Chapter 5)

561. **5.4.2** There should be a review of the legislative procedures including a review of national and regional parliamentary sessions, operating procedures and restructuring of standing committees, to promote an improved institutional framework for public decision-making. There should be a clear right of access to the parliamentary legislative procedures

to allow inputs from interested parties. There should be a Code of Conduct for members of the National and Regional Assemblies.

562. The national legislative authority as vested in Parliament a) confers on the national assembly the power: i) to amend the *Constitution*; ii) to pass legislation with regard to any matter' including matter within a functional area listed in Schedule 4, but excluding, subject to subsection (2), a matter within a functional area listed in the Schedule 5... Parliament may intervene, by passing legislation in accordance with section 76(1), with regard to a matter falling within a functional are listed in Schedule 5, when it is necessary a) to maintain national security; b) to maintain economic unity; c) to maintain essential national standards; d) to establish minimum standards required for the rendering services; or e) to prevent unreasonable action taken by a province which prejudicial to the interest of another province or to the country as a whole... The National Assembly must... facilitate public involvement in the legislative and other processes... and committees... and conduct its business in an open manner, and hold its sittings... in public. (*Constitution*, 44.1,44.2,59)

Powers include the investigation of maladministration in connection with the affairs of any state institution, of the abuse of power, of unfair and improper conduct, of improper and unlawful enrichment and acts and omissions resulting in prejudice. (*Public Protector Act 23 of 1994*, 182)

The President must publish a code of ethics prescribing standards and rules aimed at promoting open, democratic and accountable government and with which Cabinet members, Deputy Ministers and MECs must comply in performing their official responsibilities... (The code must include provisions requiring them) at all times to act in good faith... in the best interests of good governance. (*Executive Members' Ethics Act 62 of 1998*)

563. **5.5.2** Grants-in-aid strategies must be built into the RDP to ensure that all provinces receive an equitable share of revenue collected nationally. The Financial and Fiscal Commission must determine criteria for the allocation of inter-governmental grants.

564. 227(1) Local government and each province a) is entitled to an equitable share of revenue raised nationally to enable it to provide basic services and perform the functions allocated to it; and b) may receive other allocations from national government revenue, either conditionally or unconditionally. (*Constitution*, Chapter 13)

565. The Financial and Fiscal Commission established by section 220 of the *Constitution* is a juristic person... The Commission acts as a consultative body for, and makes recommendations and gives advice to, organs of state in the national, provincial and local spheres of government on financial and fiscal matters. (*Financial and Fiscal Commission Act*, 1997, p. 3)

2. (1) There is a Budget Council consisting of—(a) the Minister; (b) the MEC for finance of each province... 3. The Budget Council is a body in which the national government and the provincial governments consult on (a) any fiscal, budgetary or financial matter affecting the provincial sphere of government; (b) any proposed legislation or policy which has a financial implication for the provinces; (c) any matter concerning the financial

am.

management, or the monitoring of the finances, of the provinces, or of any specific province or provinces; or (d) any other matter which the Minister has referred to the Council...
5. There is a Local Government Budget Forum consisting of—(a) the Minister; (b) the MEC for finance of each province; (c) five representatives nominated by each provincial organisation recognised in terms of that *Act*... 6. The Budget Forum is a body in which the national government, the provincial government, and organised local government consult on—(a) any fiscal, budgetary or financial matter affecting the local sphere of government; (b) any proposed legislation or policy which has a financial implication for local government; (c) any matter concerning the financial management, or the monitoring of the finances, of local government; or (d) any other matter which the minister has referred to the Forum... 10. [After receiving recommendations from the Fiscal and financial Commission] the Minister must introduce in the National Assembly a Division of Revenue Bill for the financial year to which that budget relates. (2) The Division of Revenue Bill must specify-(a) the share of each sphere of government of the revenue raised nationally for the relevant financial year; (b) each province's share of the provincial share of that revenue; and (c) any other allocations to the provinces, local government or municipalities from the national government's share of that revenue, and any conditions on which those allocations are or must be made. (*Intergovernmental Fiscal Relations Act*, pp.2-4)
A provincial government shall not commit itself to any financial project, other than bridging finance, loans or such other product as may prescribed, which creates an interest or any other exposure of a financial or equivalent kind... Loans raised in the Republic and denominated in rand shall, subject to this *Act*, be obtained by provincial government—(i) through the conclusion of loan agreements with the national government, with the concurrence of the Minister, and the Minister may advise the provincial government to raise a loan in terms of subparagraph (ii) or (iii);... or (iii) by- (aa) entering into loan agreements with banks or financial institutions; (bb) making issues of public stock and bonds; or (cc) entering into loan agreements through the issue of financial instruments... (8) Any moneys borrowed by the responsible member, and the interest thereon, shall be the financial obligation of the provincial government concerned and shall be chargeable to and payable from the revenues and assets of that provincial government. (*Borrowing Powers of Provincial Governments Act*, 3.2,6e).

566. **5.5.3** The reincorporation of the TBVC states (Transkei, Bophuthatswana, Venda, Ciskei) and the self-governing territories requires urgent attention. All government departments at national level must be rationalised to end duplications due to racial divisions. Single ministries should be created at national and provincial level in each sector of operation. At the provincial level, government institutions must be constructed and rationalised out of existing regional structures. The role, function and mission of government departments should be reviewed with the aim of introducing a clear development focus for the democratic government administration. Policies of affirmative action, development and training must be applied in all areas.

567. To coordinate and plan the RDP requires the establishment of effective RDP structures in Government at National, Provincial and Local levels, as well as substantial restructuring of present planning processes and a rationalisation of the complex, racist and fragmented structures that exist. (*White Paper on Reconstruction and Development*, 1.5.1)

568. **5.6.1** The defence force, the police and intelligence services must be firmly under civilian control, in the first place through the relevant civilian ministry answerable to parliament. These security forces must uphold the democratic constitution, they must be non-partisan, and they must be bound by clear codes of conduct.

569. The Defence Force is non-partisan; it is subject to the control and oversight of the elected civilian authority; and it is obliged to perform its functions in accordance with law. (*White Paper on National Defence for the Republic of South Africa*, Introduction)

570. The 1996/97 period under review has been marked by consolidation and expansion of the Defense Secretariat. Considerable movement took place towards the achievement of national consensus on the principle of Defense in a Democracy and the entrenchment of democratic civil-military relations. Civil control has been strengthened in the reorganized Defense Force with the transfer of the Head of Department role and Accounting Officer function to the Secretary for Defense on 1 April 1997. The Secretary for Defence and the Chief of the National Defence Force will operate on the same hierarchical level under the direction of the Minister of Defence as his departmental policy and military advisors respectively. In essence, and in terms of day to day management, this means that the Defence Force is no longer both player and referee. The Secretary for Defence becomes the referee on behalf of the Minister and Parliament. (*Annual Report*, Department of Defence, 1997, p.10)

571. **5.6.2** The size, character and doctrines of the new defence force must be appropriate to a country engaged in a major programme of socio-economic reconstruction and development. The rights of soldiers must be clearly defined and protected.

572. The RDP is the principal long-term means of promoting the security of the citizens and thereby, the stability of the country. There is consequently a compelling need to reallocate state resources to the RDP. From the perspective of the Ministry of Defence, the challenge is to rationalise the Defence Force and contain military spending without undermining the country's core defence capability in the short- to long-term... 2.1 National security shall be sought primarily through efforts to meet the political, economic, social and cultural rights and needs of South Africa's people... 2.6 South Africa's force levels, armaments and military expenditure shall be determined by defence policy which derives from an analysis of the external and internal security environment and takes account of the RDP imperative... 2.12 Defence policy and military activities shall be sufficiently transparent to enable meaningful parliamentary and public scrutiny and debate... 2.13 The SANDF shall be non-partisan with respect to political parties... 2.14 The SANDF shall endeavour to develop a non-racial, non-sexist and non-discriminatory institutional culture... 2.15 The SANDF shall respect the rights and dignity of its members within the normal constraints of military discipline and training. (*White Paper on Defence for the Republic of South Africa*, Chapter 2)

573. The Secretariat has been extensively engaged in the preparation of the Defence Review. It presented the options with respect to the size, posture, roles, structure, equipment and design of the new DoD, addressed the applications of its primarily

defensive nature, and incorporated detailed and well- motivated budgetary forecast. (*Annual Report*, Department of Defence, 1997, p.10)

574. **5.6.3** The police service must be transformed, with special attention to representivity, and gender and human rights sensitivity. National standards and training must be combined with community-based structures to ensure answerability to the communities served.

575. An Independent Complaints Directorate is being established and will receive and process complaints from the public. Control measures are being implemented to prevent the theft of police dockets in the Justice sector and investigations into corruption are underway in the Department of Welfare. (*National Crime Prevention Strategy*, p.8)

576. **5.7.1** The system of justice should be made accessible and affordable to all people. It must be credible and legitimate. The legal processes and institutions should be reformed by simplifying the language and procedures used in the court, recognising and regulating community and customary courts, and professionalising the Attorney-General's office. The public defence system must be promoted and the prosecution system reformed. The pool of judicial officers should be increased through the promotion of lay officials, scrapping the divided bar and giving the right of appearance to paralegals... **5.7.3** A legal aid fund for women to test their rights in court must be established.

577. **5.7.2** ...Tripartite institutions should have a say in determining appointments to the Industrial and Labour Appeal Courts.

578. Everyone has the right to have any dispute that can be resolved by the application of law decided in a fair public hearing before a court or, where appropriate, another independent and impartial tribunal or forum... 165(1) The judicial authority of the Republic is vested in the courts... 165(2) The courts are independent and subject only to the *Constitution* and the law, which they must apply impartially and without fear, favour or prejudice... 165(3) No person or organ of state may interfere with the functioning of the courts... 165(4) Organs of state, through legislative and other measures, must assist and protect the courts to ensure the independence, impartiality, dignity, accessibility and effectiveness of the courts... 165(5) An order or decision issued by a court binds all persons to whom and organs of state to which it applies. (*Constitution*, Chapter 8)

579. **5.8.1** The staffing of the prison service must be based on non-racial and non-sexist principles. Prison staff will need to be trained to reflect this approach and to transform the present military command structure of the prison service.

580. The Affirmative Action Programme has proved successful in creating mechanisms to address exiting imbalances and ensure equal opportunities. Our target in creating a representative personnel corps was effectively achieved by the end of 1997 in favour of the previously disadvantage groups who now constitute 70% of the total personnel establish. Our management team is representative of all personnel of all races and also reflects gender quality. The first National Conference on Women's Rights and Gender Equality arranged

by the Department was held in April. (*In Review*, Department of Correctional Services, 1997, p.v)

581. **5.8.2** Prisoners must enjoy human rights and must be fully protected by the constitution. **5.8.3** The prison service must play its part, not simply in restraining convicted persons, but in rehabilitating and training them. Adequate resources must be made available for the humane accommodation of prisoners.

582. Rights and Obligations of offenders. The rights of prisoners already recognised, are *inter alia:* the right to be provided with food which has an adequate nutritional value... the right to receive special diet where the medical officer deems it necessary for medical reasons or where religious beliefs dictate; the right to have medical treatment at state expense; or to consult a private medical practitioner or physiotherapist chosen by the prisoner at own expense; the right of access to legal representative; all rights stipulated in the *Constitution* or which may be conferred by, for instance, the Constitutional Court... The treatment, development and training of offenders are approached as follows: involvement of the various professionals is determined according to the individual needs, circumstances and risk factors of offenders; opportunities are provided and offenders are actively encouraged to participate in appropriate programmes; offenders are informed of the various programmmes and should be active participants in decisions affecting them. They are also provided with the opportunity for redress; the various programmes are continually evaluated and the needs of offenders are addressed to determine and ensure effective approaches and programmes... The Department of Correctional Services believes that every prisoner and probationer, as a prerequisite for eventual rehabilitation, should have a basic education. The Department is thus committed to eliminating illiteracy amongst all offenders. (*White Paper on the Policy of the Department of Correctional Services in the New South Africa*, 3.2.1,3.3.1,3.3.4)

583. (1) Every prisoner is required to accept the authority and to obey the lawful instructions of the Commissioner and correctional officials of the Department. (2)(a) The Department must take such steps as are necessary to ensure the safe custody of every prisoner and to maintain security and good order in every prison... (c) the minimum rights of prisoners entrenched in this *Act* may not be violated or restricted for disciplinary or other purposes. (*Correctional Services Act*, p.10)

584. Any law which authorises corporal punishment by a court of law, including a court of traditional healers, is hereby repealed to the extent that it authorises such punishment. (*Abolition of Corporal Punishment Act*, p.2)

585. On 1 June 1997 a new disciplinary procedure was implemented which differs substantially from the previous procedure. This new procedure will also help to ensure that we maintain a disciplined and accountable personnel corps... Copies of the *Constitution of the Republic of South Africa, 1996* (Act No 108 of 1996) were distributed to all area managers for further distribution to personnel and prisoners during Human Rights Week. Various human rights organisations and individuals were invited to address both prisoners and personnel celebrating Human Rights Day on 21 March... Basic needs for

maintenance of an acceptable level of existence (right to life, food, clothing, medical care, hygienic facilities and contact with family) are provided for regardless of the behavior and attitude of the prisoner... Qualified educationists, assisted by selected trained functional personnel, present educational and training programmes at 64 prisons countrywide. There are 264 qualified educationists in the Department. Where no qualified educational personnel are available, supportive education and training programmes which focus on literacy and recreation, are presented by functional personnel as well as external educationist and trainers. (*In Review*, Department of Correctional Services, 1997, pp.5,12)

586. **5.8.6** Disciplinary codes within prison must be changed, and forms of punishment which infringe basic human rights (solitary confinement and dietary punishment) must be ended.

587. A penalty of solitary confinement must be referred to the Inspecting Judge for review. The Inspecting Judge must within three days confirm or set aside the decision or penalty and substitute an appropriate order for it; The penalty of solitary confinement may only be implemented when the Inspecting Judge has confirmed such penalty; A prisoner in solitary confinement must be visited at least once every six hours by a correctional official, once a day by the Head of Prison, and a registered nurse or psychologist or a medical officer; Solitary confinement must be discontinued if in the view of the medical officer it poses a danger to the physical or mental health of the prisoner. (*Correctional Services Act*, 25.1-34)

588. **5.8.4** The law dealing with children in custody must be reformed. Practices which infringe even the existing laws (such as the accommodation of children and juvenile prisoners in cells with adults) must be ended.

589. It is the Department's conviction that unconvicted children under the age of eighteen years who are accused of having committed an offence, should not be admitted to prisons. (*White Paper on the Policy of the Department of Correctional Services in the New South Africa*, 3.4.1)

590. (Amendment of section 29 of *Act 8 of 1959*, as substituted by section 1 of *Act 17 of 1994*, regarding unconvicted youth): A person referred to in paragraph (a) or (b) of subsection (1) may be detained in a police cell or lock-up after his or her arrest until he or she is brought before a court within a period not exceeding 24 hours in respect of a person referred to in paragraph (a) of that subsection and not exceeding 48 hours in respect of a person referred to in paragraph (b) of that subsection... A person referred to in subsection (1)(b)... shall not be detained in a prison or police cell or lock-up unless the presiding officer has reason to believe that his or her detention is necessary in the interests of the administration of justice and the safety and protection of the public and no secure place of safety, within a reasonable distance from the court mentioned in section 28 of the *Child Care Act*, 1983 is available for his or her detention... (5)(b) The Minister of Correctional Services shall as soon as possible after the commencement of this *Act*, ensure that regulations regarding the treatment and conditions of detention awaiting trial persons

under the age of 18 years are brought into line with relevant internationally recognised human rights standards and norms. (*Correctional Services Amendment Act*)

591. (1)(a) Every prisoner who is a child and is subject to compulsory education must attend and have access to such educational programmes; (b) Where practicable, all children who are prisoners not subject to compulsory education must be allowed access to educational programmes; (2) The Commissioner must provide every prisoner who is a child with social work services, religious care, recreational programmes, and psychological services; (3) The Commissioner must, if practicable, ensure that prisoners who are children remain in contact with their families through additional visits and by other means. (*Correctional Services Act*, p.13-14)

592. The Department regard all persons under the age of 21 as juveniles and those under the age of 18 as children. Since they are regarded as a separate category, their needs are specifically addressed... The Department has representation on committees such as the Inter-Ministerial Committee on Young People at Risk, the National Plan of Action for Children in South Africa, the Coordination of the Management of Juveniles Awaiting Trial and the National Youth Commission... Youth Correctional institutions such as Hawequa, Victor Verster, Brandvlei (Western Cape) Barberton (Mpumalanga), Groenpunt (Free State), Boksburg, Leeuwkop (Gauteng) and Rustenburg (North-West) and Durban (KwaZulu-Natal) provide separate accommodation for juveniles. The department is planning other youth development centres based on the unit management concept which advocates more direct supervision and interaction between offenders and personnel. (*In Review*, Department of Correctional Services, 1997, p.14)

593. **5.8.5** Pregnant women and mothers with small children in prison must be held in conditions which are appropriate for their specific physical and psychological requirements.

594. The *Correctional Services Act*, 1959, makes provision for a female prisoner to have her child with her in prison during the period of lactation and for such further period deemed necessary. (*White Paper on the Policy of the Department of Correctional Services in the New South Africa*, 3.4.2)
A female prisoner may be permitted, subject to such conditions as may be prescribed, to have her child with her until such child is five years of age; (2) The Department is responsible for food, clothing, health care and facilities for the sound development of the child for the period that such child remains in prison; (3) Where practicable, the Commissioner must ensure that a mother and child unit is available for the accommodation of female prisoners and the children whom they may be permitted to have with them. (*Correctional Services Act*, 20.1)

595. The accommodation of a baby or a child in the prison remains an interim measure... Although the Department is of the opinion that suitable placement should be actively addressed at the outset, a female prisoner who, upon admission to prison, is accompanied by her baby or young child or who gives birth to a whilst in detention, may be permitted to care for such a child for such a period as is deemed necessary... The Department is currently in the process of drafting a policy which complies with the directives as

contained in the Convention on the Rights of the Child. This policy pertaining to young children in custody within their mothers makes provision for the admittance of a baby or young child with a mother provided no other suitable accommodation and care is available at that point in time. Mothers with babies or young children are accommodated in a separate Mother and Child Unit in a prison. (*In Review*, Department of Correctional Services, 1997, p.15)

596. **5.8.7** The public has the right to be informed about prison conditions. The Prison Act must, accordingly, be substantially reformed... **5.8.8** Prisons must be monitored by an independent prison ombuds, appointed by the State President, but working independently of ministerial control.

597. The Role of the Public Protector. The envisaged appointment of a Public Protector and Provincial Public Protectors is welcomed by the Department. These are further independent and autonomous channels to investigate, amongst others, grievances of prisoners. As is the case with the Ombudsman, prisoners will have unhindered access to such offices. The Department undertakes to give its full co-operation to enable the Public Protectors to perform their functions effectively. (*White Paper on the Policy of the Department of Correctional Services in the New South Africa*, 3.7.6)
The Judicial Inspectorate of Prisons is an independent office under the control of the Inspecting Judge; The object of the Judicial Inspectorate is to facilitate the inspection of prisons in order that the Inspecting Judge may report on the treatment of prisoners in prisons and on conditions an any corrupt or dishonest practices in prisons... The Inspecting Judge may, after publicly calling for nominations and consulting with community organisations, appoint an Independent Prison Visitor for any prison or prisons... An Independent Visitor shall deal with the complaints of prisoners by (a) regular visits; (b) interviewing prisoners in private; (c) recording complaints in an official diary and monitoring the manner in which they have been dealt with; (d) discussing complaints with the Head of Prison, or the relevant subordinate correctional official, with a view to resolving the issues internally. (*Correctional Services Act*, 86,93,94)

598. **5.9.1** South Africa has a large public sector with many resources. The public sector consists of the public service, the police and defence forces, the intelligence service, parastatals, public corporations and advisory bodies, which are together some of the most important delivery and empowerment mechanisms for the RDP. Staffing levels in and budgetary allocations to government departments and institutions must match the requirements for service delivery, and the operational requirements for women's empowerment, within the constraints of the budget. A defined quota of all new employees should come from groups that were disadvantaged on the basis of race and gender, and should be given access to appropriate training and support systems. This should be evaluated each year to determine the progress made and identify problems which arise. By the turn of the century, the personnel composition of the public sector, including parastatals, must have changed to reflect the national distribution of race and gender. Such progress will enhance the full utilisation of the country's labour power and productivity... **5.10.3** While the public service must be based on merit, career principles, suitability, skills, competence and qualifications, these standards should not be interpreted to further

minority interests, as in the past. An extensive programme of affirmative action must be embarked on to achieve the kind of public service that is truly reflective of our society, particularly at the level of management and senior employees. Such an affirmative action programme must include training and support to those who have previously been excluded from holding responsible positions. Within two years of the implementation of the programme, recruitment and training should reflect South African society, in terms of race, class and gender. Mechanisms must be put in place to monitor implementation of the programme. A programme of monitoring and retraining for all those willing to serve loyally under a democratic government should be instituted.

599. 195 (1) ...Public administration must be governed by the democratic values and principles enshrined in the *Constitution*, including the following principles: (a) A high standard of professional ethics must be promoted and maintained. (b) Efficient, economic and effective use of resources must be promoted. (c) Public administration must be development oriented. (d) Services must be provided impartially, fairly, equitably and without bias. (e) People's needs must be responded to, and the public must be encouraged to participate in policy-making. (f) Public administration must be accountable. (g) Transparency must be fostered by providing the public with timely, accessible and accurate information. (h) Good human-resource management and career development practices, to maximise human potential must be cultivated. (i) Public administration must be broadly representative of the South African people, with employment and personnel management practices based on ability, objectivity, fairness and the need to redress the imbalances of the past to achieve broad representation. (*Constitution*, Chapter 10)

600. The government must introduce a law, that will integrate all former apartheid structures as unified national public service, under the *Public Service Act* of 1994. This service should be transformed into a coherent, representative and democratic instrument for implementing government policies and meeting the needs of all South Africans... National Norms and Standards for the Rationalisation Process:... the appointment of persons from outside the public service in order to promote greater representivity, after all available internal human resources have been considered and with due regard to the objective of a leaner service... The main target group for affirmative action programmes will be black people, women and people with disabilities. In developing appropriate affirmative programmes, it will be important to take into account the specific and distinct needs of these groups... The Government remains committed to the objective of a broadly representative services by the end of the current decade... Within four years all departmental establishments must endeavour to be at least 50% black at management level. During the same period at least 30% of new recruits to the middle and senior management echelons should be women. Within ten years, people with disabilities should comprise 2% of public service personnel. (*Public Service White Paper*, 1.1,8.1.2,10.4,10.6)

601. Following the introduction in 1995 of policy framework on Representative and Affirmative Action, national departments and provincial administrations were required to develop an and register their own unique policies with the Department Chapter BVII of the Public Service Staff Code, which is the policy framework, also dictates that Department reports to the Minister and the Parliament on the progress of such registration

and its consequent impact in transforming the workforce of the Public Service into the representative one at all levels and occupational classes. (*Annual Report*, Department of Public Service and Administration, 1997)

602. **5.10.1** The Public Service Commission established in terms of the interim *Constitution* must be responsible for matters relating to appointments, promoting efficiency and effectiveness in departments, establishing and monitoring a Code of Conduct for the public service and introducing a programme of affirmative action and other appropriate techniques to eliminate historical inequities in employment. The Code of Conduct must incorporate the principles of the new South African public service as outlined in the RDP. The ethos should be professional, in the most positive sense of the word; the public service must internalise the concept of 'serving the people.' This Code should be enforced and annual evaluation of personnel should take into account compliance with the Code.

603. The Commission may inspect departments and other organisational components in the public service, and has access to such official documents or may obtain such information from heads of those departments or organisational components or from other officers in the service of those departments or other components as may be necessary for the performance of the functions of the Commission under the *Constitution* or the *Public Service Act*. (*Public Service Commission Act*, p.3)

604. A project was initiated in 1997 to improve service delivery in the public sector. The project has been named Batho Pele ("batho pele" is Sesotho adage meaning people first) and aims to introduce a customer-orientated approach to transforming service delivery, primarily in the Public Service. (*Annual Report*, Department of Public Service and Administration, 1997, p.15)
A *White Paper on Service Delivery*, entitled *Batho Pele*, will be the basis of action during 1998 to transform Public Service delivery in ways that put the people first. The report of the Presidential Review Commission will assist in planning for long-term changes in the public sector. (*The Building has Begun!*, p.23)

605. **5.10.4** The Civil Service Training Institute must be transformed to train and retrain public service employees in line with the priorities of the RDP. One of the priorities of this Institute must be to ensure that a cadre of public servants is developed to transform the public service effectively, with attention to excellence and high levels of service delivery. The Institute must be provided with the necessary resources and cater for at least four levels of training: lateral entry for progressive academics, activists, organisers and NGO workers; top-level management development; promotion within the public service, and retraining of present incumbents of posts.

606. The Public Service Commission is restructuring the Training Institute, focusing on research and development, training and international comparative programmes. Modules will be developed to meet the needs of both the Public Service and the wider society. Critical to this will be the introduction of educational programmes in project management and the introduction of administrative and human rights law issues, so as to enhance implementation and management of the RDP. This will entail widening the availability of

Institute training facilities so as to extend into civil society, and also extending the skills taught so that they become transferable between Government and civil society. Accreditation of Institute training programmes will occur within the context of the National Qualifications Framework. (*White Paper on Reconstruction and Development*, 5.5.1)

607. The year 1997 saw the *Green Paper on Public Service Training and Education* evolving into a *White Paper on Public Service Training and Education* (WPPSTE) which was adopted by Cabinet on 6 August 1997. The aim objectives of the WPPSTE are to: provide a coherent Public Service Training policy; provide for strategies planning and better co-ordination of training and education in the Public Service, and for the purpose, provide for the establishment of a Public Service Education and Training Authority (PSETA); provide for the introduction of Capacity Development Standard (CDS) training award system which will provide an incentive for national departments and provincial administrations to speedily adopt and implement the integrated approach to training and education proposed by the WPPSTE. (*Annual Report*, Department of Public Service and Administration, 1997)

608. **5.10.5** A sound labour relations philosophy, policy and practice is an essential requirement for building a motivated, committed cadre of personnel who have a clear vision of their development goals. Labour relations policy must also provide for dealing systematically with corruption, mismanagement and victimisation in public institutions. Labour policy must permit the participation of public sector workers and their organisations in decision-making at various levels in this sector. This will require amendment of existing labour legislation and a review of management practice in the public sector.

609. Measures to prevent discrimination generally use fairly standard techniques to make decision-making more open and accountable. (*Green Paper: Policy Proposals for a New Employment and Occupational Equity Statute*, p.26)

610. **5.11.1** Parastatals, public corporations and advisory boards must be structured and run in a manner that reinforces and supports the RDP. Civil society must be adequately represented on the boards of parastatals and public corporations. Institutions must be transparent and open in both structure and decision-making. They should act within the framework of public policy and there must be a duty to inform the general public as well as to account to parliament. **5.11.2** To ensure effective civil participation of these bodies, governance councils should be composed of mandated representatives of appropriate organisations, not appointed individuals.

611. **5.11.3** All bodies must run on full cost accounting. All subsidies paid or received must be the result of an explicit and transparent decision. In addition, parastatals which receive 20 per cent of their funding or R20 million (whichever is less) from government, should submit an annual director's report to the relevant ministry, showing how allocated funds were used given the objectives agreed to. Every ministry and parastatal should have an office that periodically reviews its activities and measures performance as well as appraising staff performance. Rationalisation of the activities and resources of parastatals should take

place to promote efficiency and effectiveness. Parastatals should have a public consciousness.

612. Objectives of Restructuring. The initiative to restructure State Assets is part of the process of implementing the Government has concretised some of these objectives in its so-called 'six pack' programme namely: belt tightening; reprioritisation of state expenditure; restructuring of state assets and enterprises; restructuring of the public service; building new inter-governmental relations; developing an internal monitoring capacity for the above programmes... The main objectives of restructuring are... increase economic growth and employment, meeting basic needs, redeployment of assets for growth, infrastructural development by mobilising and redirecting private sector capital, reduce state debt, enhance competitiveness and efficiency of state enterprises, finance growth and requirements for competitiveness and develop human resources... Organised labour in general and employees of the relevant public enterprises should participate in policy formulation processes... Historically disadvantaged groups. The capacity of the historically disadvantaged communities to participate and benefit fully in the restructuring programmes should be ascertained and enhanced. Participation and transparency. All key stakeholders should be full participants in the policy-making process, Boards of Directors and other appropriate decision-making structures at an agreed level. (*National Framework Agreement*, 4,5.3,5.5,5.6)

613. Legal and regulatory. South Africa has already begun this process by developing White Papers to cover the broad range of regulatory reforms and to ensure that the process of public sector restructuring is transparent and leaves no ambiguity in the implementation... appropriate legislation and constitutional mechanisms to facilitate the restructuring process at national and provincial levels should be provided. Regulatory structures should be staffed by knowledgeable persons and operate autonomously. (*National Framework Agreement*, 5.2)

614. **5.11.4** Control of funds set aside specifically for development purposes (be they from contracts, the democratic government or the public domain) should vest in a competent and legitimate government agency, which could include representation from civil society.

615. Progress has been made over the past year regarding the restructuring of development finance institutions. A strong emphasis has been placed on ensuring financial sustainability. It is envisaged that grant components of project finance should be channeled through the fiscus in a transparent manner and that loan terms should be market-related. (*Growth, Employment and Redistribution*, Appendix 1)

616. **5.12.1** Local government is critical to the RDP. It is the level of representative democracy closest to the people. Local government will often be involved in the allocation of resources directly affecting communities. Local government should be structured on a democratic, non-racial and non-sexist basis. The *Local Government Transition Act* provides for the start of this process with the establishment of transitional councils, and the creation of a framework for the first non-racial local government elections... **5.12.13** A developmental culture among local government administrations should be encouraged. The

actions of councilors and officials should be open and transparent, with councilors subject to an enforceable Code of Conduct.

617. 156(1) A municipality has executive authority in respect of, and has the right to administer (a) the local government matters listed in Part B of Schedule 4 and Part B of Schedule 5; and (b) any other matter assigned to it by national or provincial legislation. 156(2) A municipality may make and administer by-laws for the effective administration of matters which it has the right to administer. 156(3) Subject to section 151 (4), a by-law that conflicts with national or provincial legislation is invalid... 156(5) A municipality has the right to exercise any power concerning a matter reasonably necessary for, or incidental to, the effective performance of its functions. (*Constitution*, Chapter 7)

618. **5.12.2** The constitutional and legal arrangements which provide for councils of local unity for the transitional phase, should be removed from the final *Constitution* to make local government more democratic. Existing local government legislation, including the *Local Government Transition Act* and the Provincial Ordinances, should be amended or repealed where necessary by a competent legislative authority.

619. 152(1) The objects of local government are... to provide democratic and accountable government for local communities... (*Constitution*, Chapter 7)

620. Any transitional local council or transitional metropolitan substructure or other such body for the pre-interim phase for which no election has been held before or on 31 August 1996 may be dissolved by the Minister by notice in the Provincial Gazette on a day specified therein... The establishment of a transitional local council for rural area of government not falling within the area of jurisdiction of a transitional council or transitional local council... all the members of which shall be elected in accordance with a system of proportional representation or of ward representation or of both proportional representation and ward representation. (*Local Government Transition Act Amendment Act*)

621. There are the following types of local municipalities: Local simple type, i.e. a type of municipality characterised by a municipal council that does not have more than 9 members; Local executive committee type, i.e. a type of municipality characterised by an executive committee system; Local executive mayor type. (*Municipal Structure Act*, p.9)

622. **5.12.3** An estimated 800 segregated local authorities must be amalgamated into approximately 300 new local authorities with non-racial boundaries. The existing grading system for local authorities should be revised to reflect needs of people, and not just existing consumption of services. **5.12.4** The demarcation of boundaries of local authorities should ensure that informal settlements on the outskirts of towns and cities, and urban settlements displaced behind homeland boundaries, are incorporated into the jurisdiction of new local authorities.

623. At present there are 843 municipalities and 11 300 Councilors in South Africa. The number of municipalities and Councilors should be reduced so that municipalities can

provide better services at lower cost. (*Local Government Information Series 1: A Short Guide to the White Paper on Local Government*, p.23)

624. The function of the [Municipal Demarcation] Board is to determine municipal boundaries for the whole of the territory of the Republic... When the Board determines a municipal boundary its objective must be to establish an area that would—(a) enable the municipality for that area to fulfil its constitutional obligations, including- (i) the provision of democratic and accountable government for the local communities; (ii) the provision of services to the communities in a sustainable manner; (iii) the promotion of social and economic development; and (iv) the promotion of a safe and healthy environment; (b) enable effective local governance; (c) enable integrated social and economic planning and development; and (d) have a tax base as inclusive as possible of users of municipal services in the municipality. When the Board determines a municipal boundary it must take into account—(a) the interdependence of people, communities, and economies... (b) the financial and administrative capacity of the municipality... (c) the financial viability of the municipality; (d) the need to share and redistribute financial and administrative resources; (e) existing functional boundaries;... j) the need to establish a single, cohesive unfragmented area, and more specifically to- (ii) include a rural area in a municipality which has a town as its core if that town has a strong social and economic linkage with that rural area and functions primarily as a service center for that rural area; or (iii) include in a municipality which has a city or large town as its core, any formal or informal settlements or industrial or commercial developments on the fringe of that city of town. (*Local Government: Municipal Demarcation Act*, pp.4,9-10)

625. **5.12.5** Elected local government, with responsibility for the delivery of services, should be extended into rural areas, including traditional authority areas. Rural district councils that incorporate a number of primary local councils must have a key role in rural local government.

626. Local authority structures will form the crucial first link with communities, and thus form a part of the vision towards which we strive, while their initial inadequacy forms a part of the reality we must encompass as communities endeavour to put their needs onto the development agenda. (*Rural Development Strategy*, p.12)

627. The establishment of local government is a lengthy process. In most rural areas no such institution has existed in the past. People are having to learn governance skills for the first time... The *Local Government White Paper* is expected to define the number of local authorities, how they can become financially viable, and describe an efficient model for rural local government. With some local variation, together both District and Local Councils are expected to provide the services set out below. It is expected that primary rural councils will have responsibility for: providing basic services... for rural development... identifying special local needs and applying to the District Councils and other sources for the funds to meet them. It is likely that District rural councils will undertake the following: establish and support primary local government structures... act as a conduit for the inter-governmental grants... appoint and employ personnel who will serve more than one primary local authority, set guidelines on levels of services to be

applied throughout the district according to the framework established by national and provincial government... provide technical assistance to primary local government for the planning of local economic and infrastructure development, and services, strengthen the capacity of primary councils... [and] establish Land Development Objectives and formulate an integrated development plan for its area of jurisdiction. (*Rural Development Framework*, pp.11,14)

628. There is hereby established a council to be known as the Council of Traditional Leaders... The objects of the council shall be (a) to promote the role of traditional leadership within a democratic constitutional dispensation; (b) to enhance unity and understanding among traditional communities; and (c) to enhance co-operation between the Council and the various Houses with a view to addressing matters of common interest. (*Council of Traditional Leaders Act*, 2.1,7.1)

629. Traditional authorities that observe a system of customary law in the area of a district or local municipality may in accordance with subsections (2) and (3) participate in the proceedings of the district or local council, and those leaders must be allowed to attend and participate in any meeting of the council... The number of traditional leaders participating in the proceedings of the district or local council in terms of subsection (1) may not exceed ten per cent of the total number of councilors of the district or local council, but if a district has fewer than ten members, one traditional leader may so participate. (*Municipal Structures Act*, p.28)

630. The National Council of Traditional Leaders, established last year, will help find the best ways of integrating traditional authority in the new democratic system, including building their capacity and encouraging their participation in local government, community empowerment, development and land administration. (*The Building has Begun!*, p.22)

631. **5.12.6** In major urban centres, strong metropolitan government should be established to assist in the integration and coordination of the urban economies.

632. 155(2) National legislation must define the different types of municipality that may be established within each category. (*Constitution of the Republic of South Africa 1996*) Metropolitan areas must have metropolitan municipalities, i.e. category A municipalities. Areas other than metropolitan areas must have both district and local municipalities... There are the following types of metropolitan municipalities: Metropolitan executive committee type, i.e. a type of municipality characterised by an executive committee system; Metropolitan executive committee (are committees) type, i.e. a type of municipality characterised by an executive committee system with an area committee system; Metropolitan executive mayor type; and Metropolitan executive mayor (area committees), i.e. a type of municipality characterised by an executive mayor system combined with an area committee system. (*Municipal Structure Act*, p.9)

633. Metropolitan areas are large urban areas with large population. There are six metropolitan areas in South Africa: Greater Johannesburg, Greater Pretoria, Cape Town,

Durban, Lekoa-Vaal and Kayalami. (*Local Government Information Series 1: A Short Guide to the White Paper on Local Government*, p.17)

634. **5.12.7** Separate budgets and financial systems must be integrated on the basis of 'one municipality, one tax base.' The arrears and debts of the black local authorities, estimated at R1,8 billion, should be written off by a competent legislature.

635. Government will take steps to ensure that sufficient resources are made available for the extension and upgrading of municipal services, and for capacity-building to permit community-based structures to assist in local planning and implementation of the upgrading. Local Government will need additional sources of revenue for operating, maintenance and subsidy expenses, as well as staff retraining and some new capital expenditure... RDP funding will be made available only if amalgamation of different jurisdictions is proceeding effectively, if single budgets are adopted for a single municipal area, and if the Local Government electoral process is underway. The transitional Local Authority will gain access to increased resources only if it becomes developmental in its orientation, proactive in winning the trust of all local residents, sensitive to issues of affordability, creative about financing, and more efficient in delivery of services. Local Authorities must demonstrate that they are already, in the transitional phase, shifting resources (staff, management, equipment, skills), switching their spending priorities, freezing clearly inappropriate projects, and engaging in consultation with community groups. Through such means, it will be feasible to build new local institutions which will take the RDP forward. (*White Paper on Reconstruction and Development*, 274,275)

636. Municipal finances must be based on the principle of one municipality, one tax base... Institutional debts of black local authorities which they cannot repay, shall be assumed by the state. (*Agreement on Local Government Finances and Services*)

637. **5.12.8** All local authorities should embark on programmes to restore, maintain, upgrade and extend networks of services. Within a local authority, the total body of consumers should be responsible for the cost of the service, including capital improvements, thus allowing for cross-subsidisation of new consumers. Tariff structures should be structured on a progressive basis to address problems of affordability. Within this framework, all consumers should pay for services consumed. **5.12.9** Local authorities should be assisted to deal with the existing backlog of municipal services through inter-governmental transfers from central and provincial government, according to criteria established by the Financial and Fiscal Commission.

638. A municipality must a) structure and manage its administration, and budgeting and planning processes to give priority to the basic needs of the community, and to promote the social and economic development of the community; and b) participate in national and provincial development programmes... Local government and each province is entitled to an equitable share of revenue raised nationally to enable it to provide basic services and perform the functions allocated to it. (*Constitution*, 153,227)

639. Intergovernmental transfers should promote the constitutional and governmental goal of ensuring that all South African have access to basic services. (*The Introduction of an Equitable Share of National Raised Revenue for Local Government*)

640. **5.12.10** Separate local authority administrations must be amalgamated, reorganised and rationalised, after consultation between employer and employee bodies. A centralised system of collective bargaining for municipal employees should be established.

641. Promote collective bargaining. The new legislation will promote the role of collective bargaining as a means of varying employment standards. In particular, the proposals stress the role of collective bargaining in introducing flexible working arrangements. (*Green Paper: Policy Proposals for a new Employment Standards Statute*, 5.3)

642. Municipal trade unions and organised local government have a key role to play in ensuring good employer-employee relations and a sound a labor relation system. The South African Local Government Bargaining Council (SALGBC) will play a role in developing a partnership between municipal trade unions, management and Councils and a framework for resolving disputes. A priority will be to negotiate common conditions of service for municipal staff and a municipal job evaluation system, improve performance and create a sound basis for transformation. (*Local Government Information Series 1: A Short Guide to the White Paper on Local Government*, p.31)

643. **5.12.11** The Training Board for Local Government Bodies should be restructured to provide more effective training for employees of local authorities. The entrance criteria of professional bodies such as the Institute of Town Clerks and the Institute of Municipal Treasurers and Accountants should be broadened to ensure better access for all South Africans to these professions.

644. **5.12.12** At local government level a women's portfolio should be established with powers to scrutinise local authority programmes and budgets for gender sensitivity. Local authorities can play a role in the implementation of affirmative action with the private sector through special criteria for local government contracts.

645. **5.12.14** Local authority administrations should be structured in such a way as to ensure maximum participation of civil society and communities in decision-making and developmental initiatives of local authorities.

646. 160(7) A Municipal Council must conduct its business in an open manner; and may close its sittings, or those of its committees, only when it is reasonable to do so having regard to the nature of the business being transacted. (*Constitution*, Chapter 7)

647. **5.13.2** Many social movements and CBOs will be faced with the challenge of transforming their activities from a largely oppositional mode into a more developmental one. To play their full role these formations will require capacity-building assistance. This should be developed with democratic government facilitation and funded through a variety of sources. A set of rigorous criteria must be established to ensure that beneficiaries deserve

the assistance and use it for the designated purposes. Every effort must be made to extend organisation into marginalised communities and sectors like, for instance, rural black women... **5.13.5** Institutions of civil society should be encouraged to improve their accountability to their various constituencies and to the public at large. There should be no restriction on the right of the organisations to function effectively. Measures should be introduced to create an enabling environment for social movements, CBOs and NGOs in close consultation with those bodies and to promote donations to the non-profit sector. This should include funding of Legal Advice Centres and paralegals.

648. Government must ensure that its service arms are accessible to civil society, especially mass organisations with limited resources, and that they are able to provide an unbiased service even in areas (such as industrial strategy, development planning or other areas of multi-partite negotiation) where interests may be opposed to current Government policies... the resources of Government (especially in the area of research) must be made available to mass organisations as they are to business and other constituencies... Future Government support for NGOs will be based on their role in taking forward the RDP, a process that can be assisted and evaluated through some form of accreditation for all such NGOs which receive Government funds. Rationalisation of service delivery to communities is a general guideline for donors. However, it is both necessary and desirable for healthy, efficient and effective community-based development organisations and NGOs to exist. Government should not have a monopoly of resources in this area. Organisations of civil society should continue to have the choice of access to alternative sources of services such as policy research so that it is not completely dependent on Government. In addition, community-based development organisations will receive more extensive financial and logistical support once representivity, accountability and effectiveness are confirmed... The RDP envisages a social partnership and Government should therefore provide services and support to all sectors, especially organised labour, the civics, business, women's groups and the churches. Moreover, Government has a duty in terms of the RDP to encourage independent organisation where it does not exist, such as rural areas. Strong consumer and environmental movements are essential in a modern industrial society and should be facilitated by Government... Government must therefore provide resources in an open and transparent manner and in compliance with clear and explicit criteria to mass organisations to ensure that they are able to develop or maintain the ability to effectively participate as negotiation partners of Government. (*White Paper on Reconstruction and Development*, 7.6.1,7.6.3,7.6.4,7.6.7,7.6.8)

649. **5.13.3** Trade unions and other mass organisations must be actively involved in democratic public policy-making. This should include involvement in negotiations ranging from the composition of the Constitutional Court to international trade and loan agreements. Education about trade unions and other mass organisations should also be promoted in school curricula and through publicly-funded media.

650. Increasingly, organisations of civil society will be involved in planning and policy-making through a variety of advisory boards, commissions, forums and other venues by which experience is gained and skills are acquired. (*White Paper on Reconstruction and Development*, 7.6.1)

651. **5.13.4** Delivery or enforcement mechanisms for social and economic rights must not focus only on the constitution, courts and judicial review, but must include agencies which have the involvement of members and organisations of civil society as means of enforcing social justice. In this regard, a revamped Human Rights Commission, with wider popular involvement, should have its mandate extended to ensure that social and economic rights are being met.

652. The Human rights Commission must a) promote respect for human rights and a culture of human rights; b) promote the protection, development and attainment of human rights; and c) monitor and assess the observance of human rights in the Republic... Each year, the Human Rights Commission must require relevant organs of state to provide the Commission with the information on the measures that they have taken towards the realisation of the rights in the Bill of Rights concerning housing, health care, food, water, social security, education and the environment. (*Constitution,* 184.1,184.3)

653. **5.13.7** Multipartite policy forums (like the present National Economic Forum) representing the major role players in different sectors should be established and existing forums restructured to promote efficient and effective participation of civil society in decision-making. Such forums must exist at the national, provincial and local levels. **5.13.8** Forums such as the National Economic Forum constitute important opportunities for organs of civil society to participate in and influence policy-making. Similarly they provide the democratic government with an important mechanism for broad consultation on policy matters. They need to be assisted (and sometimes restructured) to improve their effectiveness, representivity and accountability.

654. A variety of sectoral negotiating forums have developed a participatory approach to policy formulation. National line Departments will be encouraged, where appropriate, to continue ongoing policy interaction with sectoral forums, which comprise key sectoral stakeholders and technical experts. Forums will advise Ministers either on request or pro-actively. (*White Paper on Reconstruction and Development,* 7.4.1)

655. **5.14.1** Open debate and transparency in government and society are crucial elements of reconstruction and development. This requires an information policy which guarantees active exchange of information and opinion among all members of society. Without the free flow of accurate and comprehensive information, the RDP will lack the mass input necessary for its success... **5.14.2** The new information policy must aim at facilitating exchange of information within and among communities and between the democratic government and society as a two-way process. It must also ensure that media play an important role in facilitating projects in such areas as education and health... **5.14.7** To ensure free flow of information--within the broad parameters of the Bill of Rights--the *Freedom of Information Act* must be broadened... **5.14.8** The democratic government must have a major role to play in the introduction of a new information policy. This must, however, be limited to facilitation rather than dabbling in editorial content of media enterprises. Further, a deliberate policy must be followed to prevent unwarranted state intervention in levelling the media playing field or in preserving privileged status for

government information. The Bill of Rights and, if necessary, legislation will be crucial in this regard.

656. Government will introduce a *Freedom of Information Act* that will: describe what information the public can have access to and according to what time period; outline the procedures for obtaining that information; publicise what information must be published by public bodies on a regular basis; outline the consultation process public bodies must engage in decision processes, and outline the specific powers of parliamentary standing committees... The *Constitution* guarantees the right to this information, which is a major departure from past practice. Precise guidelines are therefore required. (*White Paper on Reconstruction and Development*, 5.7.1,5.7.2)

657. 32 (1) Everyone has the right of access to (a) any information held by the state; and (b) any information that is held by another person and that is required for the exercise or protection of any rights. (2) National legislation must be enacted to give effect to this right, and may provide for reasonable measures to alleviate the administrative and financial burden on the state (*Constitution*, Chapter 2)

658. Among other programmes and activities, the *Open Democracy Bill* which Cabinet will table in this august Assembly in the next few weeks, speaks of the commitment of this government to openness, accountability and transparency. Government knows too keenly that an informed public is the best driver of social transformation; it is a sure guarantee to the consultation of our democracy; and it is the most effective builder of a better life. (*Opening Speech by Deputy Minister Essop Pahad*, National Assembly, Budget Vote no.29, 18 May, 1998)

659. **5.14.3** The democratic government must encourage the development of all three tiers of media – public, community and private. However, it must seek to correct the skewed legacy of apartheid where public media were turned into instruments of National Party policy; where community media were repressed; where private media are concentrated in the hands of a few monopolies, and where a few individuals from the white community determine the content of media. New voices at national, regional and local levels, and genuine competition rather than a monopoly of ideas, must be encouraged. **5.14.4** An affirmative action programme, consistent with the best experiences in the world, must be put into place to empower communities and individuals from previously disadvantaged sectors of society. This must include: mechanisms to make available resources needed to set up broadcasting and printing enterprises at a range of levels; training and upgrading, and civic education to ensure that communities and individuals recognise and exercise their media rights. **5.14.5** Measures must be undertaken to limit monopoly control of the media. Cross-ownership of print and broadcast media must be subject to strict limitations determined in a public and transparent manner. The democratic government must encourage unbundling of the existing media monopolies. This includes monopolies in the areas of publishing and distribution. Where necessary, anti-trust legislation must be brought to bear on these monopolies. **5.14.6** The democratic government must set aside funds for training of journalists and community-based media and, at the same time, encourage media institutions to do the same.

Notes

197

660. The government of South Africa supports affirmative action as a conscious strategy to correct the social and gender imbalances in our society. The telecommunications industry is no exception, and can play a vital role. (*Telecommunications Green Paper*, p.61)

661. Education and training for the information age is a high priority. This means creating what some people call a "learning nation" to empower citizens with the skills and understanding for participation and innovation in the IS. (*The Information Society and the Developing World: A South African Approach*, p.18)

662. This is why the Independent Broadcasting Authority is guided by legislation which prescribes a three-tier structure of ownership–public, private and community–and it uses criteria, in granting licenses, which take the issue of diversity into account. Fully appreciative of this, Government Communications is working closely with this Department in the launch of tele-centres, and with community structures in the development of Multi-purpose Community Centres. The key input GCIS hopes to make in this regard is to identify community information needs and provide as much of the information as possible. At the same time, the strategic nature of these centres as means through which citizens can communicate with government will be promoted. (*Opening Speech by Deputy Minister Essop Pahad*, National Assembly, Budget Vote no.29, 18 May, 1998)

663. **5.14.9** The South African Communications Services (SACS) must be restructured in order to undertake two important tasks: the provision of objective information about the activities of the state and other role players, and the facilitation of the new information policy. **5.14.10** To carry out these two functions, two distinct structures will be necessary. At the same time, the information arms of various ministries, especially those dealing with reconstruction and development, must be strengthened.

664. The birth of the Government Communication and Information System (GCIS) shall be traced to this day when Dr Essop Pahad, Deputy Minister in the Office of the Deputy President, rises in Parliament for the Communications Budget Vote and formally declares the books of GCIS open. The GCIS is coming into being after a lengthy investigation into government communications. This examination, led by what come to be known as the Comtask Team, involved a large number of institutions of civil society as well as individuals from academia, media and the advertising world. This broad-based approach has helped strengthen the GCIS mandate to communicate on behalf of government. This mandate is primarily drawn from Section 16 of the Bill of Rights which guarantees citizens freedom of speech. The consequence of this is their right not only to receive information about government, but also themselves to communicate their views and activities. (*Birth of a New Government Communications Order*, 18 May 1998)

665. **5.14.11** All these measures require institutional mechanisms independent of the democratic government and representative of society as a whole. Some of the more crucial ones are:
Information Development Trust: made up of civil society, media role players, especially

community-based ones, the democratic government and political interests, to work out detailed criteria and mechanisms for assisting relevant media enterprises.

Independent Broadcasting Authority (IBA): appointed in a transparent and participatory process. Made up of persons of integrity and experts in the broadcasting field. Responsible for the issuing of broadcasting licenses and other broadcasting regulations.

Public Broadcaster Board: appointed in a similar manner to give broad direction to the public broadcaster, without undermining editorial independence.

Voluntary regulatory mechanisms: for private media enterprise, and representative of all role players, including media workers. Within broadcasting, the voluntary regulations should be within the framework provided by the IBA.

Independent unions of media workers and associations of owners of media institutions.

666. 192. National legislation must establish an independent authority to regulate broadcasting in the public interest, and to ensure fairness and a diversity of views broadly representing South African society. (*Constitution*, p.104)

667. Speech by ANC President Thabo Mbeki to the SACP Congress, 2 July, 1998.

668. One indication of RDP priorities was RDP Fund allocations (the following list is merely a departmental/functional breakdown, with particular projects too numerous and complex to describe or even summarise):

DEPARTMENTS:
    Agriculture: R7 384 000
    Arts, Culture, Science and Technology: R20 000 000
    Constitutional Development: R2 040 832 000
    Correctional Services: R21 905 000
    Education: R925 699 000
    Health: R2 050 800 000
    Housing: R2 897 000 000
    Justice: R65 752 000
    Land Affairs: R703 628 000
    Minerals and Energy: R101 599 000
    Public Works: 350 000 000
    SA Police Service: R195 000 000
    State Expenditure: R1 068 000
    Transport : R365 100 000
    Water Affairs and Forestry: R1 334 037 000
    Trade and Industry: R2 020 000
    Welfare: 25 484 000
    Sport and Recreation: R 20 000 000
    Subtotal: R11 127 308 000

ADDITIONAL BENEFICIARIES
    Provincial Administrations: R4 163 582 000
    Executive Deputy President: R701 000
    Dept of Finance: R3 139 000
    Parliament: R34 052 000

Public Service Commission: R5 000 000
Promoting the RDP: R39 131 000
Subtotal: R 4 345 605 000
Total: R15 472 913 000

(*Interpellations, Questions and Replies of the National Assembly*, First Session, Second Parliament, 9–19 June 1997, *Hansard*, p.1546)